THE WANDERINGS
OF
EDWARD ELY

THE
WANDERINGS OF
EDWARD
ELY

A Mid-19th Century Seafarer's Diary
Edited by
ANTHONY and *ALLISON SIRNA*

HASTINGS HOUSE   PUBLISHERS   NEW YORK

Printed in the United States of America
Library of Congress Catalog Card No.: 54-7598

9717

TO

MEREDITH and CORINNE

INTRODUCTION

N A SOUTHERN FAMILY, legends have a way of becoming real. They are perpetuated, sometimes even embroidered, handed down from generation to generation, until some maiden aunt, sitting in the seclusion of her parlor finalizes the legend by writing down her version. In our family there are stories steeped in the drama of the Revolutionary War, of Andrew Jackson's day, of Nashville before the War Between the States, of Augusta afterwards. Most of these are accepted on faith, a few are documented by letters which somehow resisted yellowing inroads of time. It remained for a Pennsylvanian, one of the most romantic figures in our family, to provide a truly authentic chronicle of his adventures. This is the diary of Edward Ely, physician, diplomat, adventurer.

Jonathan Ely and his wife Mary Lee, living in the family homestead in Solebury, Bucks County, Pennsylvania, had seven children, and tragically survived all of them. Only one, Edward, born in 1827, managed to live beyond maturity, and he died suddenly in 1858. Into his thirty-one years however, he succeeded in crowding more drama than most men

1

who culminate a long life embarking on the final journey while lying peacefully in bed.

From all we can discover today, Edward's childhood was the usual one for a son of a successful Bucks County farmer. Jonathan spent part of each year in Harrisburg as a member of the State Legislature, a connection which was to be extremely important to his son. As Edward grew older he studied medicine under his uncle, Doctor Ralph Lee, of New Town, but one profession was not sufficient for a man of Edward's imagination and drive. A wanderer at heart, he began to travel when only in his teens, visiting such metropolises as Cincinnati, where he attended a scientific convention, New York, Boston, and on one occasion, voyaging to England, and then the Continent.

In the March 16th, 1858 issue of the Bucks County *Intelligencer*, the issue reporting his death, there appears the following description of Edward:

. . . He was a young man of much more than ordinary intellect, of an active temperament, fond of reading and study, and industrious and persevering in all his undertakings; and, as a consequence, in addition to acquiring a thorough knowledge of the medical science, he stored his mind with an ample fund of general literature. This, added to his amiability of temper and manners, modest and retiring disposition, high sense of honor, and zeal and pride in his profession, at once made him hosts of friends and brought him into an extensive practice as a physician, upon his location at Forestville, soon after graduating.

Judging from his own writings, Edward did not possess an amiability of temper, nor a modest and retiring disposition, yet the Bombay *Telegraph and Courier* of January 18th, 1858 reported as follows:

. . . Doctor Ely had only been a few years amongst us, but during that time he had endeared himself to many. He was a gentleman of quiet and retiring manners, but his calm exterior veiled talents as high as they were varied . . . It will . . . be consoling to his friends in America to know that he did not die amongst strangers. His good qualities had endeared him to many . . . the last respect will be shewn to

2

his remains in such a manner as will not only testify to his intrinsic worth, but be in keeping with the dignity of the nation which he had the honor of representing.

The only other contemporary description of Edward Ely is perhaps the most accurate, for it is the one to be gleaned from reading his *Journal*. While biased, and, we are certain, edited by the conscience of its author, the diary provides an insight into the character of a man who played his small role in the history of his country with dignity, remarkable wisdom for one so young, and great courage.

In 1850, according to the *Intelligencer*, Ely, his health so seriously impaired as to cause strong doubts of his recovery, on the ". . . urgent advice of his friends and medical gentlemen . . . was induced to abandon his practice and visit India, hoping by extensive sea travel and a short residence in a more congenial climate, to regain his health."

A voyage half-way 'round the world was not to be undertaken lightly, and for a young man of twenty-three without any income or savings, required financial arrangements that would have discouraged many a present day voyager. But Edward was an aggressive individual and succeeded in securing passage for himself by serving as ship's doctor on the small schooner, *Delia Maria*. Enlisting the aid of his father and influential friends, he petitioned President Fillmore, and secured the position of United States Consul to Bombay, a post he held until his death.

The Senate Report of the First Session of the 36th Congress, April 17th, 1860, states ". . . [Ely] had discharged his official duties with ability, and to the entire satisfaction of the general government . . . It appears from the letter of the Honorable Charles E. Mix, at the time acting commissioner of Indian Affairs, that the services . . . were faithfully performed. . . ."

What happened in the eight years of his "wandering adventures" is told by Edward himself in his journals, his letters to Presidents Fillmore and Pierce and the Secretary of State, his consular reports, and the articles he wrote for the Bucks County *Intelligencer*. Fortunately, he was a man of culture and education, gifted with a novelist's eye for detail and atmosphere, as well as a novelist's understanding and appreciation of people. The diary, while intensely personal and filled with introspective passages, was written for posterity, as its author plainly tells his readers. Through his eyes we are enabled to see the Port of New York at Christmastime in the mid-nineteenth century, experience the rigors of a sea journey under sail around Cape Horn, visit California during the Gold Rush, witness the growing pains of San Francisco, and yes, even take a voyage by primitive steamship.

The portion of the *Journal* published here covers the period beginning in New York and ending as he arrives in India. To our knowledge, it is the only one of several volumes that survived, having been brought back to this country by Edward on a brief visit home just one hundred years ago. We feel honored to have the privilege of transcribing and editing the volume, a task its author would most certainly have encouraged.

Now, let's embark on this voyage with Edward Ely, with "stout heart, strong hands, and willing mind . . . [for] . . . many a storm and tempest must . . . [we] . . . encounter before . . . [we] . . . reach that distant land of the east."

ANTHONY AND ALLISON SIRNA

Riverdale-on-the-Hudson
December 1st, 1953.

4

JOURNAL OF MY

WANDERING ADVENTURES

COMMENCING:

NEW YORK, 11TH OF DECEMBER, 1850

RELENTLESS FATE! How surely do thy ministers perform their alloted work, how steadily does thy sister Time progress in her onward course. A few fleeting seasons ago, and I had settled as I thought for life, in a quiet country place, as a healer of the sick, and comforter of the suffering. All brilliant were my prospects then, all sanguine of success and pleasure and happiness for I thought I had done forever with the dark care that had so long obscured the sun of my life, and that henceforth, life alone should be my only care. If an inward voice ever arose in warning, or a painful thought of the past ever pointed to the future, I checked it with the conscious strength of freedom, and youth, for what is warning to the young and sanguine, what is experience wisely told to the man whose wisdom is yet to purchase.

But the time has flown. Those few fleeting seasons are gone, with all their early hopes, all their anxious cares and all their final disappointments, and now I am again, as it were, in the beginning of a new life. Suffice it to say that through exposure, both necessary and unecessary, and the constant operation of a restless mind, aggravated by the seperate and sore trials of which I was a sufferer, my health which had not been sound for several years, at length commenced to decline rapidly, and this, with other considerations, determined me to seek in the sunny land of distant India, that restoration which was entirely hopeless in my own fickle climate.

I had received offers from Duharnel Brothers & Co. of Batavia, which I had accepted, both on account of their liberality and because I should be near my own "Mary," but having seen from my interview with President Fillmore an opportunity of obtaining the appointment of Consul of the United States at Bombay, I determined upon making that remote place the Theatre of my Indian adventures and perhaps my home. My affairs at home being settled, and everything in readiness for the voyage, I bid my family a long and sorrowful farewell and with a heavy heart, left, perhaps forever, the hearthstone of home, and the sorrowing hearts that were still to remain around it. This was only yesterday morning, and I have not yet recovered from the trying scene, which I could not even appreciate until I had finally parted with my dear father who had accompanied me to Trenton, and was whirling away towards Boston in the cars. Then, only, could I realize all my sorrow, all my loss, all my loneliness.

I am writing from French's Hotel where I am staying, instead, as I had expected, of being in Boston this morning and perhaps just on the eve of sailing. My plans are all knocked in the head too, as regards my arrangements with the *Delia Maria,* for she is now in New York having come around here to finish loading day before yesterday, and Captain Burleigh tells me that he will not be able to spare his ladies' cabin which I had engaged for Mary, because his wife, and wife's cousin are going with him. I can however be well accomodated with a cabin in the gentlemen's cabin, but I think that if I can find another ship, I will do so. Capt. B. gave me a letter from Mary, who says that there is one of George L. Lyman's ships going direct to Calcutta that we

6

might obtain passage on board. I shall go to Boston this evening and endeavor to arrange the matter.

New York, 13th December, 1850
I have just returned from Boston, and our plans are settled. I could learn of no suitable chance of our getting to India together, in a favorable manner, as I had arranged with Captain Burleigh, and unless I went by the overland route via England, I should have to make this weary voyage alone. I could not afford to go in that manner, and after many propositions it was arranged that Mary should sail in the steamer of the next month for Southampton, and thence overland by Genoa, Malta, and Suez, arriving in Calcutta after visiting the intermediate places in about four or five months, while I alone and deserted should still fulfill my part of the agreement with Captain B. who now that the ladies are going wishes me more than ever to go with him. Mary will be attended by an old female servant of her mother, and I pray a just providence to bring her in safety and health to her destination.

New York, 14th December, 1850
I am on board the splendid ship *Delia Maria* fixed and settled in a comfortable cabin, for a voyage of many months. I came on board this morning, and now (3 p.m.) have got things as snug as possible, and have sat down to write some letters and also to note on this very offhand journal my few and unfertile ideas of the ship. Well, the table I am writing upon, the sofas, chairs, lockers, mirrors, and everything else in fact are of splendid workmanship, but are lashed and fast and firm as the mainmast itself and give a curious idea to the novice in nautical life, who has no thought that all this splendid palace of wood and rigging may in a few hours be tossed and whirled in the eddies of some noisy mountain torrent. The stove too which burns so cheerily this cold afternoon, and almost makes one forget the whistling wind, that sweeps through the lofty hamper with such a melancholy noise, is lashed to strong bolts in the deck so firmly that a Hercules himself might not wrench it from its place. Then with this strong preparation for the approaching strife is all the softness of luxury pleasingly blended; the rich Brussels carpets, the magnificent chande-

7

liers, and the damask and velvet curtains set off these handsome salons, and I only want my Mary here to enjoy our coming ocean life. When I look at the lovely cabin which was to have been hers, and remember her far less comfortable quarters aboard a steamer, I almost wish some accident would detain Mrs. B. in time for us yet to execute our original intention.

But that is impossible, we sail in a few days, and the Captain has even now gone to Berwick for the ladies. Mr. Bishop, the chief officer, is on the wharf attending to the cargo as it comes down; Mr. Bickford, the second officer with a few boys and old Carpenter, is reeving off the running rigging and bending the sails, while I alone am sitting here, as I said, holding communion with those I love by silent pen.

I have told Captain Burleigh that I should assist in working the ship, and for the purpose of exercise take an active part in all the operations carried on. I have therefore provided myself with all the necessaries of a sailor and have already quite a collection of marlinspikes, prickers, sail needles, palms, fids, knives, and c. and c. together with my old epitome and a new quadrant. I hope we shall sail before many days for I feel very, very bad. But the cargo comes slow because there are so many vessels here for California, and I think that if the ship had remained in Boston she would have been ready by this time.

New York, 21st Dec., 1850

Another week has gone by and here we are still. And now I am in earnest very sorry that I have been deceived into leaving home almost before I was ready, to wait and wait in this cold, damp, disagreeable city, while I might have spent all this time so happily with my dear parents. I think it will be another week yet before we are ready to sail, and I feel that it will be too late for poor me. Last Wednesday was a very cold and disagreeable day and I had been assisting Mr. Bishop with the cargo. I was in the boat in the afternoon, I had finished, and coming around the counter of the ship *William Wharton* someone, without looking, hove a whole barrel of water from off the deck, wetting me and the carpenter to the skin. I changed as soon as possible, but the next morning I was much worse, and I went ashore to Rogers' Hotel in Fulton where I might be out of the way, and in case I got sick, that I need not have to be removed when the vessel sailed. But I am better now and able to knock about once more.

I am writing, now, most impatient to bid adieu to these cold and snow-clad shores. Yet I cannot allow my parents to think any longer that I am suffering here, and although it will cost me a deception and also the end of our correspondence, yet I will write this very night, and say that we sail tomorrow. I would go home again but there would be little gained by again repeating the scene that had already well nigh caused me to give up my hopes and prospects to return to the bosom of my family, there either to die in the midst, or to lead a life of quietness and peace. Yes, I will write a letter and say I am gone.

New York, 25th December, 1850
It is the happy Christmas day, and all in the great city are seemingly merry and careless. Oh, my dear little brothers, how forcibly I have been reminded of you this day. This day is particularly a welcome anniversary to children, and I humbly trust that its sports and pastimes are being enjoyed by you with as much innocent pleasure as they were by me a long time ago when I too was a little boy of your ages.

New York, 26th December, 1850
We do not pass a day or an hour of our lives without something to attract unusual attention, either novel, ludicrous or terrible. Yesterday, I was so lucky as to find a New York shopkeeper, honest enough to run after me with a dollar which I had paid too much for an article I had bought. I was really astonished to find a man in this city of "Peter Funks" and mock auctions, honest enough to act in this generous manner, and for the public good I shall record his name that others may know that at least one honest man lives in Gotham. His name is Robert King, nautical instrument maker, corner of Front and Beekman Streets.

A few evenings ago I was attracted by the appearance of a poor wretch, who had sometime previously been in a fight and got his lips cut almost off and his teeth knocked out,

9

so that he could not drink except through a tube. This man tottered into a rumhole and calling for some Santa Cruz poured out about half a tumbler, had some sugar put in it, and then filled up with hot water, when he drew a pipe stem from his pocket, and exhausted the contents as speedily as possible. Oh! human nature, to what a depth of degradation hast thou fallen.

On Saturday last, one of the stevedores engaged upon our ship, while swinging a huge cask of brandy inboard, missed his guard and fell from the upper deck, striking his head upon the coamings of the lower hatch, and killing himself instantly on the casks in the hold. The death of this poor fellow had no effect upon his comrades. They found that life was forever extinct, and after slinging him and hooking him on the same rope by whose means he was killed, he was hoisted up by the horse, put in an empty dray that was at hand, sent away, and the work proceeded as regularly as before.

A few days ago, the 21st, a most lovely and mild afternoon for the season, tempted me to quit the crowded city and seek in the solemn woods and hills of the country a few hours repose from the busy strife of business and passion. I crossed the East River to Brooklyn, and getting into Greenwood omnibus, was soon skirting the roads of the open country of Long Island. We arrived at the quiet little village of Greenwood about two o'clock and here I left the coach. I was three miles from the town of Brooklyn and everything was as quiet as if I had been in the very center of our American forests. The relief from the painful and eternal din of the metropolis was great and striking indeed, and I rambled out into the deep woods, to enjoy in solitude the pleasure I felt. I was reminded of the many happy days that I had spent in wandering over my native hills.

The sky was blue over my head and the few fleecy clouds that were floating away seemed more like those of happy May, than the wintry vapors of the North. The gentle and mild breeze was just strong enough to rustle the dried leaves upon the grass, and then to go sighing and moaning away among the old oak and ash trees on the hills, while the ground was dry and pleasant to walk upon. I could hear the distant note of the partridge as he was calling his mate, and the cock from the neighboring yard crowed to the warm afternoon sun. Everything was still, so still that I could hear the echo of these familiar sounds from all the surrounding hills and at times too, as the wind would come from that direction, I could just distinguish the busy hum of the distant city.

Towards evening I came to the proud Golgotha of the neighboring city, and Oh! what a lovely spot has been chosen, by the living of New York, for the site of the city of their dead. Greenwood Cemetery occupies an area of more than two hundred and fifty acres, and it is far more nobly adorned by nature, than it ever will be by the hand of man. Deep and noble woodland, with sunny vistas here and there presenting the distant view of the bay or the heights of New Jersey, grassy hillocks and gently sloping banks; quiet and retired valleys, and tranquilly sleeping lakes, whose banks are fringed with the sad weeping willow, and whose glassy bosom reflects as in a mirror, the quiet scenes around. And then the tombs, the silent, awful, tombs. There is no crowding here, as in the confined grounds of Laurel Hill at Philadelphia, or Green Mont at Baltimore; all is free and open and roomy. The magnificent monument is not made to blush by the near proximity of the humble headstone, and the grand column of wealth and affluence stands alone in its melancholy glory.

The slanting rays of the evening sun and the lengthening shadows of the hills warned me that the short winter day was drawing to a close, while the wind from the sea becoming cooler and cooler spoke of the change that was soon to set in and again wrap these fair scenes in the gloom of winter.

It is New Year's Eve. The church bells are ringing, the sleigh bells are jingling, and the happy children are shouting and singing their joy through the gay streets. New York never saw as merry a New Year's Eve as this. There is fine sleighing, and the fine warm days that we have been having are succeeded by a hard and severe frost. I had been out almost all day, and the keen air had given me a fine glow and a keen appetite, but it was so cold that the frost seemed to take hold of my poor weak lungs at every breath I drew.

For the last week or two I have been taking lessons in navigation at the Nautical Academy, of Professor Vale, who teaches some shorthand and easy methods of working Lunars and Occulations, which I had never learned before, and also gives instruction in the principles and reasons of certain nautical and astronomical phenomena, which however for all practical purposes of navigation might be termed useless, but I am not sure of these superficial skimmers who go no further into the merits of a science than to gain sufficient knowledge for practical purposes.

I often think of the stupidity of the old Dutch captain, who although he knew well enough that the sea ebbs and flows twice in every twenty-four hours could give no other reason for it than the following: "Well, so ish, and it can't be no udder."

We have had several fires here this winter, some of them close to our ship so that we were all ready to "cut and run" several times. Last night as I was taking a walk with my friend Alfred Ridley in search of a barber's shop, a very large warehouse burst out in flames close by us. We were the first on the grounds but paid dearly for our pains. The street was narrow and was soon blocked up by people on either end so that we could not get out. The engines too, began to play their water and from the haste of the firemen and the confusion, the spectators in the street received about as much of it as the burning building. The dense smoke from the burning goods in the store was insufferable, and what with a good smoking and a good drenching and being crowded almost to death, I received my full share of the ills of a New York fire.

I have to visit several fine ships today, all going to California. They are Clippers generally, among which the *Stag Hound, Ino, Witchcraft,* and *Gamecock* may be reckoned the finest. I would not however leave my old palace for any of these new-fangled and swift-footed skimmers.

And now it is almost seven o'clock, I must get ready to go to my favorite church (the Mariners Bethel Ship) in the North River. I have been a pretty constant attendant here for the time I have been in this city, and although the preaching is simple in its meaning and phraseology, yet the word of God is none the less holy because it is not spoken in the costly church, and by the soft spoken hirelings of the congregation.

New York, January 2, 1851.

I have got my life insured. Well! one must not expect from this that I shall never die now, for this is not the object. I feel no stronger nor no healthier since, than I did before and indeed were I to tell the truth I should be obliged to say that day by day I feel myself growing weaker and weaker, and should I not get away from this city and inhospitable shore, ere long, I must fear that I should never leave it at all.

But why did I insure my life? Because gaunt poverty is my present hard lot, and to render safe my friend M.V.L. of whom I had drawn 1,000 dollars, I effected an insurance on my frail earthly existence in the sum of one thousand dollars. I have sent my father the policy, so if I die that no one will lose money by me, while if I live, I trust in God that I shall be able to pay all that I owe.

Had I had, instead of being in debt, several hundred dollars I should have declared to my parents my long attachment to Mary Elliot, and ere this been united to her. Failing in this, had I been able just to pay my debts, I should not of course, have married, but not one word of my poverty should my family ever have heard, and I should have gone forth into the world penniless and destitute and buffeted my way either to independence or the grave. But no, I was hundreds of dollars in debt, and I must tell my father for the purpose of arranging my debts. Oh! heavens, this was a bitter moment, and I shall never forget it.

I have been getting two more daguerreotypes of myself taken for my friends S. W. Kirk and Wm. M. Kirk. They are not so large or so well executed as those I got done in Boston, for my parents and other friends, but they are nevertheless correct, and will serve the purpose intended, my remembrance. I have also procured an Odd Fellows offering for Good Intent Lodge of Ib, OF to present to my old friend Martha Kirk. Mrs. Kirk had taken a great interest in the finishing of the new hall and our Lodge had desired me to procure her some little token of its esteem. I procured her this as the most appropriate memento I could think of, having her name stamped in gold on the back. I have sent them all together in my old black trunk which has seen so much service, to S.W.Kirk, and the key I have sent in a letter. God be with them all.

New York, Jan. 4th, 1851

Who can say that the cigar girl of the Fulton Market is not beautiful. I have just come on board from a walk in the city and I encountered her at the pier. She is free with everybody, and will sometimes talk too free. Her dress is always of beautiful silk, and her jewels are worth hundreds of dollars. She owns several houses of her own in New York and Brooklyn, and by most people is acknowledged to be the prettiest girl in New York. But in spite of all this she still takes delight in selling and giving away her cigars. If you pass her by she will call you back, and if she cannot sell you a shilling's worth, she will be sure to give you a half a dozen. I have been much amused with her lately for having become very well known to her I am the especial mark of her exertions as I go to and return from the ship.

Poor girl! She is a native of Cuba and although education has not shed her beam upon her mind, yet she is nevertheless pure at least from actual vice. God knows how long in this rotten city she will remain so, but still she looks so young, and sweet, and pure that one can hardly help saying, "God Bless Her."

I have had a curious adventure, in buying an article for a certain Secret Society that I belong to, and owing to the nature of the case must be kept from being known. The price of the article at the importers is about $30, and the first place I inquired at they had not got it, but told me to call again, when thinking that I might not be able to find one anywhere else to suit, I told them I would do so. The second place I called at was in the same predicament, and I went through the same form. The third place also had not got the article and I was there too to call the next day. Well, in the afternoon, having heard of a friend where I might find a good assortment, I went, and was surprised to find several gentlemen there, looking at the very same article that I had come in search of. They did not see me until each had bought a ——, when I also asked the dealer for a good ——. One turned around upon me and said: "Why you are the man for whom I have just bought a ——, of Mr. Johnson here." No. 2 spoke up and said I also had engaged a —— at their store this morning, while No. 3 also began to put in his voice in the matter and say that I was the very man for whom he had made his present purchase and that he expected me to take it at the stated cost. Well, I was a little confused as might be supposed, for here it had so happened that each of the men I had called upon in the morning, had on their way from dinner stopped at Mr. Johnson's to order a —— for me, each one supposing that he had a separate customer to supply; in persuance of my usual good luck, happened to fall into the whole of this nest. Each one seemed to think in the end that I ought to take the article I had ordered from himself and in fact I thought so too, but, as that was impossible, I put on a bold face and told them that I did not consider, from the few and indefinite words that passed between us, that I had in any way bound myself, and that to satisfy all I would not take either of the ones I had ordered, but would do as they had done, and patronize Mr. Johnson. This man had been looking on us now from behind his counter with great glee, and now with the very best humor proceded to furnish me with a beautiful article at the wholesale price of $25. I am very sure that it has never occurred before, for Mr. Johnson to sell four in the same day.

I have just paid $35 out of my little stock of money for some necessary operations on my teeth. Really if we do not get to sea before long I shall be penniless.

Jan. 10th, 1851
Well! Although it is late at night, I cannot resist taking advantage of the quietness of the ship and the comfortable fire and light in the cabin to write a little, especially as I have passed through a very laughable scene tonight. For some days my friend Alf had been bothered by a fellow by the name of Joseph DeSousa to come with him to his house and spend the evening. This evening after tea Alf came to me and asked if I would take a walk in the city, and upon assenting, we sallied forth and on the way he explained where he was going. We soon met Joe (he went by the name of Portuguese Joe) who first took us to a house in some out-of-the-way lane, and intro-

duced us to two very neat looking girls. I soon found out however that this was not his house and although the young ladies were agreeable, and entertained us as well as they were able, yet I thought that they certainly were not acquaintances I should like to cultivate.

Alf and I soon intimated to Joe that we would go, and he accordingly left with us. The next place was the second story of a house in a more ambiguous locality still than the first. There we found a young woman and family of small children and one poor pale looking boy who was writing at a table and who seemed about fifteen years old. The woman however was very quiet but seemed well informed but it being rather dull, I soon left and our friend Joe must needs leave with me. I asked him what he meant by taking me into these houses, and he told me that he did it to show us his friends. If they had been gay girls or even of the appearance of courtesans, I should not have wondered so much, but they were all quite respectable people, although quite poor.

I began at length however to distrust my friend Joe, and when we had wound our way a little out of the crowded and awful looking vicinity, I told Alfred that as I did not feel well I should return to the ship, but that I would not take him away.

I left these two together feeling quite sure that they would get into some scrape before long especially as Joe was already half drunk.

Well, I wandered along slowly towards Wall Street, every now and then passing the door of some underground brothel, whence issued the noise of wild mirth and revelry and in the intervals of gloom in the badly lighted streets, I stumbled frequently upon groups of half drunken sailors or noisy females, whose rude salutations grated harshly on the ear of refinement and modesty. When I arrived in Wall Street it was yet early and I thought I would take a turn up Broadway and back just for a walk, but when in Broadway, I recollected that I wanted some dungaree and thread, so off I put, down towards the North River, and into Greenwich Street. There I soon got what I wanted and indeed rather more, for the fellow persuaded me to take a whole piece of blue dungaree saying that if I did not want it I was sure to find someone on board that did, so I bought about fourty-five yards at fifteen cents a yard, and a pound of patent thread, some needles, scissors, etc. etc. These things made quite a load but just as I was going, the jolly dutchman, who had set before me some excellent rose cordial, thought that I ought to take a little to sea with me, just to take off the edge of the keen norwesters that we should experience for a few days. But I told him that I did not drink much, and besides I could carry no more to the ship. But—"Oh! bless your soul," said he, "my boy will carry it for you." So I thought I would just get a gallon of his excellent cordial, and then away I went. Crossing Broadway again I met a friend, and nothing would do but I must go to Frenches and take lunch, and so off I started again, making my boy follow, for I did not dare trust him to the ship himself.

We had hardly got set down and warmed by the great stove, when who should come in but my friend Alf with Joe, and two others whom they had picked up. I wished to remain unobserved by them, so drawing our curtains we could hear all that passed and not be seen. They entered the next recess to us and I soon found out that all hands were comfortably drunk, and that poor Alf was paymaster general, I knew that before I should see him aboard, that all the money he had with him should find its way to the tills of the publicans or into the pockets of some miserable wretches in South Street, but I would not now interfere in so select a party. I was only amused by their conversation, part of which referred to our adventures earlier in the evening, and the rest to the laughable scene they had just passed through. I laughed till I was obliged to leave the place, and bidding good night to my friend I sought my ship.

I am afraid my poor little boy will be given up for lost or at least be shut out of his home, for I had forgotten all about him while I was at Frenches, and now it is just one o'clock. Whew, I must turn in.

New York, Jan. 19th, 1851
I have been assisting in rigging the ship for sea. Poor Alf is penniless so that his evenings are dull enough. It appears that

he spent the whole of his last $20 goldpiece the night we were
out together about a week ago, and besides that he received
a present from the fair ladies of South St. by general contribution I rather think, that will amuse him for some time to
come. Our poor old carpenter who has been working aboard
since I have joined the ship, was yesterday discharged and he
is now ranging the streets without money, clothes, or a chance
of work. So much for a kind, honest, foolish Jack Tar. I gave
him a dollar to get something to eat and told him that if he
would come to me this evening or after he had got a ship I
would give him some clothes.

The Packet ship *Southampton* from London has just
arrived in twenty-eight days from Gravesend. One of the
young officers was aboard yesterday to see Alf. His name is
Dunbar Moodie, and he is from the same town in Canada as
my friend. He says they have had very rough weather this
last passage and the captain, a young man, has almost knocked
the ship to pieces [by] carrying [full sail.] I noticed myself that
their figurehead was carried away and that her cutwater was
fairly knocked to one side.

Oh! how I long to leave this horrid place. But the cold
is yet intense and every day I see the ships coming into port,
so encrusted with ice that one can hardly make out what they
are. They look like vast bodies of white ice with the masts of
the ship stuck into them. The poor sailors, too, have their
fingers and their face all frozen, and are nearly dead when
they arrive. It is an awful winter and I dread our adventure
into the wild sea, yet I pray for its speedy occurrence.

New York, Jan. 31st, 1851
It is night, and thank God it is the eve of our departure.
Everything is on board, our pilot is engaged and we sail
tomorrow morning. It is most intensely cold, the thermometer
is below zero and we are obliged to keep one hand going
constantly the rounds of the deck and churning the water
casks with a stick through the bunghole, to prevent them
freezing solid and bursting. This operation keeps a vent open
at the bung so the water may escape as the inside of the cask
becomes thicker and thicker with ice. We are losing a great

18

deal of water but it can't be helped and we have no more time to get a fresh supply. We have changed our berth, having hauled out to the end of pier 11 early this morning.

Our steward, a quadroon of the West Indies has prevailed upon Captain B. to allow him to take what he calls his wife along to act as stewardess and wait upon the ladies. I think upon the whole that it is a long-headed arrangement of his for the girl is a Creole and is very pretty, but as for being his wife, I myself am not a martinet although Mrs. Burleigh thinks it is all gospel.

We had some difficulty in getting her on board this morning as the ship had altered her berth before she came down. However the lifting etc. gave some of our young men an opportunity to show their gallantry.

We have to all appearances an excellent crew. They are strong and young men, but are all on their last spree tonight as it is altogether useless to carry any money to sea with them since we are going directly to the land of gold. Poor Jack! If your life is a hard one and a short one you are determined to make it a merry one.

For my own part I have taken my last walk in New York, and have bidden the bright and gay scenes farewell for years, perhaps forever.

I have been here now more than seven weeks, a time vastly longer that I had ever expected when I arrived, and had I any idea of it I should have at once gone home again. But Mailler and Son have been saying that "a few days more, next week, next Saturday," etc. etc. ever since the ship came round and I have thus been hoaxed into spending near two months in waiting for my ship to sail, even within a hundred miles from home.

But I am glad that my parents think that I am on the sea, for they would worry, did they know that I was here yet. And they would grieve much more did they know what a poor weak skeleton I have become and what a hollow cough racks my frame from morning till night and from night until morning. I really fear that I shall only leave my native land to find a grave in the wide and lonely ocean.

I wish very much to hear a last word from them before I leave in all probability forever, but I will not break their happy delusion by writing now.

Day before yesterday, Mailler and Son came on board the ship to me, and shaking me by the hand, offered their congratulations upon my being appointed Consul to Bombay by the President. I must confess I was a little pleased, for I had not been certain that I should receive the appointment, and if it never did me any good at all, still the honor of the thing was something, especially for a stranger in a strange place, as I should be in Bombay. I have received, too, a letter from my dear Mary who has sailed for England on the steamer *Baltic*. God bless her and temper the waves of the sea and the rude touch of the world to her delicate frame.

Ship *Delia Maria,* Sandy Hook
February 1, 1851

We left New York this morning in tow of the little steam tug *Pilot,* and arrived off the anchorage about one o'clock p.m. but there was no wind and we were obliged to come to anchor here, until we get it. There is now however a S.E. on but this is directly ahead and there is no use going to sea with a head wind. The pilot is yet on board, and of course will remain there till we get fairly to sea, when he will be taken off by one of the numerous pilot schooners that are constantly cruising off Sandy Hook.

A few days ago, Mailler and Son, received a letter from my father inquiring what were their agents in San Francisco so that he might forward to me there some letters he had received. They showed it to me, and I dictated an answer that would not lead them to suppose that I was still here.

Again last Thursday I sent my trunk home in a manner that would deceive them. I thought that my trunk which is a superior and costly one would get moulded and rotten by a sea voyage, and as it did not fit in my stateroom as well as a common sea chest, I determined to send it home, for my father and procure a chest. Well I got my friend Alf to write a letter, purporting to come from a gentleman from New York to whom I had given it in charge when I sailed but who had neglected to send it before. I hope the deception will answer the innocent purpose for which it is intended.

Ship *Delia Maria* at Sea
February 11th, 1851
Lat 22 N. Lon 35 W.

We are in the midst of the Atlantic ocean more than a thousand miles from any land, and outside the Gulf Stream. Thank heaven we are yet alive, for we have had very tempestuous weather since we have been out and sometimes very hard work. I should not much like the idea of keeping away to the northward again as in going to England, for it has been one of the hardest winters on the Atlantic for many years. We have reason however to thank providence, for all the winds have been favorable and although wild and furious we have kept on our way unharmed, except by the loss of a few light spars. What with assisting with reefing and steering and in working at the pumps I have been busy and hard at work, and have got as lean as a cat, but at the same time a great deal tougher and stronger than when I left. The ladies have been sick ever since we have been out, and Miss Sullivan has only been on deck for a few minutes one moderate morning, but the waves ran so high and the ship rocked so much as if it were going to plunge into the dark depths of the mad waters that she was so frightened that she went below and has not been out of her bed since.

Our poor steward who has served us so faithfully and who had made so many arrangements of his own for the voyage, was consigned to a sailor's grave yesterday morning. He was a clever fellow, and was liked by everybody on board. The sickness lasted but three days when he was gathered to his last rest. I had attended him faithfully from the first but every remedy proved of no avail. It was an inflamation of the stomach caused by drinking brandy and getting wet in the terrible storms we have had, and no wonder, for many times we have been up all night and day in the cold and furious blast. The inflamation passed into mortification and he became delirious. From ten o'clock night before last till three yesterday morning, I never saw such an awful sight or heard such wild imprecations. At these, he threw himself out of his berth, and before I could take hold of him, a tremendous roll of the ship pitched him through the stateroom door and through the cabin and when I went with one of the men to put him in his hammock, he was just breathing his last. The last effort of a delirious mind had broken the slender thread of life and he died.

The men sewed him up in his hammock and lashed him to the booby hatch until all hands were called, when he was carried to the gangway and after the funeral service was read his body, yet warm, and unstiffened, was launched into the sea. A plunge and a gurgle and the body plunged into the coral depths of the mariners' grave.

It was a solemn scene, that little body of shipmates collected just at the grey dawn of morning to pay the last tribute of respect to one of their number. The stormy winds were howling over the sea and howling among the rigging and masts of the laboring ship. The huge waves were constantly breaking over our bows, and tossing their spray far above the lower yards, and we were obliged to hold to the ropes while the service was said which it was almost impossible to hear. We had collected to commit one of our members to the deep, but we knew not at what hour our own wholesale destruction might not take place.

But it is all over now and we are in milder weather. The air is getting warmer and our trousers and jackets with which we endeavored to defend ourselves from the snow and hail and sleet of the latitude of 40 are in this one of 22 getting too heavy, even at night. I hope we have no other stormy weather.

Ship *Delia Maria* at Sea,
Feb. 16th
Lat 10 1 N. Lon 25 16 W.
Sunday evening. I am sitting under the shade of the sails for the western sun is yet warm and bright. It will soon be sunset, and already the sea has begun to dress in the evening glows.

We have been running down the North East Trades for six days, but as we approach the line, the wind, heretofore strong and fresh is diminishing in strength, and the weather is becoming stronger every day. Our time passes very quickly. The ladies have got over their sickness, and we form a very pleasant party beneath the awnings. There are no more storms, no rain, no hail and snow, and the sea, which but a few days ago, was dark and wild and fearful to look upon, is now tranquil and smiling.

We read or converse during the day, and in the balmy evenings dance on the quarter deck, sing songs, listen to Mr. Bishop's accordion, or play at cards in the cabin. Last evening we were dancing, Capt. Burleigh, Mr. Bishop, Mr. St. Julien, (a passenger) and myself, and Mrs. B. and Miss Gillman. I have in a great measure regained my usual health, my cough is almost gone, and I feel new strength, new vigor, and new life flowing into my veins every day.

We are not far from the coast of Africa, and I can almost fancy that the air contains a scent of its spicy plains. The sea is covered by marine plants and weeds that have been washed from its rocky islands and birds from the land sail round our ship, rest their weary wings awhile, then fly away toward the rising sun. The waters are sparkling with the tribes of the deep. The seaweed attracts these scaly dabblers and we can count hundreds of dolphin, baneta, skipjacks, porpoise, flying fish, and many others we do not know.

Tuesday, 18th February-51
Lat. 3 20 N. Lon. 24 40 W.

This has been a very warm day indeed. The sea has been a perfect sheet of glass or molten silver and not a ripple to break its surface, not a breath of a breeze to cool the feverish brow or regale the oppressed, has moved in all the long day. Now the tropical sun of the Equator is pouring his fierce beams down upon our heads and broiling the pitch out of our sides and the turpentine out of our decks. Our men have been engaged in setting up the standing rigging, and they are as black as coal heaves with the tar which has fried out of the ropes.

We are but one good day's sail from the line, yet we shall probably be a week in making it, as in the interval between the trades there is nothing but thunder squalls.

We have all got our harpoons and other fishing tackle in readiness now, but the fish seem to be aware of our intentions upon them, for they are now shy and scarce. A shark is playing about under the ship's bottom and a flock of flying fish are skipping and glancing about in the setting sun, but no

23

chance can we get to entrap any of the finny tribes which were erewhile so tame. The setting sun has coaxed a gentle breeze to spring up and it is now rippling the blue sea and sighing through the sails and rigging.

The first sail we have seen since we have been out was this morning, but it was so far off that we could not make it out. There are now however an English ship and a Norwegian one directly ahead of us and not more than twelve miles distant. We shall speak to them in the night if the wind continues the way it is.

The twilight in these latitudes is so short, that it is only at best a shadowy transition from broad day to deep night. When the sun sets, darkness falls upon the face of the waters in a few minutes, we have some of that lingering light in the western sky to which we look with so much pleasure in a temperate region, but the sun sinking perpendicularly down is soon so far below the horizon that the darkness of night might be said to suddenly extinguish the light of day. It is the same way in the morning. The eastern sky is scarcely tinged with red, and the horizon is hardly marked by the early dawn before the glorious orb is peeping above it, as if to surprise the sleeping world, in bed.

Feb. 20th, 1851
Lat 3 2 S. Lon. 25 30 W.

We have crossed the great equatorial line of the earth, and are now in the southern hemisphere of our globe. I am realizing the early dream of my childhood, the dream of my waking and sleeping hours, that I should visit every quarter of the world, roam over every ocean and press with my foot the soil of every land. We have been fortunate in meeting with fair winds and fine weather for the last two days, for it is very unusual that the mariner encounters between the latitude of 4 South and 4 North anything but calms and catspaws.

This morning having come on deck to enjoy as much of the freshness of the day as possible, I discovered on the southern seaboard a small white speck, no longer than the wing of a gull. I soon discovered it by means of the telescope to be a sail standing towards us. When the captain came on deck, he ordered that the ship be close hauled, and by nine o'clock we had come abreast of her. Our boat was lowered, and as I had scribbled a few lines to send home I got into the boat with Mr. Bishop and in a few minutes was upon the strangers' decks. She was the *Lady Saunders* of London, Capt. Beaumont, a neat tidy craft and a gentleman commander. We spent half an hour in conversation, entrusted our letters to him, and as the *Delia* had already placed several miles of water between us, we were obliged to say goodbye, and leave. We had a long pull to reach the ship which had hove to for us.

I had forgotten to say that the barque was from Columbio, in the Island of Ceylon, laden with pepper and sugar and bound home. It will be a long while ere my hasty missive reaches its destination, but it will however, if no accident occurs, be the first that my parents hear from me since leaving New York. I will write again from St. Catherine where we are going to stop for water.

Evening

Oh! Murder! How hot it is, I am sitting under the foresail which like a great fan is swaying about, in the calm, and driving a little air to my nostrils, but it is still insufferably warm. I have on scarcely enough clothes to cover my body, but it is like an oven yet. Yesterday afternoon it was quite cool and the sky was overcast with clouds, but at night they swept away and the evening sunset was as bright and fiery and peculiar as ever. God, send us wind.

March 1st, 1851
Lat. s 20 South Lon 25 23 W.

Blow ye winds O! blow. Blow good breezes, blow. Here we have been six blessed days without change giving our position a single degree, and God only knows when we will out of these longitudes. Yesterday it rained all the morning, and until about 2 p.m. yes, it rained, but, my eyes! I never saw water poured down before in that manner and be called rain. I should have supposed that the clerk of the weather had forgotten his function, and left the bung itself out, or else had capsized the whole affair altogether, for the water did not come down in drops, or streams, or bucketfuls, but it came down in torrents, such as it only rains between the Trades. Some idea may form as to the quantity of water fallen, when it is known that in the space of two hours our men caught and saved nearly a thousand gallons of clean pure rain water off the house deck, which is only eighteen by twenty-three feet. We were out in it all the time, and as there was no wind, we had nothing to do, but enjoy a good fresh-water wash, a luxury, by the by, which does not usually occur on a long voyage of many months. We stripped off, lathered ourselves from head to foot with soap and washed off the debris of a month's collection in a very few minutes. After we had put on our drawers, we challenged the ladies to come out and have a game of heaving water with us. They would not however, and so we commenced drenching each other with bucketfuls of water dipped from the main deck which was knee deep.

Well, we have no need to stop anywhere for water now, for we have enough to last to San Francisco even if we do not get another drop.

The sailors too had a regular frolic during the rain and had a regular go-ashore wash, as they say, and indeed they look much the cleaner for it today. A good smart shower is sometimes a blessing to poor Jack, who always improves the occasion, to have a clean wash and shower and shave, and to put all his dirty clothes in soak in a barrel or bucket. Poor Jack!

It is now 8 a.m. of the first day of March. The sky looks fiery and red and the sun looks like a huge globe of molten copper, suspended directly above our heads. In the morning he rises hissing and boiling from the sea, through the day he scorches every vaporing cloud from his track, and in the evening he kindles a fierce conflagration in the western sky, the funeral pile of his departing glory. A hurricane, a tempest, a typhoon, would be preferable to this intolerable, motionless, burning Sirocco, which scorches us up, like shorn grass in the noon-day sun. The evenings and mornings are the only tolerable portions of the day, and we improve them with all the pastimes with which we are conversant. Indeed, our chief care seems to be now how to keep cool by day, and how to enjoy ourselves by night, and in the latter particularly one might judge of our success by the merry laugh, the glad music and the joyous song, which breaks the deep solitude of the nights, and disturbs the slumber of the sea nymphs upon their cradling pillows. When we retire to rest, which is not generally till past midnight, each one seeks a soft place on deck, places a stray coil of rope under his head for a pillow, and with naught but a moonbeam for covering, he sleeps as sweet as the sea maid herself. The ladies of course are excepted in this group, but they nevertheless make themselves as comfortable as possible, and a few mornings ago I wandered into their cabin a little earlier than common (quite thoughtlessly) and oh! what a sight of sleeping innocence and unstudied attitude. I tried to retreat unseen, but Mrs. B's quick ear caught the sound and then, whew! what a scattering and screaming. Mrs. B says I shall not expose them, but Miss Gilman has seen my papers, and it is all up with me now, far as peace and quietness goes.

Well I am rapidly improving my health, and what with warm weather, warm friends, plenty of good exercise and sea air, together with sleeping on deck myself, and laughing until I cannot stand, with the women, in their dishabille, doing the same, I think I shall soon be a second Sampson.

This morning I fished up a sun-squall in a bucket, and was much amused with it. They are a species of the Mucosae and without knowing them to posess animal life one would think them nothing more than a mere mass of soft clear brown jelly. But touch this dead inert mass, and if it does not look very formidable it will be found a most potent agent of pain and suffering. The part becomes inflamed and feels as though a thousand needles were eating their way into the bone; the effect is somewhat similar to the stinging nettles of marshes and swamps. These animals are from the size of a pea up to that of a hogshead.

The sea here seems strangely destitute of fish. I have not seen a fin for a week, and we are all becoming quite fish hungry again. I suppose they have given us up as a hopeless case and have gone to search for some other vessel so fortunate as to have a wind.

The gulls too, with the exception of an occasional Mother Carey's chicken are all gone. They have gone in search of wind also, I suppose, and I wish heartily they had taken me along.

Captain Burleigh has a novel idea of electricity in his head, if one may judge by the means he has employed to protect the ship from lightning. He has had a wooden staff seized on each royal masthead, with a tapering end, so that it will enter the mouth of an inverted bottle, which is stuck on each one. The staff projects about six inches above the trunk and the whole concern looks more like boys' play than anything reasonable.

Indeed, even the captain can not explain the manner in which they are supposed to be of use, all he knows is that they have been recommended by a friend of his, and that in the absence of the conductors he will try them. Try them, indeed! I hope we shall not be so fortunate, or unfortunate rather as to have an opportunity of testing their efficiency. They appear to me to be a sign that says as plainly as it can speak, "not another drop in the jug."

Sunday March 2nd, 1851
Lat. 30 N. Lon. 25 12 W

What a delightful morning! The power of the sun is diminished by a broad curtain of haze in the sky, and a gentle, westerly breeze just ripples the water. In spite of our slow progress we enjoy ourselves and do not often complain. It will be seen from our position today that we have again crossed the line to the northward. This of course was quite against our wishes but we have been so unfortunate as to get into a stormy N.W. current and it has been so calm for a few days that we have been helpless as a log. We are now within one-hundred and fifty miles of the island of St. Pauls and may perchance seek that land if the wind does not favor us. We have occasionally much fun with our pigs. They are turned loose every morning, when after sunning about the decks all day and making a great deal of dirt and bother they are caught at night and put back again in their pens. All hands are required for this and it is amusing to see the frolic of the sailors in the chase. Away they go, around the decks, and under the spars, shouting and laughing, and sometimes half a dozen of them tumbling down among the pigs, and sometimes struggling singly with a resolute porker. Nothing the sailors like better than their daily pig chase. We have lost three pigs overboard and about eight chickens, and if the captain turns the chickens out on deck, as he purposes, I think he will lose a few more. There is a ship and a barque in sight, but so far off that we cannot make them out very well. I think from the appearance of the barque that she is French.

Wednesday, March 5th 1851
Lat. 32 N. Lon 26 10 W.

We are yet to the northward of the line but we have got out of the adverse current, and have now a very good prospect of getting again to the south. We have a constant succession of scorching heat, deluges of rain, and provoking catspaws. The currents have set in far to the northward, but we have been drawing a little also to the westward and have now caught the rascal we have been looking for for so many days. I mean the southeast trade wind. We shall cross the line for the third time this afternoon. And should it please God I shall not again see the North Atlantic for a long, long time.

We have had quite a row in the ship this morning. Since the steward died, the woman who came on board as his wife, and who was to wait upon the ladies, has carried rather a high hand. The mate, and the second mate have already had quite a few disputes on her account; and she has assumed so much dignity and had abused her post as stewardess so much to the crew, that she has been called by them a perfect hell-cat. Four successive men have undertaken to do the cooking for the ship, and they have each been obliged to give it up on her account. This morning the fourth one left the galley and swore that he would starve rather than cook, and at the same time act as her servant and dishwasher. This infernal woman has caused ill feeling fore and aft and I heartily wish she was at the bottom of the sea, or in some other warm place of worship. Bill Chapin, a young man-of-wars-man has undertaken the galley now, and as he has been quite a favorite with the stewardess, I hope we shall get along better.

Yesterday I went to have a look around, and I counted nine sail of vessel in sight. Some of these were off two or three miles, and others just in sight on the horizon. This morning however there is not a yard of canvas in sight except that which hangs from our own yards. Some of the old sailors say, that they have seen as many as thirty sail of ships in the sea at one time. The reason for this is that all the vessels that cross the line either north or south, must be detoured here for a long while and like driftwood in the eddies of a swollen river, they float about in great numbers until they either catch the southern or northern trade winds and go off to give room for others. We have been constantly followed by a huge shark for nearly a week, and the superstition of some of the tars must needs have it that someone must be a victim to his maw before he leaves us. I hope not, but still there is a probability of it, for one of our poor fellows has been very sick for a long time and in spite of everything I can do, he seems sinking daily. He is a Prussian named Charles Miller, and his disease is inflammation of the liver and lungs. I hope we shall soon be into cooler weather where he will have a better chance, otherwise he must sink under his disease and in reality become a prey to the monsters of the deep like our poor old steward.

A few hours ago, one of the men was fishing from the jib boom when Mr. Shark made his appearance and snapping at the white rag on the hook carried hook, line and all away. In ten minutes he was back again without the line, (I suppose he had chewed it off) when the cook heaved the dolphin grains into him, but it made a plunge and tore them out again. Bad luck to him. I wish he was at the devil, or somewhere else, for I like not his company.

Sunday Afternoon, March 9th 1851
Lat 8 40 S. Lon 27 20 W.

Huzza! for Cape Horn! Our good ship is driving the foam from her bows in thundering cateracts, to the impulse of the fresh South East Wind, and we have left for good the burning heat of the equatorial calms. I am sitting under the quarter deck awning writing at intervals upon the top of the skylight, and at intervals enjoying the refreshing breeze. Oh! how delightful is this cool wind, after being broiled for so long under the fierce heat of the line. Everything is set alow and aloft that will draw, and everything bears a heavy strain.

Plunge on you noble courser, and bear us speedily to the regions of southern winter.

We have not been favored by a visit from Neptune in crossing the line, which by the way is rather strange, since this is the first time the ship has ever been in the south seas; many hints were thrown out while upon the line, about having the ship shaved, but the captain did not, or would not take with the fun, so poor Jack has missed his frolic and his grog.

Yesterday in the afternoon we made a sail, astern, bearing right down upon us, upon the same tack and going the same course. She was a fast sailor, and overhauled us fast, but night set in before we made her out. During the night we kept a strict lookout but somehow we lost her in the darkness and this morning at daylight there was nothing in sight, from the royal yard. She must have altered her course several points, or else have been the flying dutchman. I suppose her to have been a Brazilian slaver, and consequently anxious to avoid company.

We are off Pernambuco, and if we are lucky it will not be later than the middle of June when we reach San Francisco. Go it old boat, and stave in your bows if you will, but do not be longer than three months in giving us a sight of California.

March 11th 1851
Lat 12 18 S Lon 31 4 W

Just through another tremendous gale of wind. We have been driven by an awful storm for twenty hours and our poor ship has groaned in the agony. But it is over now, with no other loss than a few spars and with the sunshine and the breeze, all is again forgotten.

March 12 [1851]
Lat 13 15 S. Lon 32 W

The morning has been showery, and the sun breaking out at intervals has been most oppressively hot. Everything has looked (as much as a sea landscape can beseem a rural one) like a sultry morning in the dog days of Pennsylvania, only a great deal warmer. One can almost fancy that he smells the

31

perfume of the summer flowers, or that of the ripe grain fields in every hot breath of the wind.

Mr. St. Julien has just gone aloft with a spyglass to see if he can't make out Sandy Hook lighthouse and the hills of Long Island, and I should not wonder if he does because he is gifted with the most extraordinary obliquity of vision I have ever seen, and a squint around Cape Horn or over the Rocky Mountains would be no very wonderful feat for him. Mr. St. Julien is a great man in his way, and he is the jester in our party, or rather the subject of our jokes. He can only spit clear of his chin, and even then he must make a considerable effort, for all he is thirty years old, and notwithstanding the generality of the Jews are so wide awake, yet it takes Mr. St. Julien (who is by the way a Jew) quite two hours to get his eyes wide open in the mornings. But Mr. St. Julien is rich, (no great wonder) and he is a great favorite with the ladies because of his droll and comic speeches, and then too he is liberal which is a great treat for all of us. Many a good bottle of Medoc and Sillery have Mr. Bishop and myself drained for him, and yet his stock is never exhausted, and he has almost twenty thousand cigars yet left of the choicest flavors, most of which he expected to have smoked on the passage, so it will be seen that Mr. St. Julien is a very necessary man to one's amusement and comfort on this long voyage.

I was much amused at him the other evening, during the second day watch, endeavoring to find the North Star, which of course has been behind the horizon ever since the Latitude of 9 N. We at length showed him the great Southern Cross, and told him that it was now our only star. He has just now come down from aloft with his glass saying that he can not see Sandy Hook.

No, I guess it is now as hard to see as the North Star.

And now it is evening again, the sun is just sinking behind the western waves, while the whole vault of heaven is lit up with a crimson glow, like a vast conflagration. The deep blue sky has been so clear that the brighter stars have been visible all day long, and now a few fleecy clouds have floated over with the wind and are lying low in the western seaboard like the variegated touches of a spiritual pencil upon that vast blue field.

We have had showers all the afternoon, and the air is now most refreshingly cool and exhilarating. We have nothing to do but read and write, talk and sing, watch the evolutions of the tiny nautilus or listen to the music of the sighing winds.

But one question is forever rising up in my mind that prevents entire contentment. How are all at home? Mr. Bishop had just commenced playing our favorite air "Sweet Home," and as it is too dark to write any longer, I will lay by my pen, and gaze upon the rising moon, think of my own sweet home and its beloved inmates.

March 15th 1851
Lat 17 30 S. Lon 34 W.

What medicine is so potent to the broken constitution and the weary spirit as the change of climate, freedom from care, and entertainment and excitement of the mind. I am surprised myself at the rapid recovery I have experienced from almost hopeless disease. I am now healthy, hearty and strong and I can without uttering a falsehood say that "I am well in health and happy in mind." I have never been in any situation where all my tastes and fancies were so well suited as here.

Last evening, I came near catching a nautilus, which had shaped his devious course directly alongside of us, but he was too slippery for me, and away he went dancing over the blue waters, towards the setting sun looking more like a creation of fairyland than a real terrestrial inhabitant.

The morning is fresh and fair, and the ship is running smoothly along before the gentle northerly wind. By day the awnings protect us from the sun and we pass the hours in uninterrupted reading etc., by night the full tropical moon sheds her silver light over the waters illuminating the ship and the sea with glorious brightness in which we dance or play or sail and gaze silently upon the majestic scene.

Sleep is quite a secondary consideration with us; I have not slept below for nearly a month, but take the open deck for it, where the free air may not be wanting and the planks give to the frame that elasticity and lightness that is never derived from the couch of down, and pillow of luxury. If it rains, I remain awake until it stops, for the loss of sleep is nothing here, where the night and day is all the same.

This morning I went overboard altogether and had a regular swimming bath. I had made fast a rope to the lower part of the martingale, and took several knots in it so that I might hold on the better and haul myself up by it.

Well I got a regular keelhauling for my pains, for the ship was lifting and pitching, so that before I could get fixed for a swim I was plunged under and jerked out of the water several times, that I was glad to cry quits and come on board again. I had like to get adrift altogether for a light breeze had filled the sails and our fleet ship was dragging me through the water at a great rate. At all events I am the first "man overboard" on the ship, and am likely to be the last, for nobody else will venture unless they tumble against their will.

There are two sails in sight, one on our weather beam standing north, and the other on our larboard quarter standing across our wake, so that we cannot speak either of them; I should be glad to have another opportunity of sending a letter home.

March 16th

It is five bells in the mid-watch and I have just been on deck writing these observations by the moon above.

Mr. Bishop has gone below, and all is still as death save the heavy tramp of Mr. Bishop as he paces the quarter-deck. The sky, since the sunset, has been perfectly cloudless and notwithstanding the brightness of the moon, is a perfect starry arch.

The mild air is so clear and pure, that one cannot help drawing deep breaths, in pure gratification of the senses alone. I have no other clothing but a cotton shirt and pants, and am very warm. There is no dampness in the night air here.

Last evening the captain's hat went overboard in a scuffle with the ladies, and as it was a fine "Panama" he did not like to lose it. He told the man at the wheel that if he would get it, he would pay him for it, but the fellow could not swim. Little Jack however, who was fast coming down the mizzen shrouds, no sooner saw the accident than he jumped first from the ratlines on the deck, and then the taffrail into the sea. He soon had the hat, but by this time he was far astern. The helm was put down, the ship luffed into the wind, her headway stopped, and Jack soon reached the rope which was thrown for him with the hat safely in his mouth. He had not been on deck five minutes before the huge shark which had been following us for so long, but which we had not seen for four or five days, came swimming about under the counter. He was evidently in quest of little Jack, who however had been smart enough to get on board before the monster smelt him. I have no doubts too, that he was not far off when I was in the water early in the morning, and had it been calm so that I had let go my rope, and swam round a while, I am sure that I should not now be writing here.

But we need not fear that monster anymore. The large harpoon was handy, and Capt. B. snatching it up we bent a pair of top-gallant-studding-sail-halyards to it up to the eye in the back of the shark. The mate got a turn with the line around the timber heads so that he could hold him, and sung out for all hands. All hands came, but they had their hands full in getting the monster on board, and when he was on board no one could go near him so wildly did he throw himself about and bite with his huge jaws everything he could snap at. He would have taken a man's leg off at one bite, so everybody was willing to stand clear of him until his death agony was over. But he had a life like a cat, and seeing no prospect of his dying, we dragged him down on the main deck by the harpoon line, which was still fast. There one of the men succeeded in spearing him in the spine, when the savage brute stretched out dead enough.

He was about ten feet long and his mouth would have conveniently taken in the body of a man; one of the men is preparing his jaw to clean, and I will obtain it for a curiosity if I can, or rather as a memorial of the monster to whose jaws I was so near a victim.

Good night, I think I can go to sleep now. At all events I will try.

Sunday Evening 16th March-51
Lat 18 S. 34 22 W.

The ship lies on the water as motionless as a log, except when lifted and pitched by a long and regular swell from the southward, which denotes a coming gale of wind. It is observed that the swell precedes a storm by many leagues, and this one is now becoming more and more heavy, and the sky is assuming a heavy laden appearance.

We are near the Brazilian coast and within a day's sail of Rio Janiero, but the adverse and calm weather might make it a week before we can reach that port. But we have caught so much water at different times that our casks are full, and we do not wish to touch either at Rio or St. Catherine.

There is a long, low, black brigantine, lying about ten miles to the northward of us, and notwithstanding it is a perfect calm, she has been moving at the rate of two knots, towards San Salvador since daylight. She is no doubt a slaver from her very look, and her motion may easily be accounted for when we recollect that these vessels in time of danger employ sweeps to propel their vessel, worked by the miserable captives on board. She is now no doubt urged forward by a double bank of oars or sweeps on the side opposite to us, because her commander is suspicious of our size and warlike appearance that we are a cruiser. We have been talking of going on board in our boats but the day is so hot that the men could hardly stand it to pull eight or ten miles in the hot sun, and back again. So we will let them go, especially as I don't think we should receive a very hearty welcome.

Thursday morning, 17th March
Lat 18 5 S. Lon. 34 24 W.

Another calm and hot morning. The sea is as red as a brick towards the surrounding horizon, although blue as ether directly under the eye. This is owing to the reflections of the burning heavens upon the surface of the dead and placid waters. The thermometer now stands at 92 and before two p.m. if the sky does not become overcast it will stand at one hundred.

Last night was, literally speaking, as light as day, and its tranquillness was only varied by an occasional catspaw which would ripple the water for a few minutes and then die away again as calm as before. At eleven o'clock, as the men were hauling upon the starboard main brace, they saw a shark directly under the counter. None of us had secured [any weapons] and the captain was on the taffrail in a moment with harpoon in hand. But the shark, having gazed upon us for a few minutes in the pale moonlight, returned again to his usual haunt under the ship's bottom, where he will probably stay till he gets his fill, in some way or another. The superstitious sailors shake their heads and declare that some one of us is a doomed man and must ere that rapacious monster leaves the ship, fall a victim to his jaws. Who will it be.

Wednesday, 19th March 1851
Lat 18 19 S. Lon 34 30 W.

Half an hour ago, a smart squall struck us aback and had like to have whipped the sticks out of us, but it has nevertheless been a great blessing for it has brought down with it the regular trades once more, which have been for the last few days, roaming about. God knows where! But now we are running away with a bouncing free wind upon our beam, and should it hold, we shall soon place many a mile of blue water between us and Rio Janeiro, ere another twenty-four hours.

There are two sails astern of us, one of which we are dropping fast but the other, which must be a man of war from her taut masts, square yards and easy sail is overhauling us rapidly. Although she is yet hull down, she will probably be up with us before night and as she is no doubt bound for Rio, I will now write some letters home, in anticipation of her boarding us.

March 21st
Lat 22 50 Lon 34 55 W

We are scudding before a northeasterly gale at the rate of ten knots. I have just come from the wheel, and it is quite as much as one man can do to keep her within two or three points of her course. Two men relieved me, and if I am not mistaken they will find it a ticklish job to keep her at all steady.

Stars alive, how it blew last night. We had everything

37

off of her except her storm sails, and yet she flew through the water like a mad courser. While putting the close reef on the main topsail, we thought we should be blown badly from the yard so powerful was the wind.

I very much fear that poor Charley's days are numbered, he must speedily change for the better or else sink under the malignity of the disease. He was a nice quiet young man and we all liked him very much. We have none too many men either now, for the ship works very heavy when the rigging is all wet, and to be short-handed off the cape is almost to scuttle the ship at once.

We did not speak the ship which was standing down upon us last Wednesday. She came within signal distance however and we made her out to be a Brazilian frigate bound to Rio. We have seen several others coming out and going in, but we have not spoken any of them. Indeed we have been quite fully employed in taking care of ourselves, and as the sky still wears a lurid and threatening appearance, I fear that we have not yet had the worst of the gale.

The sun is just upon the line too, and we may expect rough and tempestuous weather. This morning a large flamingo sailed over the ship towards the westward. He made several circumvolutions as he passed us, apparently surveying us closely, and then struck a bee line for Rio. Mr. St. Julien wished to hoist our colors that he might report us but we were obliged to content ourselves with hailing him and desiring to be reported.

The southern sky is grown wilder and darker every moment, and as we dash onward in our mad career, it seems as if we were rushing into the very battle ground of the elements.

Tuesday Morning, 25th March

Two more days are gone again, and we are four hundred miles nearer Cape Horn. How cheerily sounds the sailor's song this morning.

Blow Ye Morning Breezes
Sing Yo! heave O!

and how delightful fresh feels the air of this bright September day. The wind is off shore, and with it comes the smell of the autumn fruits of the land, and at night the heavy dews of the hill and valley fogs are swept over and upon us like a heavy rain. Although the sky may be perfectly clear and myriads of stars shining in it, yet one cannot stand on deck for half an hour after nightfall, without getting wet to the skin. Consequently our sleeping on deck is over until we have passed the coming winter and are again in the tropics on the mild Pacific. We are fast overhauling a brig ahead of us, and if we pass near enough, the captain will send aboard for fruit, as they are steering from the coast and must have plenty. A few plantains, bananas, and pine-apples would now be a great treat to us.

This fresh wind will soon bring us up with La-Plata that Hatteras of South America, where one can never pass without having the fact forever afterwards well impressed on his memory. I hope I shall not have as fearful acquaintance with this stormy spot, however, as I had six years ago, off Cape Hatteras.

I think I never saw a more perfect scene of lovliness than now greets my vision; it is sunset, and I will readily admit that all the glowing ideas I ever entertained of Italian stars and Indian scenery are far excelled by the South American landscape.

I have just had a long private conversation with Mrs. Burleigh. Poor thing, she sees so little real happiness with her husband, and has also been an almost constant prey to sea sickness. I can no longer disguise the fact that we have a great deal of ill feeling on board, and affairs are daily growing worse. In the first place our stewardess, a beautiful Creole! and as interesting a girl as ever came from the South, has raised the devil between Mr. Bishop and Mr. Bickford so that they have quarreled seriously several times. Now it seems that Captain B. too has so far forgotten himself as to seek her stateroom, during the time that his wife was sick, and Mr. St. Julien had no better sense than to tell Miss Gilman of it, so that it at last reached Mrs. Burleigh's ears. It is obvious that one woman is not enough for Capt. B. but he is to be excused in a great measure as the girl is very insinuating in her dress and seems to take delight in having a multiplicity of admirers. Then, Capt. B. is rather given to drink too much and has on several occasions quite grossly insulted Mr. Julien and Miss Gilman. He also has an impatient fault-finding disposition and is lastly, though not least, very "near" or in plainer words "damned mean" in the pecuniary sense. This last affects all hands alike. We do not get any too good fare and we have not got men enough to work the ship properly, making it very hard for the few we have. The officers are not such philosophers as Job, and they illy bear the tyrany that he seems to exercise. And the men often break out into violent demonstrations of dissatisfaction. They call Capt. B. "the blow hard," "Old Assassinator," "Old Flogag," "Old Horse Jockey," "Typhoon Jack," etc. But enough of this; it is a long day that has no sunset.

Sunday, March 30th 1851
Lat 31 28 Lon. 17 30
It is the Sabbath day once more, and a bright and lovely autumn morning it is. I have just been thinking over those beautiful lines of Bryant,

The morning wind of Autumn,
How it charms the mind!
It has a soft emollient power
Like summer twilight's pensive hour.

and I have felt that power often settle like incense upon my soul, while breathing the fresh air of my own home, as well as the no less pure breezes of the South American coast.

We are running cautiously along on account of shoals laid down on the chart hereabouts, and have hove the lead to the depth of two hundred fathoms without finding bottom. We have been sixty-two days at sea, without a single sight of land.

For the last three days we have suffered another tremendous storm. It commenced on Wednesday evening when we were in full chase of an American vessel which we supposed to be the *Nebraska;* the wind freshened and we commenced shortening sail, then the royals, flying jib, top-gallant-sails, etc. etc.; we had reduced her down to closest reefed main and foresail. This was about twelve o'clock midnight, and from that time to last evening it has blown with all the fury of the elements. We have lost much of the tools etc. that had been stored on deck, the main deck was swept by the enormous seas and everything looked as if we were soon to bid adieu to this life. The ladies, and even Capt. B. have been sea-sick, but we have had our hands full enough to keep away a much worse disease than the sea-sickness. Even Mr. St. Julien who has been to sea often before was obliged to lash himself to the rigging, where having nothing else to do but watch the storm, and the groaning ship, he several times gave up all for lost.

The ship today is filled fore and aft with the wet clothes of the ship's company which were soaked in their trunks and chest in the storm. One not accustomed to the sea life would be amused to see the men, so busily employed in exposing their articles to the sun. An occasional dispute sometimes arises as to the right of ownership to a particular sunny place, but the shifting of the sails or deviation of the ship, soon settles the difficulty by casting the place in the shade so that it is no longer of any account. Sailors are obliged to be their own servants, wash-women, tailors, shoe makers, etc. and it is amusing to see the shifts they make sometimes.

Our men are allowed watch, and watch, so that they all have time to attend to their little matters of repair etc. Their Sundays are spent in lying under the shade of the sails, reading and passing their time in rest, after the fatigues of the past week, and no one has anything to do but the man at the wheel. Some read aloud for the benefit of the others as well as themselves, some take their Bible into a quiet place and read it in silence, while others lie upon their backs telling yarns to one another or cracking jokes. All are cleanly washed, shaved and clad and all enjoy the freedom of the day.

But Monday morning must come again, and poor Jack must lay aside his Sunday togs, daub himself with tar, and go to work sewing, sizing, and serving; pitching, painting, and parceling, patching, pulling and hauling.

Thursday, April 3rd 1851
Lat 37 53 Lon 52 40 W.
Off Cape Lobos, distant one hundred fifty miles. We have left the stormy Rio de La Plata far behind, and although our

autumn weather is beginning to feel a little cool, still it simulates our November weather at home.

I caught a nautilus today with his sails furled, his sweeps hauled in and his little craft made snug altogether. Poor little fellow, this weather is growing too cool for him and instead of lying to in this fair wind he had better be making all sail to the northward.

Saturday, April 5th 1851
Lat 41 70 South Lon 58 30 W.

We are off the coast of Patagonia, and still hold the fair wind which has been steadily wafting us to the southward for the last week, but we are now on an inhospitable and savage shore, the face of nature too has assumed the wildness peculiar to the clime; the sky is leaden and glowing and the waters dark and troubled. The air is yet pleasantly cool, but should the wind haul around to the southward we should soon be shivering in the cold damps of these southern wilds. Truly everything looks as if we were plunging onward into everlasting gloom and darkness.

This morning a large school of porpoises came under our bows, numbering several hundred. Our cook, John Conrad Kouper, ran out upon the martingale with a harpoon, and at the first heave drove it through the body of a large bull. There were but few men upon the line however and the porpoise succeeded in wrenching himself off the iron before he could be got off the water, and started off as fast as he could swim. The whole school followed him and soon put an end to his life by [attacking him] with their sharp noses; it is the habit of these fish to kill any of their number who are so unfortunate as to become injured in any way. Thus it is with everything inhuman as well as human; once become the prey of misfortune and all our fellows and previous friends are at once willing and ready to put the foot of oppression on our necks. After completing their work of death, the porpoises returned to the ship in about half an hour. The cook was again successful in striking one, and this time he was hoisted high and dry before he had time to turn himself in the water. He weighed upwards of two hundred pounds and will feed the ship's company for two or three days.

Great numbers of birds people these waters, and their noises, in calling to each other in the fogs are dismal and startling. The most numerous are the black and white gulls, boatswains, pellicans, goneys, boobies, albatross, and penguins. These last cannot fly, and when once at sea are obliged to buffet the waves as well as the wind. Their cry is loud, plaintive and startling, at times, while at others it is confused and muttering, like a boy endeavoring to shout and sing, with a mouth full of plums or marbles.

I was exceedingly astonished, and then amused yesterday evening by the apparition of one of our men dressed up in a British red coat and a high conical sheepskin hat, wool outside, come aft to the wheel. Of all the ludicrous spectacles I ever saw, this man was the most laughable. His coat which was a splendid one was too short for him, and the little tails hardly covered his posteriorum. The trouser legs were also too short and his legs were thrust through almost to the knees, and his sheepskin cap was the wildest looking thing imaginable. Last, not least, the sober face he wore rendered him an object that rendered the most boisterous laughter.

We are obliged to maneuver in various ways to kill the heavy time, and no landsman can believe to what shifts a sailor can turn himself in an emergency. It is curious to see them mending their shoes, and boots, and cutting out their clothes etc. etc. without rule or tools, and if a sailor can get a few pieces of cloth, no matter how odd the colors, he will turn to and make a very passable cap or waistcoat. They eat, sleep, and wash without any of the conveniences or even necessities of life, and indeed it may be said that the entire life of a sailor is a life of emergencies and his whole occupation is the strife with and shifts to overcome these emergencies. Truly, the sailor is a being different from all his species.

Thursday, 10th April 1851

No observation for two days. The sky has been overcast, and the surface of the ocean shrouded in so dense a fog, that it has been impossible at times to see the end of the ship. But all the time there has been a gentle breeze and this afternoon the fog has lifted entirely and we are thundering onward before a stormy north wind, like a wild thing with everything singing and crackling and a young Niagara under our bows. With the fog has gone the wild fowl, and we are startled no more by the screaming of the gull as he wakes from his billowy cradle or a plunging sea horse rushing away from us as from a devouring monster.

There are two sails in sight, one a brig, hull down on our lee quarter and the other a ship on our weather beam. I hope we shall speak one or the other, because I am exceeding dubious about our longitudes. Capt. B. has been so drunk for the last two or three days, that really I think he has lost all reckoning of the ship, and as he had let the chronometer run down, and was drunk last evening when we set it by a lunar, I cannot depend upon that either. Yesterday afternoon he gave us an exact specimen of the "Coast of Guinea Skipper" or in other words made himself as drunk as a loon. They had been overhauling the ships stores which was stowed in one of the vacant staterooms in the gentlemen's cabin, and he opened a box of gin. This was in the morning, and before noon he was so wild that he knew next to nothing. In coming off the quarter deck, he fell from a water cask on the deck, broke his quadrant, and capsized a barrel of water upon him. With this he rolled down into the lee scuppers where his wife who had been sitting on the after sky-light weeping as if her heart was breaking, went to him, and took him into the cabin. He was not long there before he was out again, singing out to clear up the royals, when they had not been set all day, ordering the helmsman to luff, when the sails were already shaking in the wind, and then the ship was taken aback, and Mr. Bishop was obliged to take the command. Ah! Damnation! I hate a drunken man anywhere, but a drunken captain is more to be feared than to be pitied.

Sunday, 13th April 1851
Lat 46 10 S. 62 55 W.

It is the gloomy evening of a gloomy day. Since Thursday last we have had nothing but a succession of gales dense fogs, and sharp squalls of rain, and during all this I have virtually commanded the ship. Mr. Bishop who has been ill at times, ever since we have been out, so that either the carpenter who is a tolerable sailor, but no navigator, or myself have been obliged to keep his watch, was again day before yesterday confined to his bed with a violent inflammatory rheumatism and fever, and it appears that the captain must have hurt himself seriously last Wednesday afternoon, for since Thursday morning he has not been able to sit up in his berth, much less to come on deck. I suppose he has given his back a severe wrench, for it is that of which he most complains, being unable to turn himself and roaring like a lion's cage with the pain, at every pitch of the ship, and now what would become of us did I not fortunately possess a good knowledge of navigation. Neither the second mate nor any of the other sailors are able to take a simple meridian altitude of the sun, or to work the chronometers. Mr. Bickford and the carpenter might be able to keep the ship a given course, by her sails, but who is to give that course, and who is to keep her position amid all these fierce gales, and powerful currents. Truly we are now in danger, and although I have ample confidence in my own judgement, and feel able to take charge of the ship under any circumstances, yet I have no one to consult, and not even enough men to man the huge ship properly, and those that are yet able to do duty are weakened from hard work and almost constant exposure to the storms. My best support in these trials (next to God) is Mrs. Burleigh, who not only keeps up her own spirits under her severe suffering, and also takes off the time for me from the chronometer and cheers me in the discharge of my hard duty.

It will soon be eight bells again, and I will have another long and stormy night. Farewell to all; may God preserve us.

Thursday Afternoon April 17th
Lat 49 20 S. Lon 62 20 W.
Thank Heavens I have at last got an observation for longitude, but as for latitude I must guess. And thank Heaven no less that we are still alive and safe, after being tossed by the worst gale I have ever experienced. It set in last Thursday morning from the southwest—and in twenty minutes from the time it commenced to blow, we had already our close-reefed topsails furled, and the ship hove to under her fore

top-mast, stay sail, and main spencer. We are still hove to, but the gale has abated considerably and I have had the close-reefed fore and main topsail set, to prevent her from rolling so heavily. There is yet however too much sea to make much headway, especially as it is ahead and the wind is ahead. The clouds broke away about an hour ago and as I said I have got an observation for longitude, but I can hardly depend upon it for I do not know an exact latitude, not having had an observation since last Tuesday week.

I have put her down as above, and if I am right we cannot be more than three hundred miles from Staten Land. Good God! the prospect is dark before us. We have fearful weather here, and what will it be if I am so fortunate as to get to the southward of the Staten Land and off the Cape. There is no prospect of either Capt. Burleigh or Mr. Bishop getting out for weeks, and here I am, with an ignorant second mate, that I cannot trust, and a handful of worn out seamen.

Day before yesterday we passed close to the ship Tagus of New York, but the noises of the storm prevented anyone from being heard on our own decks, let alone hailing another ship. I was anxious to know her longitude however, and when we were just opposite her, I chalked my longitude on the head board of the bows and held it up to him. He soon answered my number by giving me his longitude. We differed 22 miles, but I think I am right. The Tagus has lost both her top and main gallant masts and her mizen top mast. Thank heaven I have lost none of our more important spars yet and I hope I may not. All the sound that I could hear from the ship as we shot past her, was the barking of a dog from her quarter deck.

Saturday afternoon, 19th April-51
I cannot put down any latitude for I do not know where we are. Ever since last Thursday afternoon when the gale abated, we have been enveloped in one of the same kind of fogs that we experienced off the Falkland Islands and although we have had but a faint wind, we have had tremendous currents setting to the S.S.W. We are like a blind man for we cannot get sight of the sun, nor can we see the land even if we made it, until we were too close to avoid the beaches. All is done that

46

can be done, but what can mortal man do with a ship in a dense fog, no wind, and a current of unknown velocity, setting you cannot tell where. Oh! God! send me storms, gales, hurricanes, but lift up this blindfolding fog, that I may know where I am.

Every one on board is alarmed and anxious, but everyone confides entirely in me. Have mercy upon us, oh, Thou Eternal Father, for we are in Thy hands, the powers and skill and experience of man is nothing and of no use here. I feel almost exhausted with watching and fatigue, and although we have had such a long spell of calms and everybody on board is much refreshed by it yet for me there is no rest. I know our imminent danger and I have no rest or peace.

Ship *Delia Maria* at Sea.
Pacific Ocean Lat 57 28S. Lon 70 4 W.
Wednesday 30th April 1851

Yes, Pacific Ocean, Thank God! and Cape Horn with all its stormy terrors, treacherous currents, and wild skies is far behind us. Could I summon up resolution to give description of all that I have suffered, all that I have felt since last I had an opportunity of writing in this journal, eleven days ago, I should spend the whole evening in the task, but as I am not different from most other human beings, and soon forget dangers and difficulties when once past, I will not attempt a full description of the dangers and the difficulties of the past eleven days other than note my progress.

All night long on the night of the 19th we contrived to be enveloped in an impenetrable gloom, and although there was a heavy sea which became more angry towards morning yet there was no wind to lift the fearful fog from the water. Sunday morning dawned without much change and as soon as it was light I went to bed to try to get a little sleep, giving strict orders to be called if there was any wind or if the fog lifted. I fully expected another gale of wind, and as the heavy seas were coming from the northeast I was fearful of it coming from that quarter, because if we got a strong N.E. gale now that we were embayed between Staten Land and Terra-Del-Fuego, and with only a narrow strait between them I was painfully impressed with the great hazard in attempting to enter the straits and likewise of the utter impossibility of clearing the eastern part of Staten Land, with the ship on a wind. At breakfast time the stewardess came to call me to eat, but I was not hungry and turned over to go to sleep again, but before I closed my eyes, I heard the second mate on deck, singing out to let go the top-gallant-haul-yards fore and aft. Not knowing what was the matter, I ran on deck, and there beheld as appalling a sight as I ever witnessed. The fog to the northward was boiling and rolling down upon us in vast pyramids and before we could start a sheet or man a clew line the squall was upon us. It struck us on our starboard side and the ship was on her beams end in a moment. "Let go everything," I roared, and my orders were obeyed as fast as the nature of the case would allow, but it was too late to have the desired effect, and our sails instead of easing the ship only flapped in thunder to the wind and one by one were going to pieces and flying away like feathers. The jib alone stood and as the men could not get on the forecastle, to let go the sheet, it was the only means of our salvation besides the last resort of cutting away the line. The ship logged as she was paid off before the squall, and continued to go round until the wind was on her lee quarter, when she righted with such a roll as I expected would spring every mast in her. We were then running right before the wind about south by west, and as soon as possible we secured our heavy sails and stowed all but the fore-topsail and fore-top-mast-stay-sail. We had lost only our royals and top-gallant-sails, and carried away the starboard fore and main braces. This was pretty well, considering our narrow escape, and in spite of our danger I could not help a smile at the fright of Mr. St. Julien and Miss Gilman, who both came to the cabin door as the ship went over for the last struggle. Poor Mr. Bishop was just able to raise up and look out the window at the scene, while the stewardess still showed her love for him by remaining in his stateroom the whole time. Capt. B. was thrown out of his berth by the shock, and was obliged to be lifted back again by two of my men and Mrs. Burleigh. All the breakfast dishes and half those in the pantry and all the cook's boilers etc. went over to leeward with a crash, and there was nothing removable on the deck but went overboard altogether.

48

Amidst all the trouble I was perhaps best pleased because the fog was cleared off and I could see around us. Depending upon Providence for success, I determined against the judgement, but with the consent of Capt. B. to run at a venture for the Straits of Le Main between Terra del Fuego and Staten Land. I kept her away S.W. and for about six or seven hours ran her at the rate of ten knots, right through the seas, instead of over them.

About two o'clock in the afternoon the gale seemed to abate, and although nothing could be seen from the topsail yard, yet I was afraid of another of the treacherous calms, in which I might be swept far off my course by currents. Mr. St. Julien, Miss Gilman, and Mr. Bickford however were so free from care that they commenced fishing for the cape pigeons, albatross etc. which the late continued gales had rendered so hungry that they flocked around us in thousands. They caught two large albatross, and a dozen pigeons in about half an hour, with a hook and line baited with a small piece of pork; the pigeons were fat as butter and if we could have had an opportunity, they would have made us a splendid pot pie for supper. One of the albatross was over ten feet from tip to tip.

We had hardly got the damage of the squall in the morning repaired as well as possible, and the new sails bent, before the wind hauled around to the west and commenced freshening again into another gale. The carpenter had sounded the pumps, and found nearly two feet of water in the hold but before we could reduce it one quarter, we were obliged to shorten sail again, and brace sharp up on the starboard tack. The wind however increased again with such fury that we were soon obliged to heave to, for it would be madness to run south directly upon a lee shore, it would hardly be advisable to run south before it to the east, and there was nothing for it again but to heave to. This I did under nothing but the main spencer so that she would not lay over so as to prevent pumping. All hands were now called to the pumps. We worked nearly an hour and then sounded the hold again. *She had 21 inches.* Every man looked worn out, and despair sat in every countenance. The second mate too, who should have lent me all the aid possible, quit the pumps in a pet say-

ing "There is no use, let her go." "Let her go where?" said
I, "to the bottom or on an iron bound and savage shore." I
took hold of the pumps myself and endeavored with every
argument to cheer the men. This was about five o'clock, and
the gloom of night was again settling over the troubled deep.
As is the usual custom before the nightfall, I sent a man aloft
to look around. He had not gone ten ratlines from the deck
when he sung out "Land o!"

If I had been shot, I could not have felt such a shock.
There was no use in asking where the land bore for I knew
it was to leeward, and sure enough as soon as we had looked
we could see the black and dismal cliffs, of Staten Land, with
more fearful breakers not five miles under our lee.

"Great God!" ejaculated everyone and well might that
ship's company appeal in earnest to their maker for deliver-
ance. And what did I, young, inexperienced, exhausted, the
master of a huge ship, with a small crew in a living and terrific gale, that threatened at every moment to wrench the
masts out of her groaning hull, and that hull a mere wreck,
half full of water.

I sent the men from the pumps, and they knew as well
as I did what alone was to be done. We must make sail on our
already laboring ship and drive her into the teeth of that
furious tempest or in less than two hours drift on rocks
where the surf broke a hundred feet in height, and where
escape was impossible.

Before I started anything, I went into the cabin and
told Capt. B. our situation and on what part of the coast we
were, asking him which tack I should put the ship upon.

He thought we had better run to the east, and get
clear of the land if possible, because it was a most uncertain
experiment and last resource, to try to enter the straits in
this gale.

I told him that it was the next thing to an impossibility that the ship would keep afloat long enough to clear
the land even if we could weather it, and that as all prospects
were so dark, I for my own part, would rather undertake to
run into the straits where we might let go our anchors under
the lee of the land, and keep her afloat until the gale abated
or at worst perish in the attempt.

Capt. Burleigh turned to his wife, who all along had maintained a composure most astonishing for a woman. Bursting into tears, for the first time, she said, "Leave it to him John and we will pray for the best."

I waited for no more, but going on deck, placed two men at the wheel. We had furled our topsails with all the reefs in and now I sent all hands to the weather-main-top-sail sheet.

"Let go!" Away went the sail flapping and thundering like a cannon, but our fellows were working for life and they succeeded in hauling both sheets home. In like manner we set the close-reefed fore-top sail and then the fore-top mast stay-sail. We had been lying with our head to the south west, and consequently were not obliged to wear. As the ship gained headway, she began to labor so much that I feared she would either go to pieces, or go to the bottom from the leak, before we could get into an anchorage, and now I knew what it was to be firm. Every eye was upon mine, and every mad plunge, Mr. Bickford would say, "She can't stand it—she will never bear it," etc., etc. I told him she must either carry the sail or go ashore, and he seemed to give up everything. The poor fellows had all come aft for the whole forward part of the ship was almost constantly under water. It was almost dark, and no one in this whole world can imagine my feelings as I thus blindly ran my ship seemingly to utter destruction. How was I to know in the darkness of Egypt that was soon to fall upon us, where was the narrow strait, or when I was in it. I called everyone aft and told them that they had little to expect because we were on a lee shore where if we struck, no power on earth could save a single living thing nor even God Almighty could befriend us in this awful place. Even if we gained the shore we could not survive the cold and storms for a single day. Not a tree or shrub grew upon the land, and every hill and plain was covered with frozen snow. "Boys," said I, "you must lay aside sickness and weakness tonight. Every man in the ship, stand by the stations. Exert yourselves for a few hours and we will either be in safety in the straits or we shall be in eternity." Every man seemed to know his danger and everyone promised to do his duty to the last ounce of his strength. I took one of the men away from the wheel and placed old "Jim Taylor" at the weather spokes in his place, where I lashed them both.

All this time I was fearful at every plunge, that she would either go down, or jerk the mast out of her, when death would soon have been our fate. I was standing in the weather rigging watching our bending masts with almost hopeless feelings, when one of the men I had stationed in the slings of the fore yard sung out, "Breakers under the lee bow." "O God!" cried everyone. "How far on the bow?" I asked. "About three points" answered the man. "Can you see any land?" "I can see land about four points on the bow and one high rock just in the breakers." "Loose the fore-sail." "Ay ay sir." Mr. Bickford came up and said that it was not possible that she could stand the foresail; it would shortly carry away the mast. "Loose the main-sail" I shouted, "she *must* stand them both, or we must go ashore. She makes more than three points leeway with this short sail, and it is impossible for us now to go about, we should be on the rocks before we should get her half round and besides she is settling fast and must go down in less than four hours if we keep her in this sea for we cannot pump her while the gale lasts and there is no appearance of that tonight; and lastly I believe that that point, under our lee bow is Cape Del-Medio, and that if we can weather it, we shall be past all further immediate danger, and can keep her off two or three points, besides easing her of her tremendous press of sail. All hands to the fore-tack." The second mate was convinced of the necessity of carrying the sail, but was also convinced that the masts would go over the sides. The old sailors also shook their heads and looked at our already creaking and strained masts. *It is our only chance* I shouted. *Bear a hand or we are on the rocks.*

Amidst torrents of water pouring on deck and wood and boards floating about, the whole crew went forward, took the tack to the capstan and in a moment, more of the huge sail fell from the yard and went flapping like thunder in the wind. Every man did his best but before the tack was half down, a tremendous blast laid us almost on our beam ends, and tore the sail in thunder from the yard. "Lay aft," I shouted, but they could not hear. A cannon might have been fired, and the noise of that thundering Niagara over our bows, would have drowned the sound. But they knew their duty, and clinging to the weather rail made their way aft. "Down main tack—ease away the buntlines!" and in a moment more the huge sheet was thundering in the wind and I confidently expected to see it share the same fate with the foresail and be blown away. But it was a new sail, and although its thrashing shook the ship to her very keelson, yet they succeeded in getting it set in a few minutes almost drowned in the lee scuppers while hauling aft the sheet. There had been no reef taken in this huge sail and now the sorely pressed ship seemed driven beyond all strength of wood and copper. Instead of lifting to the heavy seas, as she had been doing, she now plunged bodily through them, and every one swept her decks from the knight heads to the quarter deck. Whatever had not gone overboard before, now was torn from its lashings and swept away. Pig pens, coal crates, harness, casks, spare spars and empty water casks went over the lee rail in a mass, the lee bulwark was torn away and no one could set foot upon the main deck without the most imminent danger of being lost. All this time I had been too much engaged to attend to the steering of the ship or to the bearing of the rocks. I had called the lookout down from aloft, and we were all collected on the quarter deck.

We could now see the milk white foam of the breakers not more than three points on the bow and seemingly not a mile distant. "How is her head?" said I. "The lamp is out," shouted the helmsman, and thus we were without compass in that awful situation for we could not light it then. "Keep her full, Jim, but don't run her off." "Ay, ay," said the poor fellow who was already bruised almost to a jelly by the violence of the wheel, which it was sometimes impossible for the two men to hold, and it would fly round like a top, striking and bruising the hands and arms of the poor helmsmen. We had nothing more to do, and each one watched his fate, with almost suspended breath. The tempest roared with the noise of ten thousand Niagaras, the huge ship groaned and shrieked in every timber, and the tall masts and heavy yards bent like reeds in the gale. No voice, or trumpet sound could be heard at five steps distant, no one could quit his hold and our only dependence for life in this world was upon the strained and creaking masts and their sails and rigging, and upon the direction of the gale.

If everything held for a few minutes longer, and if the wind did not head us, we should be safe, if the least thing gave way, if a lanyard or rope-yarn parted, or if the wind headed us off a half point, we should every soul of us be in eternity in five minutes, and our noble ship a scattered and shattered drift of fragments. Great God! what a moment. Every man was prepared to meet his fate, and every man offered up a silent prayer to his maker for his salvation. The lights were out in the cabin, and everyone there was awaiting in fearful suspense, the outcome of the crisis. Already the roar of the surf on the black cliff began to drown even the fearful noise of the storm around us, and in a moment more we should shoot past the rock. At that moment the sails flapped and thundered in the wind. I shouted at the top of my voice, "Hard up," for I knew that ere we could fall off we should either strike on a sunken rock or be past the point. The order was heard and obeyed but before another word could be said, or before a motion could be made, the black mass of rock and foam shot by us like an arrow and we were past the point. Every one took a deep breath and uttered an inward, "Thank God." And our strength which had hitherto supported us failed at once and several poor fellows sunk down on the deck. But now we had another duty to perform. To take off the sail from the ship, and endeavor to start the pumps.

But the ship had hardly payed off to fill her sails, before the main-sail split into a thousand ribbons and went fluttering away to leeward. We had been steering S.W. b S. to clear the cape, but now I kept her away S. b W. and we hauled up both topsails, and left nothing upon her but spencer and fore top-mast stay-sail. The gale seemed to abate also, and the puff that blew away our mainsail was the last we received, for we were now under shelter of the high shore of the opposite side of the straits which we were just entering, and the tremendous sea was also changed for the comparatively smooth straits.

The carpenter sounded the well and found seven and a half feet of water. I sent eight men to the pumps and the rest to the anchors to clear them away ready for coming to. In half an hour, we had almost a dead calm, and as there was but little sea, we could work all the pumps and soon gained on the water. I had thought of anchoring, but to do this, we must make sail, for there was nearly sixty fathoms of water where we lay and this would be hard work. I then determined to free her of water if possible where she was, but before turning all hands on the pumps, I went into the cabin and told the stewardess to bring out some bread and a whole cheese, and I took the liberty of opening the same case of gin which had been the first cause of Capt. B.'s sickness and my own trouble.

I brought out four quart bottles and set them out on deck, with the bread and cheese and sat myself with the men, to eating and drinking. After the exposure all night to the bitter cold, and the driving sleet and hail, and the relentless wind, such a repast was indeed a feast to all of us. This was about one o'clock in the morning and although it was almost entirely calm, and a favorable tide was setting us into the straits, I could do nothing to guide our course or to prevent our drifting upon the numerous rocky points of the shores. Indeed so hopeless had been our condition but two hours before, that this minor danger, seemed now of little importance.

At two o'clock, the whole ships company, cook, passengers, officers, and all, commenced the serious task of freeing a large ship of almost seven feet of water. All four of the pumps were manned, and from this till daylight at about half past five we worked constantly at our task, at this time we had reduced the water to about sixteen inches, and the bilge pump sucked, and half an hour later the main pump sucked, and the ship was free. We were satisfied that the leak was not very serious and that much of the water had been made through her strained and open seams, during the gale. At daylight we discovered our position about seven or eight miles in the straits of Le-Haire, and close to the Patagonia side. Oh! what a thrill goes through the human frame, when after a long passage upon a cheerless sea with nothing to relieve the eye from that everlasting world of sky and water, and naught to attract the attention from the regular occurrence of calm, breeze, and tempest, you are suddenly aroused by the cry of land.

But what are the feelings of a storm-beaten handful of men, when in the midst of a terrific gale that warning cry proclaims that an ironbound coast is under our lee. Should anyone who has experienced the horrors of the ocean in all its forms, ever read these lines, he shall know how to feel for our dangers that night of darkness and dangers, and to sympathize in our joy, when as the morning dawned, we found ourself safe and free from present danger, and in a favorable condition for repairing our damages. I had the pleasure of receiving sufficient commendation from Capt. B. and Mr. Bishop for my able handling of the ship, and the far more sweet and grateful thanks from the ladies.

Now that we were in safety, we were in no hurry to get out of our present landlocked berth, and all day was occupied in passing under easy sail those friendly straits. The men had bent new sails, repaired the rigging, and set things to right on the deck. The carpenter had found the leak where we had supposed we had taken in the most water and had stopped it up, and we had nothing more to do but watch for adjoining mountains and rest and recruit ourselves after our hardship and prepare for new.

How different are these shores from those of my native land. Every feature of nature is so bold that distant objects appear hard by. The high mountains, bare of all trees and vegetation, are covered with ice and snow, and the high and rocky cliffs that skirt the shore have been beaten by storms of an eternal winter and are dark, dreary and forboding. Not a sign of vegetable or animal life can be seen in the range of telescope vision, and the whole appearance of these southern wilds is one vast scene of desolation.

Before evening set in, (Monday the 22nd) we had gained the southern end of the straits and were again becalmed in too deep water to anchor. Not a breath of air stirred the water which was here still and calm as a mill pond and soon one of those sulphurous fogs, so peculiar to Cape Horn first spread itself over the surface of the water and then enveloped both sea and land in its impenetrable folds. These fogs are almost always succeded by a gale, such as we had just experienced and I again felt uneasy less we should be caught again. But the night wore away, and no sign of a gale showed. In the morning a light breeze from the north sprang up and rolling away the fog, showed us for the first time in many days a clear sky and bright sun. I improved this fair morning by sending down our lofty top-gallant masts which I had so near lost in the late gale and in making several other dispositions for continued hard weather; I had nearly driven everything to pieces on Sunday night, and water had penetrated everywhere. The cabin windows of my cabin were stowed in, and everything completely flooded with the sea; this day I dried as much as I could, and had the carpenter to replace the windows. Mr. Bishop was able this morning to come on deck a little while for the first time. Both he and Capt. Burleigh were much better.

During the morning we made four sail of vessels. Two ships apparently coming from the eastward from the southward end of Staten Land, and two coming through the strait of La Mare. Those from the east passed far to the southward, but the other two came in our wake. One of them soon fell behind as the wind grew fresher, but we made her out to be the *Tagus* which we had spoken on the 15th and which had escaped the difficulties we had encountered in being far behind us, and having plenty of sea room, during the last gale, and yesterday while we were becalmed in the straits she had had a fresh and fair wind, made the straits and almost overhauled us. Thus it is in life, the slowest and most indolent often go the safest.

The other vessel, having the light sails set soon came up with us. She was the French barque *Ville de Founiens,* 72 days from Marseilles and also bound for San Francisco. The Frenchman run so close under my lee that owing to a slight sheer he took his fore-top-mast studding-sail-boom, caught in the lee leach of our foresail, and carried his boom away. I did not pity his misfortune as it was done through his own carelessness. He said he had avoided the heaviest of the gale we had, being two hundred miles north on Sunday night and had only had a double reefed topsail breeze.

He passed on, sailing much faster than we did because he was light, and had all his lofty sails set, royals, studding sails, etc.

"Well, well my fine fellow," said I as he went careening away as gaily as if he was on his own blue Mediterranian, "if you don't haul down some of that lofty hamper of yours, I am thinking you will be fortunate if you do not lose it."

All this day we had a fair northerly and by seven o'clock in the evening were but sixty miles eastward of Cape Horn. The wind at this time suddenly hauled around S.W. and commenced blowing in squalls. I hauled her up N.W. b W. and thought that if the wind did not head me, I should be able, with the offing I had got to weather all parts of the Cape. The wind kept on increasing, and before twelve o'clock I had single reefs in the top-sails with blasts and snowing equally. At two o'clock in the morning we close reefed the top-sails, but still kept her close to the wind which favored us a point, in the hope of weathering the Cape. At four o'clock the snow had ceased and the sky was clear. I now thought that instead of lying to until daylight as I had calculated we must be almost up with the Cape and it would be a great risk to run in the snow storms so near the land and where currents were setting in every direction so strong; that I would run on keeping a good lookout for land on the lee bow. I had not been aft two minutes after setting the watch before the lookout sung out, "Land O." "Where away?" "Directly ahead." "Whew." Here was a mess. I went forward, and not only saw land ahead, but also two or three points on the weather bow, and thought that I could distinguish at about the distance of 10 or 12 miles, the sharp peak of Hermit's Island which marks Cape Horn. I let her run into within two or three miles of the rocks because there was no appearance of immediate squalls, and I wished to get a view of the outline of the coast, so as to determine my position. I supposed that the land I had made directly ahead was Barnevelts Island, and that I had had a strong easterly current that had been setting me back almost as fast as I advanced; so that my course from the time the wind had changed at seven the evening before, was north, instead of N.W. B W. as we had steered. Well we went about at five in the morning, and stove off till light. We then went about again and now I could see by the land that we were making nothing at all, land that bore it not altering its bearings at all. This time I was sure of the land for I could see the bold, black cliffs of Hermit's Island about twelve miles to the westward, while the no less gloomy rock called Barnevelt's Island was directly under our bows. The shore is bold here, and this time I ran in, within two hundred fathoms of the rocks, so near that we could see the waterfowl sitting upon the rocks. 'Bout ship and try it again.

Oh! disagreeable of disagreeables, and terror of terrors, how can I sit here and write of all our sufferings, our exposures, our hardships, during all those long days and far longer nights, of snow storms, gales, wild squalls, head winds, and head currents that intervened between the time we made Cape Horn, (Wednesday morning 24th April) until we at length got a fair wind and passed it yesterday, 29th as I hope for good.

It has been nothing but a dead beat to windward and against a strong current and heavy sea. Every few hours a violent storm of snow and hail would come from the S.W. blending in with its sharpness, and covering the ship in snow. The men have, many of them given out, and are sick, and those that remain on duty are almost disabled by hard work and the cold and wet. It has been a divine mercy that I have been enabled to stand the hardships through which I have gone, but I feel as well now as if I had spent the time in lying under the awnings upon the tropical seas, instead of for eight, ten and 15 hours at a time remaining exposed upon deck to all the fury of these winter storms, hoarse with calling, wet to the skin, my clothes frozen, and myself almost exhausted. Had it not been for the sisterly care of Mrs. Burleigh in regard to drying my clothes, and sending me brandy, wine, etc. I think I too must have sunk under the fatigue and hardship of the duty.

Mr. Bishop is yet not able to do duty, he comes on deck in the intervals of the gales, but is careful not to get wet. Capt. Burleigh has resumed command of the ship, but still is only able to come on deck in the finest weather and in the day time. He came on deck day before yesterday for the first, and yesterday took my log book, charts, quadrant command, etc. etc. Thank heavens I am released from the forced duty I have been doing, and I say again, thank a merciful providence who gave me strength to go through all that is now past, for the good of others, and with no bad effect on my own health or strength.

We are now steering west and are far away from the Cape, and all its wild and gloomy terrors. May it please God, I never wish to pass through these scenes again, for although a storm at sea is something I sometimes delight in yet, days and weeks of cold and storm and almost dead certainty of shipwreck upon a barren and uninhabited land of rocks and snow is an exercise I shall not soon be willing to repeat.

Thursday May 1, 1851

May day! How cheerful sounds the wind, and what bright recollections of by-gone times are associated with its merry sound. This day a twelvemonth I was on my way to the western states of our union, to join in the scientific conclave that was to meet in Cincinnati to debate upon matters relative to the medical profession, and oh! how far different was that bright, blossoming, breezy day, from this cold and desolate one in the south Pacific ocean. Then, the songs of birds, the sweet rippling of murmuring streams and the sweet scent of the spring flowers were combined to fill the senses and gratify the mind. Oh! How wide is the contrast between all these pleasant memories of a happy past, and the sweeping storms of snow and dark and frowning clouds of this dreary region.

But snowstorms and tempest, cold winds and angry storms, only cause the prospect of the past to brighten in proportion to the gloom of the present. Oh! my happy home, green be thy fields and bright be thy flowers, for there are those amid thy scenes whose happiness and joy I regard far more than my own, and while I am suffering in these dreary wilds I humbly pray, and reliantly hope that they may experience all the pleasures of the season, and more than all its usual happiness. I sometimes think that ere many more seasons go round, I shall again be with them, but destiny rises up, and with her finger, points out a course of self denial and toil, extending far into future years, and although hard is the reality, yet I trust that it will only enhance the joy of our reunion, when Fate and Fortune permit. Sweet thoughts of home, adieu; I must brace me with the armor of fortitude, and indulge in thought, only to anticipate and not to regret.

Friday, 2nd May [1851]
Lat 55 48 S. Lon 75 W.

Since yesterday we have averaged a course of N.W.b W. allowing for variations and have run about 180 miles. The weather is cold and squally and the sky almost constantly overcast with black and dismal clouds. Truly we have not much more pleasant weather than when we were off the Cape. But thank God there are no violent gales here where the rocky coast is spread like a net to catch the luckless mariner. We are in sight of several vessels aft standing the same way with ourselves, but too far away to make out. I have been looking at one from the mizzen top and I think it is a French barque with his top-gallant mast either carried away or sent down. I thought the fellow would come to his sense if he caught a Cape Horn squall. The wildfowl come swarming over us as if enraged that their prey should have escaped them, and the porpoises play around us in seeming reluctance to quit the prize which was so nearly theirs! Oh! ye cannibals, not yet awhile are our bodies to be delivered over to your tender mercies.

Saturday, May 3 rd. 1851
Lat. 55 58 S. Lon 75 42 W.

We have not gained much this day and the weather is still cold and stormy. We have had a head wind and have been scudding first this way and then that way before the fierce squalls. The sea here is tremendous, and it is impossible to eat, drink, write, or read with any satisfaction. Everything is lashed and made fast, or everything would be stove to pieces. When we are in the trough, the heavy seas seem like mountains rolling down to engulf us. The sea is heavier and higher, and more regular here than I ever saw before. It comes up from the far regions from the south, and is cold and dark as the gales that accompany it.

We took another porpoise this morning, and succeeded in hooking about twenty cape pigeons which come around us in great flocks and settling upon the water wait for any offal that may be thrown overboard. A handful of grease thrown among them will cause the greatest row imaginable, and many are almost drowned by the numbers that rush to

the spot and alight upon them. Mrs. B. caught a large albatross this morning upon her line, and it had like to heave her
overboard. The man at the wheel was obliged to haul him in
for her, and he measured eleven feet six inches from tip
to tip.

Sunday 4th May [1851]
Lat. 54 48 S. Lon. 52 16 W.
Made good a distance of 218 miles since yesterday before a
whole regular tropical breeze sometimes measuring twelve
or fifteen knots an hour.

This day last year, I was also afloat but it was upon the
bosom of the river Ohio, on my way to Cincinnati. Verily,
one day knows not what another may bring forth.

I have felt quite sick and unwell today, and feel as
though I had an inflammation of the bowels or the kidneys
coming upon me. I have just bled myself and feel a little the
better for it. But my head aches and I will go and lie down.
Mr. Bishop has so far recovered as to be able to come up on
deck to keep his watch again, and so now I am free to do
and not to do.

Tuesday 13th May 1851
Lat. 35 10 S. Lon. 89 W.
On last Sunday week I was taken with rheumatism and an
inflammation of the kidneys, and for three days I suffered
the most intense and piercing pain. I dont think I could
have lived 24 hours longer; but on Wednesday morning the
pain grew less acute, and soon gave way to an uneasy aching
distress, which was almost as bad as the first. Yesterday was
the first that I felt much better, but today the fever has left
me and I have sat up for an hour or two. I must quit writing
now however, for I am much too weak to think or hold the
pen long. Thank God O, that I am better now, for a ship
is no place to be sick in. Every one is engaged at his different
duties, and it is hard to lie on one's back from morning to
noon and noon till night and all the long night, together,
with no one to speak to or ask for assistance. Mrs. Burleigh
has been very kind to me however and many a gloomy hour
has she rendered bright by her cheerful company.

To render my situation worse, we have suffered another tremendous gale of wind. It set in last Saturday morning and all day Saturday and Sunday the roaring of the wind and waters, and the pitching and tumbling of the ship, was awful indeed to me, who was not only unable to go on deck, but was obliged to lie in my berth, rolling about from side to side, where every motion was almost death. It was the most trying affliction I ever experienced. The ship is still rolling and pitching in a heavy sea, but the gale is gone, and they have got her under sail once more; but enough for the present.

Thursday 15th May, 1851
Lat 32 2 S. Lon 87 W.

Off the coast of Chile, and distant from the island of Juan Fernandes, only three hundred and twenty miles. We have been running on a wind since last date and have only been able to make a N b E course. We have all been endeavoring to persuade the captain to go into Valparaiso or Juan Fernandes, but he still keeps his course as near as possible, so that if the wind does not head us off more, we shall see no other land til we reach the California coast.

This is a good whaling ground and is chiefly occupied by the Nantucket whalers. We have seen several sperm and sulphur bottom whales, and any quantity of grampus. The weather is yet quite unsettled and wet, and some of our men who have been here fishing, tell me that such weather is very common and sometimes the wind will keep to the northward for several weeks on a stretch. I feel much better today and have been on deck. I am still however, very weak and sore. This day one year ago, I was at Quebec in lower Canada, ranging about the country which has become historical ground, from the many sanguinary conflicts that have taken place in the vicinity.

Sunday May 18th 1851
Lat 30 46 S. Lon 84 8 W.

The ways of Providence are inscrutable, and if I have committed a fault in leaving my home, I am now atoning for it and yearning for its scenes and inmates once more.

The weather here is such as I have never seen before, the sky is continually overcast with a soft smooth curtain of dun, and it neither rains, nor is there ever any rain here. It is now the season corresponding to our November but it is far different. We have left the stormy latitudes far behind us, and now it is a mild, calm and peaceful region, without hardly ever a glance of the sun, or moon or stars. We are now looking for the S.E. trades every hour, and if we are fortunate we shall reach San Francisco in the latter part of the month of June. The anticipated idea of going into Valparaiso, is exploded and we have now nothing for it but many a weary mile of the water before we can set our feet upon the solid earth.

Monday 19th
We have just had a very unpleasant occurrence on board. While Mr. Bickford and the carpenter were eating breakfast, the stewardess as is her custom sat down at a table with them. Mr. Bickford was in a bad humor about something, and turned round to her saying that she had better eat with the mate for she was not wanted here. She answered that she was as good as he was any day, whereupon Mr. B. called her a damned Creole. This exasperated her Spanish blood, and first dashing her cup of hot coffee in his face, she seized a carving knife and ran around the table towards the 2nd mate. He got out of the cabin as fast as his legs would carry him, and then commenced to tantalize her, which rendered her perfectly furious. She went forward to the galley and commenced heating a large pot full of grease, swearing she would scald his eyes out the next time he came by.

Mr. Bickford then went to the captain and told his tale, which enraged him so much that he told him to get a pair of irons and going forward took hold of the girl's arm and at one jerk brought her out of the galley on deck. He had for several days been angry with her for she would not obey orders without much quarreling and grumbling and was otherwise saucy, and he now was in a very favorable humor for pitching her over the side. He forced the handcuffs upon her wrists and locked them but she drew her hands out of them with the greatest of ease and laughed at him in his

64

face. There was not a pair of handcuffs in the ship small enough to prevent her pretty little hands from coming out of them, and if he had had irons for the ankles it would have been the same way, for I have never seen a prettier formed woman. Capt. B. then cleared out the fore-hatch house, and put her in it, locking her up, and boarding up the windows so that she could not see out. He swears he will keep her there on bread and beef until she promises to behave herself, which I do not think from her disposition she will ever do. We will miss her very much, for notwithstanding her strong passions which is more the fault of her country than her disposition she has always been very kind to us, Mr. Bickford excepted. Capt. B. after securing the stewardess turned to Mr. Bishop and told him it was his fault that the stewardess was so saucy and violent.

Thursday, 20th May 1851
Lat 28 5 S. Lon 85 W

The fracas of yesterday has made quite a general riot in the ship. Mr. Bickford after hearing the Captain censure the mate for his frequent connections with the stewardess (whose name is Alie) thought proper also to behave in a very supercilious manner to his senior officer. This afternoon when he relieved the mate at four o'clock, the mate called to him to come forward, to show him what he wanted done. Mr. Bickford did not pay any attention, when the mate called him again Mr. B. answered, "Go to H - - l." This enraged Mr. Bishop who immediately jumped off the forecastle, and came off to where he was standing. Bickford waited til he was pretty close and then stooping down, ran under him so as to throw him down, and then caught him by the hair and commenced pounding him. Mr. Bishop could do nothing, for he was underneath and held fast so that in less than half a minute he had his face, eyes and lips all cut and bleeding.

I had been steering and Miss Gilman was standing beside me talking. I saw the mate when he was coming at Bickford and told Evelyn to go tell the captain to come on deck, for I knew that the mate was sure to get the worst of it. I could not leave the wheel myself, though I itched to have a hand free to give the rough second mate a settler. But the captain rushed out of the cabin, and picking him up like a child, hurled him into the lee scuppers with great violence.

It was with the utmost difficulty that they were kept from rushing into each other again, and I am sure that we shall yet have trouble with them. At all events, Mr. Bishop is laid up for two or three days. Every one took his part for he is a gentleman and an amiable pleasant man, while Mr. Bickford is a conceited jackass, and is only jealous of the favor in which Mr. Bishop is held by the ladies, passengers, men, and last but not least by the pretty stewardess.

At tea time Capt. Burleigh told the mate that he might turn Mr. Bickford forward with the men if he liked and pick out another from the crew to fill his place if he wished. But he has not done so yet, and says that he will try him a little while longer.

Henry Walker is now steward. He gets along very well, but is rather awkward yet. Alie is singing songs and is trying to keep herself very merry in her dark prison house, and I think that Capt. B's "bread and beef" will not affect her much while the mate has a key which fits the lock to the fore-hatch house door. Last night he put in a whole pie, and a piece of cheese and I am sorry to say that he was daring enough to put himself in for half an hour also. I do not blame Mr. Bishop, for the girl is certainly attractive, and human flesh is certainly no more than mortal, after all, but I fear that if these nocturnal visits are discovered by either the captain or the 2nd mate, that there will be work.

God send us wind! wind! wind!!!

Friday, May 23rd 1851
Lat 24 26 S. Lon 57 W.

> Bounding Billows cease your motion
> Bear me not so swiftly o'er . . .

The storms and gales and dark rolling billows of an antarctic winter we have left far behind us, and now the exquisite beauties of the ever gentle Pacific, are above and around us in all their glory. Yes, tarry yet awhile my bonnie bark, and let's breathe together this fresh air, these clear and fragrant breezes. Let us enjoy the bright sunshine of life while it lasts, for oh, such loveliness cannot always exist, and life itself is too uncertain a state, to place our whole dependence upon. Then let me not shun the cold strife with the world, let me not dally with these enchanting breezes and laughing waters, for although life itself may here be robbed of half its hardships, yet—

> Ever is fancy on the wing
> For some happier era warming

and ever, I might add, is man invisibly propelled forward in the pursuit of his peculiar destiny. Yes, speed there! Speed there my gallant bark, for although we have already been a long time at sea, still we are a long way from our destined port, and instead of the four months I thought would complete the passage I find that even five or six will not be too great an allowance. Our ship has done all that we have expected of her, yet Fate in the form of headwinds, storms, and calms, has been seemingly against us. Yet I do not repine, but am rather thankful for the protected time. My health is entirely restored, and my mind improved by meditation and companions, and my pleasure, were it not for the occasional difficulties on board, would be entirely gratified.

But of late I have been thinking much of my home, and my thoughts never revert to that loved spot, but feelings of regret for my absence, and yearning for the companionship of its inmates course through my bosom. I have looked upon the miniatures of my dear parents and brothers often, and wondered if they are enjoying the health and happiness their happy home should afford.

I was looking over some papers and letters today in the bottom of my closet and found among them a copy of some sacred poetry copied by my dear mother before I came to sea. At that time the words and meaning would have been unheeded by me, but long months of absence and wandering have wrought a change in me, and I have read the lines and their accompanying exhortation with such stifled feelings as I cannot describe. Dear, dear devoted mother, how deep must be thy love for thy children.

I am becoming very anxious to hear from home, and even in my dreams I have had visions of that sweet pleasure, which on wakening causes me a sickening disappointment. I am not homesick, yet I feel that uneasiness, which I have experienced before, during a season of suspense, uncertainty or hope deferred. It is now nearly six months since I left Pennsylvania, and almost five since I have heard a single word from home.

Tuesday May 27th 1851
Lat 19 12 S. Lon 91 30 W.

We have not been fortunate in falling in with the trade winds as far south as they usually extend, 30 S. and did not take them till last Saturday in Lat 23 S. But we are making up the lost time now, running away N.W. with the yards square at the rate of about nine knots. The weather is as warm as that of Pennsylvania in rosy June, and I trust that I have seen the last of winter's cold and storms, for many a year. But still that soft curtain of clouds obscures the sky by day as well as by night, and although dense enough to sometimes descend for a while in mist, yet it cannot be called clouds. Sometimes for a little while the sun breaks through, and smiles upon the ocean and then the most beautiful rainbows are always seen. I have heard much of the circular rainbow, but never have had an opportunity of seeing it till now. From the lofty yards, when the sun is not too high there is a perfect circle, seen in the mist, opposite the sun, of the brightest and most vivid colors of the solar spectrum. The effect of this is beautiful in the extreme for the circle is doubled and trebled in such a manner that the whole appears a succession of concentric circles brighter in the center and fading gradually away in the circumference. I am afraid that the sacred historian who wrote the Bible, did not well understand the law of light, when describing the nature of the covenant made by God after the subsidence of the waters of the deluge.

Last night we obtained a short glimpse of the Ursa Major, that constellation so familiar to our northern eyes, which has been so long below the horizon. I hope it will not be many nights more, before we shall lift the North Star also, from his watery bed. Speed thee, oh speed! my bonny bark to the shores of thy destination and then, and then, I will bid thee a willing farewell. I will not give thee longer than another month to finish the passage. Will thou do it?

Wednesday, 4th June, 1851
Lat 10 20 S. Lon 102 2 W.

We have now left behind the latitude of damp and overcast skies, and are bounding over the maniac waves that dance and play in the clear sunshine, with everything that will draw, from the lofty sky-sail down to the sea-beaten water sail that is constantly dripping with the spray that is dashed from our bows.

Notwithstanding many unpleasant causes of dissatisfaction among the little family of the *Delia Maria,* yet there are hours of sunshine when all troubles are forgotten, and we enjoy each other's company with freedom. It is a pity that so small a number cannot always agree together, and by mutual effort contribute to make our long voyage as pleasant as possible; for my own part, I am on good terms with everyone on board, and would fain bring about the same understanding among all, but this it appears cannot be. Much of my own sunshine I owe to the pleasant company of the ladies and Mr. St. Julien, who so far have gotten on happily together.

We occasionally amuse ourselves with fishing, and now that our pigs and fowl are gone, the result of our sport often results in a delicate treat. There are plenty of dolphins, skipjacks, etc. besides shoals of flying fish which are too small to bother with, when there are others so much finer. It is amusing however to watch their motives and to see the efforts they make to avoid their enemies, the dolphins and sea hawks. The dolphin will dart among them, catching as many as he can, and terrify the others so much that the whole school will leave the water and take to the air sometimes flying two or three hundred yards before they are compelled by blindness to take to the water again. The sea hawk who has been sailing over the water in search of prey, watches his chance while the fish are still in the air, to pounce upon them and to provide a good meal from the flock.

Sometimes a flock will take their course directly towards the ship, and not being able to see while out of the water will strike against the sides like a storm of hail, invariably killing themselves and floating away in the water, an early prey to their pursuers.

Yesterday we caught a boneta and as it was almost tea-time the cook proceded to dress it at once, but was astonished to find in his maw, a live flying fish which must have just been caught. We put him in a bucket of water and he was soon quite lively, but while we were at tea, enjoying the flesh of his late captor our tom cat came along and being a most enterprising fisherman where there is no danger of getting much wetter, he soon succeeded in hauling the fish out of the bucket and making a meal of him.

Sunday 8th June, 1851
Lat 4 10 S. Lon 109 15 W.

Coursing onward with the same wind and the same sail; the former of which is just variable enough to give the men plenty of exercise in trimming the yards. But all hands are at present well and able to do duty for the first time since crossing the line in the Atlantic. Poor Charley Miller has recovered and is going about deck doing what light jobs are wanted. He has had a long seige of it, and not too many men have been as near the end as Charley. We are all in hopes of arriving in California before the 4th of July, but I dare not build too much upon it, for I remember the long and tedious calms on the line in the Atlantic too vividly to make any rash calculations here. I hope however that the south Pacific may prove more favorable to us.

We had another grand row on board yesterday morning, which has at length brought about the change which should have been made long ago. The second mate had the mid watch, and just about seven bells the captain came on deck and found both him and the lookout on the forecastle fast asleep. It is considered a great neglect of duty for a lookout to be caught napping for the safety of the ship and all on board from rocks, breakers and collisions, is often entrusted entirely to his vigilance. But it is far worse for the officer of the watch to sleep, for then the ship is at the mercy of any contingency that might occur, and as this was the third or fourth time that Mr. B. had been thus caught, Captain Burleigh was determined to give him a lesson.

Walking forward he procured a bucket full of water, and coming softly up to Mr. B., he dashed the whole of it over him. This roused him up quickly enough as may be supposed, when Capt. B. said to him, "You are a pretty thing to call yourself second officer of a ship,"—and was going on to tell him to go forward among the men, and not take his place in the ship as second again, when he interrupted him with, "Yes, and you are a *horse* you are a—."

"Go forward, and don't let me see you aft again; you shall do duty as a sailor, and I shall get a second officer from the men."

With this Capt. B. called one of the men and told him to take Mr. B's things out of the stateroom. But by this time Mr. B's anger had been raised, and he commenced such a tirade of abuse as I have seldom heard before. He told him of every mean or unfair thing he knew of him, and of every unfavorable opinion he had ever heard expressed against him, to all of which Capt. B listened without rejoinder or remark. I cannot say the captain did not deserve all that he got, but he certainly did right in breaking Mr. B. who has long been too disagreeable to be endured. Mrs. Burleigh declares that she will never sit at the table with him again, and I suppose that he will be discharged in California. I do not see how the captain stood his abuse, although well deserving it. Among other things he told him that he got drunk and made a fool of himself off the La Plata, and was shamming sick off Cape Horn, so that he might escape the hardship of responsibility of working the ship in that dangerous place, and that he starved everyone fore and aft the ship.

Well! we expected the thing to end here, but at six o'clock in the next watch, when the mate was washing decks, he happened to heave a bucket of water where it happened to hit Bickford where he was coming forward with some of his clothes. The old wound between them had never healed, and now Bickford's feelings highly excited, he sung out, "Mind what you are doing G-d d--n you." The mate had not seen him, and it was altogether unintentional on his part in heaving the water upon him, but being spoken to in this way he must justify himself and so he said, "Get out of the way there then." At this, Bickford threw down his clothes, and jumping on the forecastle aimed a blow at the mate's head that must have thrown him overboard, but Jim, the same man who endeavored to take Bickford off of the mate before now stepped between them again. But this time he paid dearly for his interference; Bickford picked up the harpoon which was lying near by, and poising it, in another moment would have driven it through Jim's body, but another man caught his arm from behind and while he was turning himself round he missed his footing and fell off the forecastle.

He was in a perfect fury now, and picking up a handspike hurled it with all his force at Jim's head, who was knocked down by the blow. In a moment however he was up again and with his head and face bleeding in a stream he jerked out his sheath knife, and had not Capt. B. rushed upon deck just then, there would shortly have been at least one murder done, for every man dropping his bucket and brooms was preparing for a general fight.

The Capt. caught Bickford by his throat, threw him down, and then after choking him a while, and sending all the other men off, he shoved him in the forecastle and shut the door. Really I wish that someone would give that bully his deserts and I am thinking he will yet get them if he is not careful.

Well that is another row ended, and fortunately without serious consequences. Every one who saw it expected that one of three combatants would be killed or seriously wounded, and so I believe too, had Capt. B. not been just in time to prevent it. How it will end yet, no one knows, but everyone is against Bickford.

It is fortunate for Capt. B. that he is a man of Herculean powers or he could never manage this refractory crew.

Monday, 9th June [1851]
Lat 1 27 S. Lon 114 28 W.
Sail Ho! Half an hour ago while looking at a strong current which seemed to be setting us to the S.W., we were startled by the cry of sail ho! upon the masthead. The sail was a large

ship, and was standing right down to us, but as soon as he came near enough to see that we were deeply laden, and had in all probability been out a long time, the rascal tacked ship and stood directly from us.

I suppose he was afraid we should be in want of something, and to prevent our begging he kept out of hail. Well, peace be with him, only I never like to see such selfishness as that.

We made him out to be the *Ontario*, whaler of New Bedford, and although we should not have begged anything of him, yet it would have been a great pleasure for us to have spoken to him, not having seen a human face besides our own for several months. Goodbye to you, you selfish churl, you are like the dog in the manger.

Today I applied the watch my dear father gave me when I left home to a purpose which I suppose he never dreamed of. All the watches on the ship have been broken, or are out of order, and at the request of Mr. Bishop I have allowed him to use mine to time the watches by. It is now hanging in the binnacle, an indispensable article for the ship.

I forgot to say that the stewardess had been liberated from her confinement (in the house I mean) on last Saturday week, having spent a period of 12 days "in durance vile" without in the least bringing down her high spirits or causing her to make a promise to do better. Capt. Burleigh was at length tired of attending to her, and the ladies were suffering much inconvenience on account of her absence, so one morning he came forward telling her to behave herself in the future, and took her out of the place. He told her if she did not behave he would use other and more harsh means of bringing her to her senses. At this the girl laughed, and indeed she would have been willing to remain in the prison house for six months, if she could have always been supplied with good food as during this time, and also enjoying the company of Mr. Bishop, every night. She has done very well since she has been liberated, and with the exception of having no respect whatever for the captain, is a very good stewardess. She still says that although Bickford is now forward, she will not hear one word out of his mouth but that she will either stab him or scald him to death, and I would earnestly advise him to heed her threats for she is as ardent in her hates as she is in her attachments.

Tuesday 10th June 1851
Lat 14N. 115 2 W.
Once more in the northern hemisphere! After roving for so many weeks over the southern wilds, one almost feels at home again to be in north latitude.

We crossed the line for the fourth time since leaving the United States, at ten o'clock this morning, and as I was at the wheel I have had the honor of steering her when crossing both in the Atlantic and Pacific Oceans. I rather think however that the next time she makes an equatorial transit that some one else must handle her fiddling stick. We took the N.E. trade wind yesterday afternoon without losing the breeze that we have had, the S.E. wind suddenly shifting around to the N.E. so that in less than half an hour we had taken in all our studding-sails from both sides and were braced up sharp on the starboard tack heading N.W. b N. and running off 10 and 11 knots. Hurrah! How delightful to stand on the forecastle of a gallant ship, and feel her plunge nobly and swiftly forward to her long-looked-for port. It is like the sensation caused by riding a proud and frisky steed, that pounces and cavorts in his impatience to fly rather than canter, over the free and open country. Thank fortune we shall have no calm between the trades. We hope to reach California before July.

This evening the capt. appointed one of the men from the starboard watch to act as second officer in the place of Bickford. He is a very pleasant fellow belonging to East Bergholt in England, by the name of Thomas Stollery and is far more competent an officer, and more polished a gentleman than his predecessor.

11th June, 1851
It is one of the most lovely mornings I have ever witnessed. The air is fresh and cool, and everything looks pleasant and cheerful. The sky is perfectly cloudless and of that mild and

lustrous hue, so peculiar to tropical climes, while the sea is as sparkling and clean as the water of some mossy fountain in the desert rocks.

Thousands of dolphins are gamboling around our bows, or chasing the flying fish from the water. The sun shining upon their beautiful coat of many colors, has a beautiful effect in conjunction with the depth of the ocean blue, and the pure white of the foamy billows crest.

It seems to me that Thomas Moore must have crossed the Pacific Ocean, before writing that beautiful little lyric:

Oh! had we some bright little Isle of our own
Far off in the blue summers ocean alone
Where the bee banquets on in the bright sunny bowers
And gathers sweet incense from the open blown flowers.

I too might wish for some bright spot to arise in these waters, that I might transport hither my beloved Mary, and live secluded from the cold world "evermore."

Sunday Morning, 15th June 1851
Lat 10 51 N. Lon 119 30 W
Really I think that sour grapes will taste sweet after this voyage, at least far more profitable than the tempers of some of us, are sweet. For the love of Moses, I hope that we shall not be much longer in reaching California.

This is the first ship whose crew I have ever seen holystoning the decks on Sunday. We are busy to be sure in preparing for port, painting, cleaning up, etc., etc. but sailors are used to having their Sundays off and free of all work, except a rough wash of the decks in the morning, and what necessary pulling and hauling in working the ship during the day. But here they are turned to in the morning at three bells, and from then till eight o'clock are kept hard at work at every necessary and unnecessary job that turns up. This of course is the work of the captain and together with the scanty and inferior allowances of provisions he allows the men, is not at all the kind of treatment to insure harmony and good will on board.

We had another flare-up yesterday. Mr. Bishop had his

75

watch aft cleaning the paint off the quarter deck and Mr. St. Julien having nothing else to do, commenced splashing Mr. B. with water, and bantering him to return the compliment. Mr. B. stood it for sometime, but at length caught up a bucket of water and hove it all into Mr. St. J.'s face and bosom wetting him from head to toe. Mr. B. then ran forward to escape a ducking from St. J. but the latter seizing another full bucket hove it after him but instead of wetting Mr. Bishop, the whole of it went down the after sky-light upon Mrs. Burleigh who was sitting in her cabin, working a beautiful piece of embroidery, and upon Capt. B. who was reading by her side.

Did you ever hear a lion roar? You might have heard one now. He rushed upon deck in a violent fury, asking who threw the water, and when Mr. B. went to explain, that it was all in fun, and that it was a mistake of Mr. St. Julien, I never saw a "gentleman" use such language before, in my life, and I cannot here repeat it. At length he told them if he saw any more such skylarking, that he would fetch them out of that, and they might have a trial of the forecastle for their fun. I had been sitting upon the spanker boom reading a favorite book, and saw it all. I thought I never saw as black looking a countenance as our worthy captain put on. Ten thousand devils seemed looking out of his eyes as he berated his offenders, and poor Mr. St. Julien crept away fairly frightened, and not daring to go into the cabin for dry clothes, he sat himself down on the forward sky light to dry himself in the sun. Mr. B. paid no more attention to the storm than if it had only been a monkey chattering, and as for myself I had too much fun in observing J. to pay much attention to my reading.

Instead of having regular N.E. trades here, as we ought, the wind is S.W. and W. How is that. I am sure everything is wrong with the ship.

Sunday Afternoon, 29th June 1851
Lat 29 17 N. Lon 134 W.
What a peaceful day is a Sunday at sea, in fine weather. All day long the ship has been wending her way slowly over the

blue waters, towards the northwest, with just enough breeze to breast the playful waves with feathery foam, and render the air pleasant and cool.

Everything is quiet, the sighing of the wind in the rigging, the low murmur of the waves under the bow, of the startling peal of the ship's bell, as hour after hour glides away, are all the sounds that break the deep silence of the day.

I have thought much of my home for the last few weeks, and besides my many daydreams, constant visions of that beloved place, haunt my wave-rocked pillow. My home has always been *my all* and it would go hard with me if any melancholy change should occur in it, in my absence.

We have had much and unexpected bad weather in the last two weeks, and in the place of N.E. trades, we have had a succession of N.W. winds and gales, and almost continual rain squalls. We saw a sail last Thursday, but was too far off to speak. This is the second sail we have seen in the Pacific.

The weather has been more favorable in the last few days, and now it is more settled again. The tremendous swell too, which has been rolling down from the north, has much diminished, and although it is impossible for us to now reach San Francisco by the 4th July yet we hope not to be over a week in accomplishing the distance. We are about eight hundred miles from our destination, and now we are heartily tired of the voyage. Capt. Burleigh has become very petulant and ill. He is not at all the same man I knew in Boston and New York. Poor Mrs. B. spends much of her time in tears. They do not suit each other at all, and I am sorry that so delicate and affectionate a woman should be linked for life, to such a ——, yes, I must say it, Hog. The stewardess has been at the bottom of most of this, and I wish she had been in heaven or some other place of worship before she came on board the *Delia Maria*. Everyone is tired to death, morose, and sullen, our food is, much of it, exhausted, and the remainder of a bad quality and the water is hardly fit to drink. Jonah, or the Devil must certainly be on board, and I pray for a loving gale of wind to sweep him overboard.

Ship *Delia Maria* at Sea, Pacific Ocean
July 4th, MDCCCLI
Lat 35 31 N. Lon 135 40 W.

The glorious fourth of July!! Far from our homes and our
native land, far from the land for which our fathers fought
and bled to free; in the midst of the broad Pacific Ocean; we
the company of the noble American ship, *Delia Maria,* of
Richmond in Maine, commanded by John H. Burleigh Esq.
celebrated this the seventy-fifth year of our Independence, by
—no holiday or remembrance whatever.

It is customary for American ships to give a holiday on
the fourth of July but Capt. B. can't afford to do that. They
have been painting and cleaning all day and moreover have
had the great rarity of salt horse and sea biscuit for dinner.

However we have had a little better dinner than usual
aft. Green corn, preserved tomatoes, preserved beef, together
with green peas and boulli soup. Really one might fancy himself at home, partaking of the produce of his own garden. We
also saw a sail this morning to the northward, but she is now
hull down astern. Our distance to San Francisco is but 650
miles and with a seven or eight knot breeze we should not be
more than three or four days in running it. But the wind is
ahead and light.

10th July 1851

We have just had another grand row. Poor Mr. St. Julien
always seems to be unlucky. This morning he got his pistols
out to clean, and figuring it would be fine sport to shoot at
a mark, he got one of the boys to hang a bottle on the weather
flying jib by a rope, and then commenced firing at it. Pres-
ently the mate brought his pistols out, but neither of them
could hit the bottle. The captain was just coming forward to
warn them not to cut any ropes when bang went Mr. St. J.'s
pistol and the ball cut away two of the strands of the flying
jib and there being a heavy strain on the rope, the other
remaining strand parted like a rope yarn, and the captain was
just in time to see the mischief. Whew, was there not an ex-
plosion then. Poor, poor unfortunate Mr. St. Julien.

The valiant captain's temper had not got cooled when
as the men were hurling in the brace, he saw little Jack, not

pulling as much as he might, and roaring out at him, he threatened to flog him if he did not pull. Jack answered in rather a sullen voice that he could pull no harder than he was doing, at which the Capt. sprang upon him choked him, threw him down, and would have strangled him if Jack had not been too nimble for him. He then dragged him along aft, and would have tied him up, but Jack then thought that the best policy would be to beg off. So he was let go with a good rope's ending. Ah, Captain, you have a sweet temper.

Bickford our ex-second mate is employing every means to get into the captain's favor again, and they have long conversations together. I have accidently overheard part of them and I find that Bickford is telling him everything he can remember or think of that the mate, or we, or the men have ever done or said against him. I should not be surprised if he were made second mate again in California for Mr. Stollery intends to leave the ship there.

Our little pet Allie is growing saucier every day as we come nearer to our journey's end, and were it not that every day the captain is expecting to get a fair wind so as to be in, he would shut her up again.

San Francisco, 14th July 1851

How can I bring my mind down to the task of writing, when we have only just entered our destination after a voyage of nearly six months upon blue water, without a single break. But I cannot pretend to sleep, and it being so dark, I can see nothing from deck, and too late to go ashore tonight I can do no better than to write up the occurrences of the last few days.

First, I am still in my cabin on board the *Delia,* but it is my last night and tomorrow I bid her a long farewell. We have only arrived here a few hours ago, and as I said it was too late to go ashore tonight. Notwithstanding many unpleasant circumstances that have happened on board to render ourselves uncomfortable, yet now I feel a sort of sadness in leaving the old vessel which has been my home for more than seven months, which has carried me over nineteen thousand miles of tractless waste, through danger and darkness, storm and calm, and through it all has so nobly acquitted herself.

It is not thy fault my brave bark, that I leave thy well

tried and storm beaten shelter to seek a new and perhaps less worthy ship. Thou hast fallen into bad hands my beauty, and like the stork among the sparrows I must abandon thee on account of thy company.

We struck soundings off the coast three days ago, about two hundred miles from the entrance of this bay, and in the midst of very thick weather. We had not run down all our calculated longitude however, and as it was blowing a stiff breeze we reduced our sail and ran with much caution, till about three o'clock the next morning when we hove to, being according to our reckoning not more than 70 miles from this place.

Saturday morning was still thick and it was impossible to see a hundred fathoms ahead. We ran on very carefully keeping the head going every half hour. During the day a large school of whales were flying around us, sometimes coming quite close to the ship and blowing the spray in our very faces. The ladies were very much amused in looking at them play about, until one of them rose within a few fathoms of the ship, directly to windward and giving a powerful blow, sent the water from her pipes in a shower all over them. This together with the peculiarly disagreeable smell of their breathing was quite enough, and we saw no more of the ladies on deck until after the whales had gone.

At dark on Saturday evening we again hove to for the night. The weather continued very thick and it was madness to think of making any land while this continued.

Sunday morning rose rather more clear than it had for the last few days. The sun shone out pleasantly and the sea was clear of fog. By this time we had overrun our calculated longitude, but not a speck of land could be seen from the royal masthead. We began to feel rather uneasy, because we knew not where we were, or where the currents on the coast might set us. I remembered my own troubles off Cape Horn, and began to think that what poor Bickford had seen regarding the captain's incapacity might be too true.

At 9 o'clock a.m. we spoke the barque *Madonna* of Valparaiso bound also to San Francisco. The captain informed us that he had got an observation the day before and that our longitude was at that time according to his reckoning 123

13 W. instead of being, as our famous captain had made it out, at least a hundred miles upon dry land. Well, we all thanked the stranger most heartily in our own bosoms, and as we had yet about sixty miles to run, we filled away again, and soon left our friend out of sight in the fog. The weather still continued on thick, and we were obliged when we supposed ourselves to be about twelve miles from the coast to heave to again. All night long we kept a bright lookout for land but this morning dawned and still nothing was to be seen but the dense impenetrable mist around us.

The wind all this time was fresh and puffy, and our top-gallant sails were furled. About eight o'clock we heard a large bell ringing, and supposed it to be a steamer either coming out or going in to the harbor. We had hove to in the hope of clearing the way for it till about one o'clock this afternoon, when the captain determined either to find the entrance to the bay or to run the ship ashore and gave the order to fill away.

Away we went, right onto the coast, through fog as dense as the darkness of Egypt at the rate of six knots, and I was beginning to think that we must either strike at any minute or else that the land had disappeared altogether, when a man who had been starboard on the flying jib roared out, "Sail O! hard a starboard! hard a starboard!" We all looked ahead in an instant, and there coming out of the fog not fifty yards from our bow and directly ahead was a small schooner. We were all standing on the forecastle at the time, and the captain had no sooner repeated the order of the sailor, than we were abreast of the vessel and missed running her down by only a hair's breadth. We hardly had time to breathe freely after this escape when a voice from the schooner hailed us and asked if we wanted a pilot! "Hurrah! A pilot!" burst from every tongue and in one minute our cares and troubles were at an end. In five minutes we had hove to, got our pilot on board, and were at ease. "Square away the main-yard," "Loose top-gallant and royals," "Let fall the fore-sail and main-sail," "Be handy boys, be handy," succeeded each other in rapid succession, and in ten minutes more our ship was flying through the water and mist, at the rate of nine knots. In about an hour he called out to have a bright lookout kept for the rocks, and he had no sooner spoken than I, who was standing on the weather cat-head saw the land. "Land ho!" What joyous emotions fill the breast of the storm-tossed mariner, when that cheerful sound first meets his ear. I could not help comparing my present experience to that which I experienced in that fearful night, when in the midst of all the terrors of the elements, all the uncertainty of a foundering ship, I heard that startling cry upon the wild coast of Staten Land. And oh! how earnestly have I thanked an almighty God, that he has conducted me, thus to the end of this long passage, in health, strength and safety renovating my broken constitution, so that now I am a strong, healthy, and powerful man.

We took our pilot I said about two o'clock; at half past three I discovered the land, and before sundown we had passed the narrow strait leading into the bay of San Francisco. At seven p.m. we let go an anchor off Blacks Point, and here we are, if not in the "Promised Land" we are floating upon its waters and for my own part I am only waiting the light of another day to set forth upon its shores.

But now goodnight. The midnight watch has been relieved and I must seek repose. Yes, it is the last I shall ever take on board the *Delia Maria.*

July 27th, Hotel St. Frances,
Benicia California.

Between this date and my last there is an intervening period of fourteen days. How have they been spent?

As I suppose we must all give a precise account of our time at the bar of judgment, when the last trumpet shall sound, I have been in the habit lately of reviewing my actions at least once a day, and find how true is that little verse I once learned from my mother when a child.

> How pleasant is it at the end of day
> No follies to have to repent.

I hope these few days do not contain many follies.

The next morning after our arrival in San Francisco, I told Captain Burleigh that I thought I should leave the ship, as I thought he would be detained some time, and that I wished to see California before I left it. I also said that I

82

should find some other ship to prosecute my voyage in, and as I would prefer going as an officer of a ship, rather than passenger, and as Mr. Bishop was not going to leave, and he had retained Mr. Bickford as second officer, I should look for a better chance and better pay. I expected to raise a whirlwind by this, but on the contrary Capt. B. expressed much regret that I was going and Mrs. B. really shed tears. Poor thing! I pity her case, she had made a confidant of me during the voyage, and I know that she has much to give her sorrow. Capt. B. generously invited me to make the ship my home as long as I was in San Francisco as board was very high, at the rate of five dollars per day.

The ladies seconded his invitation with so much earnestness that I consented, for to tell the truth I had become much attached to these amiable New England girls, and our intercourse during the voyage rendered us more like brothers and sisters than strangers.

Well, I now had a home without paying for it, and it was a pleasant one too. Capt. B. had put on his Boston face again and all went smoothly enough. Mr. Julien left us to seek business in this busy land. The stewardess went to a large hotel as chambermaid at $30 per month, and every man left the ship the moment she was moored at the wharf.

The mate, carpenter, and two boys, Alf, and Henry, were all that were left of the large ship's company. All the others had gone their ways to seek for that common desideratim, gold. Having nothing now to detain me on board, I spent my days and evenings on shore, viewing the city, exploring the surrounding country and visiting all the "Lions" of the place. Sometimes I accompanied my friends on an excursion among the surrounding hills, or on the steam boat to Santa Clara on the coast, a pleasant and picturesque little Spanish town, so quiet and retired that I often thought of our own rural villages at home, and sometimes we would ride horseback to the Mission Dolores of the Hacienda Martell, to enjoy as much as possible the days of our stay in San Francisco.

In this manner I spent these days, and very pleasant days they were. San Francisco, however is not the place to interest a traveler very long, and at the end of the period I have just mentioned, most people would, like myself, have seen all the attractions and novelties, and begin to tire of its busy headlong bustle, and unfinished and makeshift construction.

Situated on the eastern shore of that peninsula which separated the southern part of the bay from the Pacific, at a distance of twelve miles from the narrow mouth of the bay, San Francisco affords an example of American industry and invention, seldom seen elsewhere. A few years ago, and it was but an insignificant Spanish village. Now it is a large populous and eminently commercial city. It has a good harbor protected on the sea by a range of high hills and on the land by the high land beyond the bay, and vessels of any tonnage may safely lie at a single anchor. One year ago there were no wharves here, and now there are no less than six long piers, capable altogether of accommodating more than forty large ships. Very few ships are obliged to discharge their cargoes in lighters and the water front of San Francisco will soon present as substantial and busy a front and appearance as New York, or Boston.

There are many deserted ships, here lying either at anchor in the harbor, and used as store ships, or dismantled, and lying hemmed in by whole squares of buildings in the very heart of the town. These wanderers of the deep look melancholy in their odd berth and it is not an infrequent occurence, while walking along the streets, in the midst of the bustle and confusion of a large city to meet with the stern of a large ship abutted against the street, and occupied as a warehouse, a workshop, or a dwelling. I have noticed the *Henry Lee Salem, Bertrand, Baltimore, Salem, Kingwood, Bath* and many others without a name. These ships have been deserted by their crews when the excitement was at its height and becoming dismantled, dismasted and unseaworthy have been allowed to go to shore on the mud, and as the town has been pushed further and further into the water they have been surrounded with piles, streets and dwelling houses.

This manner of building has been necessary in San Francisco because of the shoal water reaching so far out so that some of the wharves "Long Wharf" and "California Wharf" particularly are nearly half a mile long. Several of

84

the streets that run parallel with the water are also built upon piles forming a great bridge as it were, and the houses which line them are also built over the deep water.

Of course there are no cellars here, and the people when they wish to go boating or do an errand in the harbor have only to lift the trap door in the floor of their houses and get into their boat which lies underneath. When I quit the ship the first morning after our arrival, and before she was hauled into the wharf, my boatman took me to my hotel in the very center of town, under streets, houses, stores, etc. without ever leaving the boat.

This mode of building, however handy at the moment as it may be, must have great disadvantages. But a few years will elapse, ere all these piles will be rotted off and the houses and streets will either be tumbled into the water, or some means must be taken to prevent this consequence. The Corporation therefore, seeing the threatened evil, have already commenced to fill up with sand and dirt, all that immense tract of water built over in this manner. They have built a small railroad from one of the adjacent hills, where the cars are loaded, and then descending the inclined plane discharge their contents in the most dangerous places.

An idea may be formed of the instability of these structures when I say that I have been, sitting in the counting room of "Queneau and Johnson" on Montgomery Street and have felt the concussion of every ship striking the wharves and of every steamer when coming in, as plainly as if I had been on the very spot although the distance from the point of contact might have been a quarter of a mile.

San Francisco is a great city of temporary habitations. Were New York or Philadelphia to be destroyed by fire, or otherwise, ages would be required to render them complete again, while should the same happen to this city, two months would easily repair the mischief and restore the original, if not greater beauty to the town. There are no stone buildings, and three or four of brick. The rest are all of wood or canvas. The streets are laid with plank, and generally have raised sidewalks. The handsome buildings are those devoted to gambling purposes, among which may be mentioned the "El Dorado," "La Veranda," "Diana" and the "American," all large handsome and airy buildings. There are two theaters also, one the "American" has been in successful operation for some time and the other the "Jenny Lind" has only just opened. The last mentioned edifice is a splendid structure of gray freestone and would be a credit to a far more beautiful and refined city than this.

The Plaza or public square is a disgrace to the name. It occupies the slope of a hill and might be rendered a great ornament to the city. But now it is worse than any filthy common I ever saw. It is employed as a common depository for all the offal and filth of the neighborhood, and is as dry and as dusty as the middle of the great desert. In regard to the internal accomodations of the California houses I can say but little. Two hotels, and five gambling houses, together with the very few dwellings of the richer merchants who have their families here are the only places where anything like comfort can be found; the "Oriental" and "Jones" boasted of the superior accomodations and they are perhaps on the scale of a second-rate hotel in Phila., but all the others are miserably furnished indeed. The lower story is generally in one immense room, used indiscriminately as a barroom. The upper ones are also in one, surrounded like a steamboat cabin with tiers of narrow berths ranged one over the other and barely room enough to stretch out. No beds or chairs are to be seen in the "chambers" and the latter are scant enough below. Benches are the most common seat, and indeed one may deem himself lucky if he can get a chance to sit on his own knapsack in this crowded and bustling country.

Regarding the moral condition of San Francisco, little need be said. As a general rule I have heard it remarked that where a great superabundancy of the male population existed over the female, that the social condition of the place was inferior, and I have now had an opportunity of proving the truth of this remark.

There are a hundred males here to one female, and children and youth are not to be met with at all. All the restrictive influence of fair women is here lost, and the ungoverned tempers of men run wild. There are more public houses in San Francisco than all the other buildings put together, and full half of these are gambling hells. Thousands and millions of dollars change hands here every day, upon the toss of a card, and the rattle of the dice box may be heard in every direction from morning till night and from night till morning. The grey dawn as well as the high noon hear the anxious call of the bankers in their play, and waking as well as sleeping the eternal clink of money is sounding in your ears. There is no respect paid to the Sabbath. All work and every amusement goes on here as freely on Sunday as any other day, except perchance it be that which is under the control of some rare person whose respect for religion equals his love of gold—by the by, rather an unusual occurrence in California. No one puts any guard upon his tongue, for there is no delicate ear to be shocked by profanity or vulgarity. No little children or modest little maidens. The few females there are here also are far from bettering the condition of things, for also the price of virtue here is too dear to be resisted by most of the frail sex.

The first building I entered in California was the Post Office, and to that sacred spot (the most sacred in California) I directed my steps immediately upon landing. Oh, what sweet comfort it is to receive a letter from home after long months of absence, and ignorance concerning all its beloved inmates. The poor exile in a far off land asks in a faltering voice if there is a letter for him, and waits with trembling anxiety, the answer. The letter is brought, and there is the well known postmark of his home town. Words cannot express his condition and he leaves not the spot until every word is devoured.

Thank a merciful providence that all my letters contained good news. Oh how much I dreaded to hear anything to the contrary, and my pleasure and satisfaction are only diminished by the early date of the letters. It is now the last of July and the latest dates I have received are 30th March. I shall not leave California however till I have written home and received an answer.

Having seen everything in San Francisco worth the while, having traveled over the surrounding hills and plains with my fair companions, assisted my old New York companion Alf Ridley to escape with his clothes from the ship, and also lent the boy Harry a like assistance, I bade farewell to the ship and the pleasant family on board and went to the Oriental Hotel, preparatory to setting out on a tour over the country. Here I found our old friend Allie, looking as fresh and blooming as a spring morning in her own native vales of Cuba.

I could not remain long here however, and pay $5 per day for my food and lodging, so on Wednesday evening, having given my chest and other useless and bulky articles in charge of my friends Queneau and Johnson, I started in the steamer *Union* in the direction of the gold region. I stopped at Martinas the first night, about 30 miles from San Francisco; the next day I spent in rambling about the meadows and groves of this pretty little town, and in crossing over to Benicia where I am now.

Benicia is a scattered village on the southern slope of a range of the western mountains. Its situation is lovely and it bids fair to become the fairest city of the Pacific territory. The place does not number more than one hundred houses, and everything is well finished and neat. The place is inhabited principally by people with families and is consequently much more pleasant as a residence than San Francisco. Governor MacDougal and his lady live here, and for the little time that I have been its visitor, Benicia has given me much pleasure.

This morning I had the pleasure of a visit from Capt. Burleigh and his lady and Miss Gilman. As they were going to return at two o'clock, and as the weather was cool and pleasant, I procured four fine horses, and we rode over the beautiful country around here to our hearts' content. We visited Don Suarez's hacienda about five miles back of the city and were very well received by the hospitable master. His house and surrounding buildings, walls, gates courtyard etc., etc., are all handsomely kept in repair and give one an idea of the dark chateaus of old Spain. Don Suarez has lived here nearly forty years and has witnessed many revolutions in his adopted country, without taking part in any of them. He has enough money to keep himself comfortable and to give his two black-eyed daughters a splendid portion when they marry and the gold excitement has had no effect on his sedate mind. I was much struck with the beauty of his younger daughter Maria Louise. She is almost the picture of my own Mary and within a few days of being as old. We bid these people goodbye, and mounting our horses cantered back to Benicia by the way of the United States barracks. We were only just in time for the boat, and my friends were obliged to hurry down to the hulk as soon as we had returned. I accompanied them on board, bid them another farewell, and sauntered back to my hotel to write these lines. And now I will stop, for I don't know what I shall do next, whether go on to the gold mines and try my fortune there for a few months, or after looking around the country a while, make a voyage to Oregon or the Sandwich Islands and back.

I shall make a move tomorrow.

Hotel St. Francis, Benicia, Cal.
Tuesday Morning, 29th July 1851
I have just returned from the Pacific Mail Steamship Company's depot on the river a mile above this, and I am now busy in preparing again for sea.

Truly I have become a poor lonely wanderer, when one day I do not know where I shall be the next; when I arise in the morning I do not know where I shall lay my head, the coming night.

Last Sunday evening I chanced to meet an old acquaintance, Captain Bawbee, who commanded the steamer *Saratoga* upon Lake Erie, while I was coming as passenger in her from Sandusky to Buffalo. I remembered him well after I had time to recollect him; as soon as I was introduced I recollected his somewhat odd name. I found out that he was at present chief officer of the *Oregon,* Pacific mail steamer now lying at the depot undergoing some repairs and repainting, and coaling for her passage to Panama on the 1st Proxima. It did not take us long to make an arrangement to sail together because he wanted company, and I wanted something to do, and as the office of quartermaster was vacant on board the *Oregon* I accepted it at once. I shall have a particular task to perform but it is a situation of independence and I am willing for the sake of good company to take a trip down coast. We sail on the evening of the 1st August from San Francisco, and we leave here early tomorrow morning.

Farewell to thee Benicia, I have loved thee but to leave thee.

San Francisco, 1st August 1851

All ready once more for sea. We left Benicia at daybreak day before yesterday and have been lying here at Long Wharf ever since. We shall have over five hundred passengers going down with us and if there is any more fun in having a crowd than a decent number, we shall be well amused I know. I have been engaged all morning in getting in our sea stock of fruit, vegetables, livestock, etc., and looking after the immense quantity of gold dust that has been shipped for home. We have more than three millions of dollars on board in gold, and I keep thinking what a splendid prize we should make if we chanced to be captured by an hostile force. I have also been to pay another farewell visit to my friends and as this is the third time I have taken, as I thought, a final leave I suppose it is the last. The *Delia Maria* will be gone before I leave for Panama. I also endeavored to find my own friend Alf, but he had left the place to which he had first gone and no one could tell me where he had gone. Boy Henry who I also helped off from the *Delia Maria* has had the gumption to have himself found and caught by Capt. B. and is now kept on board strict enough. I expect the ninny will lay all the blame attached to his desertion on my shoulders, but I do not care, for thank fortune I am able to bear with almost anything now, and I am not afraid of suffering in the eyes of those I care about.

I have given Mrs. B. a splendidly bound copy of Rottecks *History of the World,* and to Mr. Bishop a Colt revolver as keepsakes.

Well, I must close. We shall sail in about four hours and my duty now calls me on deck. I have had liberty this afternoon, to arrange some matters, but must now bid these shores a long farewell. I am very comfortably lodged here, in a large stateroom on the hurricane deck all to myself. There are three on each side, the surgeons, 2nd and 3rd officer, 2nd, 3rd, and 4th engineer's and my own. We are in the coolest and most airy part of the ship and now that we have such a crowd on board I would not have a cabin or state-room below under any circumstances.

Monday Afternoon 4th August [1851]
Ship *Oregon* off San Diego

It is past four o'clock p.m. and we have just left the harbor of San Diego, and are now starting away again over the quiet waters towards the southeast, and keeping close in with the shore. And how stern is this rockbound coast. The black rocks are piled into high and beetling crags, upon which this rest-less ocean heaves its troubled waters, seeking in vain to burst its shackles and, making the very earth tremble with its strength, and the air reverberate with its sullen roar. The solitary seafowl sits upon the high ledges and pinnacles of this eternal barrier, looking down upon the boiling cauldron at his feet, or scanning far and wide the boundless waters for his prey. He seems the guardian spirit of the sea, for no other living thing is to be seen, and these wild storm-beaten cliffs are his favorite home. Occasionally some high promontory extends far out into the deep blue waters as if in derision of the powers of the ocean, and champion like bearing upon its face the redoubled attack of the heavy surges. But the deep rents and ghastly chasms, on its sides and into its center, tell too plainly the approaching fate, and in a few more years, that stern feature of the coast will have crumbled away and will be lost in the depths of the relentless flood.

We did not leave the harbor of San Francisco till the day before yesterday, in the morning about four o'clock. We had it is true got all the passangers, freight, treasure, provi-sions etc. on board by seven o'clock in the evening, and not-withstanding the night was very dark and a heavy westerly gale seemed setting in, it was determined to put to sea with a huge overcrowded and encumbered ship. We accordingly let go all the warps and hawsers, which had held us to the pier, and were soon roaring and foaming our way out of the dense forest of shipping in the harbor, and making for the mouth of the bay. An ocean steamer leaving her port to launch forth upon the mighty ocean, with all her mighty paraphernalia, tremendous engines, and vast dimensions, with her immense freight of human beings, always is an object of intense interest, and as the engine made its first stroke, and the noble *Oregon* moved off from the pier, a simultaneous shout from a thousand tongues, thrice repeated our farewell, and the weary men who were returning to their homes and native hills, from their long, and in many cases sorrowful pilgrimage in the search of gold, answered the cry by a similar demonstration of their feelings. Those old hills re-echoed the sound, and for a long time the roar of waters and the escape of steam, were drowned by the deafening cheers of the fast parting friends.

Reader, were you ever on board of a noble ship, crowded with passengers and putting to sea, in a dark night, amid all the confusion of trunks, mail, baggage, and a thousand other things that have not yet found a place, and with your passengers running about in all directions like a frightened flock of sheep always in your way, and always calling, shouting, cussing, swearing, hunting baggage, or asking questions, taking your ropes to lash their chests, letting go the top-sail haulyards, or jib sheets; looking for their wives or children, hunting up all the buckets to vomit in or rolling about the decks without them, doing the necessary business in some snug corner where you are sure to find it when you are going to trim sail or let go the ropes, bothering the man at the wheel, so that he cannot steer the ship, or tumbling over the binnacle and breaking the compass and in short making such a universal noise, confusion, and uproar that your orders can neither be heard by the sailors, nor obeyed if heard, except with the greatest difficulty. Indeed you are fortunate if you can find sailors at all that night, for if Jack has not already made himself drunk on his own hook, he generally finds plenty of liquor among the passengers, who are using it in the vain hope of preventing sea-sickness.

Well! it is a mess altogether and you are happy indeed if you do not meet with some serious accident or casualty. In our case we are bothered enough, but after reaching the mouth of the bay, the weather came in so wild and thick that we could hardly see a hand before the face, and as in this case, it would have been madness to attempt the passage of the narrow and dangerous strait, we were obliged to run back to the anchorage and drop our hook till the morning.

The weather had been very fine for some time and as it was to be a warm weather passage no one thought it necessary to provide himself with any other bedclothes than the ship found. These amounted to about three hundred matresses and blankets and the remaining two hundred were obliged to lie on deck in any sheltered spot they could find. The most of these were miners and accustomed to sleeping in the open but this night was very cold and windy, and the poor fellows suffered very much. To screen themselves as much as possible from the dense mist and cold west wind, they lay down in bunches of forty and fifty, as close as possible and covered themselves with their spare coats or an occasional blanket. I had taken a party of sailors and got up a few sails and these together with the stages and guard platforms, were speedily made into a rough tent around the large smoke stack, and filled it overflowing with the shivering crowd. I went to my state room about one o'clock in the morning to catch an hour or two's sleep and what should I find there but two Spanish girls who were going to Mazatlan and who not being fortunate enough to secure a berth in the steerage, and being too poor to pay cabin fare, had been obliged like many others to take their chance on the deck. We had made a sort of room of sails by the side of the engine for the few women that were on board without accomodations, and at first I felt a little angry that my own room should have been taken possession of by these girls. My lamp was burning and I took it down looking at these two poor things. They were both lying in my berth, which was a wide one, with their arms around each other, and sound asleep. I knew them at once, because I had noticed them coming aboard in the afternoon, and in the early part of the evening they were sitting upon a settee near my room door and had seen me enter it and get my pea-jacket. They were young and pretty with black hair and eyes and seemed to belong to a respectable grade of Spanish society. After looking a few moments, my anger turned to pity, and I was just about to hang up my lamp and leave them undisturbed, to spend the night in walking the deck, when one of them awoke, and rising up commenced an apology in very broken English and rousing her sister they said they had only come in for a few minutes in the evening because when they saw me come out I had left the door open, and then they had seen me very busy all the time. They were cold and thought that I was a kind man because I had smiled at them, and had not made so much noise and swore like the other officers, and that it would do no harm to go into my room till I came in to go to bed, and that they had gone in and shut the door and waited so long and I did not come, that they were sleepy and then they lay down and went to sleep.

Well!! here I was with two pretty and black haired and black eyed Spanish maids about 16 and 17 years old in my bed, and hardly able to understand their language although I was well enough understood. I had taken notice before they awoke that they wore remarkably clean white stockings and drawers, and their underclothes were rich and trimmed with lace, and their traveling dresses which had become disarranged showed their dress to belong to respectable and neat people. Therefore I told them to lie still, that the night was still cold and that I would not want the room. They thanked me very kindly, and the oldest who looked very much like Maria Louise Suarez whom I had known at Benicia was really eloquent in her gratitude. I knew that they had not had anything to eat since coming on board in the afternoon, for it was impossible to cook any supper for the steerage passengers, so I went out and going down into the pantry told some of the stewards that I wanted something for two girls that had no supper. I brought up a waiter full of cold goose, pies, cakes and grapes, and gave it to them. I had also two dozen of Calvert in my room, and uncorking a bottle of that also, I told them to eat. I am sure that their hunger must have been sufficient excuse for them getting out of the berth and eating before me, and I trust also that the beauty and appearance of these poor unprotected things, was also sufficient excuse for me remaining and looking at them. I told the eldest one who could speak the best English to take the key of my room inside and lock the door, and in the morning I would come after we had got to sea, and see them. This was nearly three o'clock, and from that time to six I walked the deck relieving the sleepy and half-drunk fourth mate who went below and turned in. At six we roused all hands, hove up the anchor and stood out into the Pacific, enlightened now with a bright morning sun, after the damp and cold night. I was upon the quarter deck till eight, when the other quartermaster Mr. Beecraft, relieved me. Breakfast was ready in the mess room and I went to it, before going up to my room. I was saluted on all sides with a loud, "Hurrah, here you come, where are your girls?" It appeared that Mr. Hull the third mate had seen the girls in my room through the window, and as the mess room on board all government ships is the place for freedom and mirth he had told everyone in the mess of it and they all pounced upon me like a pack of wolves. They thought that the girls they had seen were "grissettes" or in other words like many other foolish men that I had given them their passage for "their company." I soon however, cleared the matter up, yet I am still solicited to introduce my friends to some of these gents, but as I thought at first and as I have since found true, they are modest and respectable girls, although, very lovely, and prefer remaining in my state-room reading my books, or sewing loose buttons on my clothes, than to walking around the crowded decks to be looked at or to be in our way. I have made our messroom boy carry their meals to them and to keep the room in order, but as to the latter, they themselves attend to it. Nikola often tells me that "Dem two sister, no very like you, you hair, you eye, no like, you parlez English, dem parlez Hispanola." I had told Nikola that they were my sisters. My time is divided into watches as usual, and I have four hours duty on the quarter deck, and four hours to myself alternately day and night. The ship is crowded with passengers, and I am always glad when I am relieved from duty. I have given my room up entirely to Annette and Nina, and as the nights are lovely and warm, I spread a mattress on deck, by my door and sleep as soundly as in my own hammock which I left in the *Delia Maria*. In my day watches below I sometimes lie down in my own berth, because the sun is too warm to lie on deck, there is too much noise, and besides the girls are much pleased when I come into my room. This morning I came in after breakfast as usual and found them both kneeling together,

95

and performing their prayers according to their holy church, but rising immediately they both seemed confused and said that I was no Catholic, I was no friend to the Virgin. I told them that I loved not only their Holy Virgin, but all good virgins like themselves. I was tired and sleepy for I did not get any rest at all in my middle watch, last night, and so I lay down on the berth that Annette had made, and was soon fast asleep. The guns which are always fired on going into a port and which at twelve o'clock, were fired in going into San Diego, woke me up. I found Nina sitting by my side, fanning me, and Annette busy making sherbert for my dinner, of some limes I had got in Monterey and loaf sugar and wine. Really, I wish that these two sisters might go the whole voyage with me, they are so gentle, kind and grateful.

But I said that we were off San Diego and I have neither mentioned that town or Monterey which we passed yesterday afternoon. And as it is almost six o'clock I shall put off any description until tomorrow afternoon. I have now been writing two hours, ever since I came below at four o'clock, and I am tired. Nina and Annette have gone on deck to look at the scenery along the coast as it is bathed in sunbeams, and I will do the same.

Tuesday Afternoon 5th Aug. [1851]
Ship *Oregon* at Sea
Lat 27 46 N. Lon 114 41
Off Morro Hermosa.

We have now been four days at sea and much of the difficulties of the vast numbers on board have been remedied and we have got a little settled down, into the regular routine of sea life. There is one thing about a steamer, among the many things that to a sailor are unpleasant and that is the constant progress to the destined port, whether it be calm or a fair wind or foul. We make about from 240 to 260 miles every day and although there is not that quiet easy and graceful motion about her that there is with a regular "winged wanderer of the deep" yet her mighty frame gives one the idea of strength and power, as she plunges over every billow with a plunge and a bound, and one soon becomes accustomed to the roaring of the steam, and the heavy jar of the engines.

We left the bay of San Francisco as I have before said on last Saturday morning, the 2nd Aug, and the ship's company were all day engaged in cleaning the ship and putting things to right in ship shape and sailor fashion. Baggage was to stow away, chairs settees and mattresses to get up from the hold and a thousand things, known only on board a large ship, to be accomplished. By the time we reached Monterey at two o'clock in the afternoon we had everything snug and as we swept proudly into its broad and beautiful bay, everyone was at leisure to regale his eyes with the peculiar beauties of the scenery.

Monterey is a modern looking town, built in the midst and on each slope of a broad valley on the southern shore of the bay. It is not a large place and is scattered over a deal of ground, but there is a degree of quiet loveliness and picturesque beauty attached to it, that very few places possess. There is no business seen going on in the quiet streets, and the inhabitants are either all in their houses or in the country beyond the hills. A few children were playing in front of the doors of some of the houses on the green grass, and at every turn a party of women might be seen engaged in the calm conversation of the Spanish people. There are few buildings of any importance yet there are none of a mean or poor appearance. The whole place lying as it did between the quiet and pineclad hills, with its pretty cottages scattered over the green slopes that stretched down over into the calm blue waters of the bay looked as pleasant and as peaceful as some of the country mansions of the green fields and woods of Pennsylvania basking in the mellow light of a fair summers Sunday afternoon.

There was an American fort to be sure on a high point at the mouth of the bay over which floated the starry banner of my country, and as we entered and discharged our two large 18 pounders, we were saluted from its walls by the thunder of a 36 pounder which rolled and reechoed from every mountain and rock on the bay. Besides this no other sounds were heard. We did not anchor, but lay quietly about a quarter of a mile from the shore until the boat which took the mails ashore could return. It was my office to go with the boat and convey the mail agent ashore, and wait till he was ready to come off again. He told me that he should be detained about half an hour which would give me ample opportunity to take a look at the place. I was back at the little jetty where we had landed before time, for although Monterey is a pleasant quiet Spanish place, yet there is nothing to be seen but the quiet streets, the neat houses, the Catholic chapel, and an occasional bright-eyed, brown-cheeked Spanish maiden.

In two hours from the time we came there, off the town we were again, dashing around the rocky and pine clad knoll that forms the southern landing of the entrance, and bidding the finely wooded and beautiful region, of that neighborhood adieu. As we generally keep within the distance of one or two miles from the shore we can see every varying feature of the landscape. Like the bay of Monterey there are several other breaks in the general ironbound coast, between San Francisco and San Diego. The lofty mountains are at all times to be seen in the distance, and at irregular intervals a wide valley or vista opens from them clean down to the sea, through which flows a pleasant brook whose banks are either skirted with a noble growth of pines and redwoods, or else the vista is one vast meadow, in which countless heads of cattle, horses, and goats are grazing, and embellished by the white walls and tiled roofs of some retired hacienda, or mission with its constant accompaniment of cottages in the background.

We arrived at San Diego yesterday at twelve m. precisely. This is a small place, inferior by far to Montery in beauty or importance. The town is situated upon the banks of a small river about four miles from the ocean, but the vessels which trade there and the steamers all stop at the barracks three miles below. The post office is also here, and several offices of mercantile business, and a dozen fishermen's huts, but that is all, and little enough too. Even the scenery of the place is uninteresting, the southern bank of the river is a low and swampy plain while the northern bank is bound by abrupt brown hills covered in some places by scanty oaks, and in others with the clay of their naked sides. As soon as we had come to anchor we lowered all the boats, for here it was that we were to obtain most of the livestock for the voyage.

As at Monterey I here also took charge of the mail boat, landed the mail and mail agent, and brought off about half a dozen passengers, and their baggage, among whom were Major Lee and his two sons Jerome and Arthur. They all belonged to the United States surveying expedition which was there in the neighborhood of San Diego, and together with three others of the same party were going home. The manner of getting bullocks on board is something novel. As soon as the steamer is seen entering the harbor, the owners of the cattle drive a herd into a large pen, near the boat landing. Here the steward or storekeeper chooses the best of them, and a long rope is immediately made fast to one's horns and twenty Mexicans and Indians get hold of it and drag it down to the water's edge. The end of the rope is then passed into a boat which lies far enough off shore to swim the bullock, who is then dove into the water and pulled up alongside and his head made fast to the front of the boat. Another is served in the same manner, and then another boat takes the first one in tow and each being well manned they are rowed off nearly half a mile to where the steamer lies. When the boats come alongside everything is ready to hoist the bullocks immediately on board. Tackles have been rove on the foreyard, and the blocks overhauled down to the water's edge. A strong strap is put around the horns, the tackle hooked in, and a dozen men at the capstan soon raise the poor bullocks twenty feet high and dry out of the water. Here they hang like a criminal upon the gallows, and bellowing awfully until a guy rope can be rove to swing them in on deck. This being done, they are landed on the main deck where for a few minutes they are unable to stand, but directly they feel better, they get upon their feet, shake their heads and if they are not well secured, you may look out for a fuss. Sometimes they have been known to break away and rushing aft among the passengers clear the decks in short order. We had no accident of the kind however, and as fast as they came on board they were led off to their berth on the port forward guard.

In this manner we got six bullocks on board, besides two or three dozen sheep, a dozen hogs, ten or twelve dozen fowl, ducks, and turkeys, two or three boat loads of potatoes, cabbages, turnips, and onions, and last but not least four or five barrels of sand for holystoning the decks.

Everything being completed, the boats hoisted, the live stock stowed away and the passengers all aboard, we hove up our anchor, fired a gun, and in a few minutes were gliding out of the river into the blue Pacific.

It may seem strange to some people that we took on board so much stock, but when they remember what a vast number of mouths we had to feed the quantity will seem small enough to last till we reach Acapulco next Tuesday morning (8 days). In the first place we have a captain, four mates, purser, surgeon, store keeper, chief engineer and four assistants, quarter master, carpenter, and carpenter's mate, boatswain, and mate-butcher and mate, two water tenders, twelve firemen, twelve coal passers, one marine store keeper, one mail agent, three express agents, twenty-two deck hands, two chief cabin stewards and four assistants, two steerage stewards and eight assistants, two pantrymen, about twenty cabin and steerage waiters, messroom steward, two barbers, five cabin cooks, two ships cooks, 380 steerage passengers, 162 cabin passengers, besides servants, boot blacks, sculleries etc. in abundance, making in all about six hundred and seventy souls, on board this immense floating palace. It is not strange therefore that we should eat one bullock, four or five sheep, two hogs, six or seven dozen of fowl besides a cartload or so of vegetables, bread, etc., etc. and drink about forty or fifty dozen of wine, brandy, or ale. Yes we do use up the good things of life, here with a perfect abandon.

Thursday Evening, 7th August [1851]
Ship *Oregon* at Sea at
Cape St Lucas

It has been said by some that Cape St Lucas is the Hatteras of our western coast, but we are now almost past it and no sign of a gale, or a squall has appeared. The weather has become quite warm, and everyone seems to enjoy himself. In the morning at seven o'clock the awnings are spread over the whole deck fore and aft, the wind sails are trimmed for the gentle breeze, and everyone is enjoying the morning breeze after the cold water bath. At eight everyone gets breakfast fore and aft, and at nine commences the business, pastimes and sports of the day. The deck hands are busied with brooms and swabs, in keeping the decks clean from dust and litter, and the crowds and passengers are busily employed in dirtying these again. Orange peels, bottle corks and cigars are the principle litter and these employ a dozen men to sweep up. Then as soon as the day grows warm, a general rush is made to the pumps and two men are obliged to stand by them to see that the water is not wasted, and the decks from being wet.

On the quarter deck the cabin passengers are sitting in knots about or are talking about things wise and unwise or writing in their notebooks. There is a party sitting around a basket of pineapples and oranges, and there is another with a plate of grapes. There are half a dozen sitting around the captain, and there are a half a dozen bottles of wine and a plate of cakes, and yonder is a waiter passing around a circle of gentlemen and ladies with eggnog, lemonade and porter-sangaree. On the forecastle are a dozen men sleeping in the cool breeze, and among them several groups of card players busily engaged in their games. On the main deck, the carpenter is busy building a coal shute, and the cooks and cabin waiters are busy preparing their utensils for dinner. The upper deck is occupied by the more quiet portion of the passengers, and here out of the noise of the ship and in the pleasant shade they pass the day in reading, writing, and conversation. My room is the pleasantest place in the ship, and on the settees in front of my door, the ladies from the cabin often come and read. My friends Annette and Nina are still with me, and as pleasant as ever. They have formed an acquaintance with two young ladies, cabin passengers for New York, the daughters of Captain Patterson of the *Golden Gate,* who are going home to join their father rather than make the voyage with him around Cape Horn. These girls visit back and forth, and have become quite intimate companions. My duties on board the ship are quite light and I have much time to devote to amusement and pleasure. Annette and her sister are always ready to enter into anything that is proposed, and it is interesting to mark the delicate feelings and the quick sensitiveness which govern the graceful movements and mark the actions of these girls. Caroline and Anna Patterson are no more accomplished or better educated than "my sisters" as every one calls them, and as for bright sparkling beauty they cannot compare. Their manners too are much more free than those of our own country, and although innocent and modest they think no harm in many things that an American girl would never think of. Thus it is not incompatible with their etiquette to occupy my room in an emergency like this, and although I sometimes have the occasion to enter it in the evening after one or both of them have put on their night dress and laid down, yet I am never greeted with any affectation of modesty or shame. Poor girls you must not expect that all the world is as sweet and as pure as your own bosoms; you have not been among its scenes long enough yet to be wary of its snares.

It is a curious scene during these bright moonlight nights to look down upon our decks covered in every direction with sleeping passengers. The weather has become so warm that many, or I might say most of them prefer sleeping on deck to sleeping in their close cabins below. Two or three hundred are ranged in close tiers fore and aft the decks with hardly room to walk among them without stepping first on a hand and then on a foot and then tumbling over three or four at a time. Yesterday as I did not feel very well, I did not go on deck, but laid down and tried to sleep it off. The surgeon came while I was asleep, and gave Nina some medicine for me to take. She would not wake me for some time and then had it all prepared for me to take. I drank it and then she fanned me to sleep again. In the evening I was much better, but I had slept so much in the day that I could not think of lying down now, and after all had gone to sleep, I passed the night in walking the hurricane deck sitting with the solitary third officer, during his lonely watch on the bridge. When he was relieved by the fourth officer at twelve, I came down to the upper deck, to get my pea-jacket out of my room, and found Caroline and Anna Patterson sitting with Annette and Nina in front of the door, enjoying the moonlight scenery of the coast. I joined them and we sat for more than two hours talking of the past and watching the dark shadows of the distant mountains, or the more evanescent shades of the passing clouds over the nearer hills and plains.

The scene was most solemn and magnificent, and high and holy thoughts crowded themselves on the mind. The time was one for deep thought, deep love, or silent sorrow. No one could look upon the eternal barrier of the rock and forest, piled mountain upon mountain in the east, upon the sloping hillsides, broad plains and deep valleys hard by, upon the broad Pacific rolling her restless waves far away to the westward, and dashing against the rocky shore, upon the whole grand solemn scene bathed in the silver light of a full moon, without acknowledging the greatness, the magnificence of Nature; and banish from her bosom the lightness, folly and affectation.

I had often told Annette that she reminds me of a dear friend that is far away, and she had been telling the others of it. They all wished me to tell them my story and to please them I did so, suppressing of course some facts that a young man would rather a young company of girls would not hear. And thus we sat talking or listening to many an adventure of by-gone days, and speaking of many a scene never to be witnessed again. Tomorrow would be the last day that Annette and her sister would be with us, and we drew from her much of her own history, simple and unvaried and calm and cloudless as her own fair brow. Caroline and Anna Patterson had seen much of the world and its vanities and had traveled considerably, seemingly evaded the thorns while they had often plucked the rose.

The bell sounded two o'clock before I knew I had sat half an hour, and we separated. Morning dawned however, before I closed my eyes, and then it was but for an hour. The men who came to wash the decks awoke me and I went into my room, where my friends were sleeping as usual in each other's arms. I did not awake them but drawing to the blinds of the open door and windows, I sat down upon the settee and was asleep in a few minutes. Oh how soundly I slept. Surely convalescence is the pleasant period to the season of sickness, so sweetly do the wings of the drowsy God, fan your eyelids to repose.

I had forgotten to say that on the day that we left

San Diego we spoke the steamer *Carolina* from Panama to San Francisco. Her commander desired us to take on board two men who had stowed away on board the *Carolina* at Panama for their passage to San Francisco and to take them back to Panama. This is the usual practice on board these steamers. When a poor fellow who has not money enough to pay his passage and cannot get a place on board to work for it, stows himself away in some snug hole, till the steamer is at sea in hopes of getting along, he is sent back by the first opportunity, to the place where he came from. So these two fellows who had been abused, knocked around by the captain and kept at work in the coal bunkers, until they were almost dead, and until they had reached within two days' sail of San Francisco, must be sent on board our ship and carried directly back. They may thank their stars that our captain (Pearson) is a rather more humane man than the captain of the *Carolina* for although they are kept at work they are used as any other man.

One of our passengers has a bear on board which he has brought from the mountains of Oregon, and is taking him home. He is the most clumsy and playful beast that I ever saw and affords a deal of fun to the people. We keep him chained to one of the cannons on top-gallant forecastle and feed him on all the offal meat of the ship. He is quite tame and will play with a man for an hour, rolling him over, hugging him and all without even biting him or hurting him.

Sunday Afternoon 10th August [1851]
Ship *Oregon* off Cape Corientes
On the Sabbath day man generally feels more at peace with himself and all the world than on any other. There is a sense of relief felt which is at once pleasant and melancholy and we feel peculiarly at leisure to review all our actions, good and bad. I have not been well today for the second time in many months, and there being nothing to do I have spent the day in the society of a lady who has become quite dear to me, the Spanish maid Annette Guion. I listened to the Episcopal service this morning for the first time since I have left New York and am happy in the belief that although the word of God was spoken by a purser, and an unordained minister,

from that nautical pulpit the capstan, yet its precepts had no [less] weight than that motley congregation. More than half the people however could not get on the quarter deck, and the remainder collected on the forecastle to listen to the discourse of a Methodist Minister who now for the first time since leaving his home in the mountains of New Hampshire had had an opportunity of opening his mouth in the service of God. As this is the first time I have had an opportunity of seeing the manner of conducting divine service on board a ship, it was a little interesting. The ship received an extra polishing in the morning. All the paint and brass were cleaned and the decks were well scoured and dried. At ten o'clock the ship was dressed in all her colors and pendants, and the large ship's bell tolled for ten or fifteen minutes. The quarter deck had been ranged into a church. The capstan was covered with the star-spangled banner, and another very large one was suspended from the awning nails as a canopy. As many chairs, settees, etc. as could be placed in hearing were arranged, and while the bell was tolling the people took their seats. When they had all become seated, the captain made a signal and the bell ceased tolling. The engine stopped and the service commenced. How solemn did the words of the preacher sound as they rose from that silent deck. No other sound could be heard except the hardly perceptible murmur of the light waves, and the occasional sighing of the wind as it rose for a moment and moaned in the rigging. The blue sea was all around us, the distant coast could just be seen on the horizon, and above all the clear blue heaven expanded its broad arch, the only, and most fitting temple of devotion. The huge ship lay still and silent as a tomb, and even the restless steam in her vast boilers, seemed to have lost its usual noisy power, and like the angry billows of Bible description, "to have been stilled by the sound of his voice." I think I never heard better singing. The bass of course prevailed because there were very few ladies to join in the hymn, but the bass was more powerful and more suitable to the solemnity of the scene. The service terminated at eleven o'clock, the bell was struck, the engine gave a puff and a groan, the wheels revolved and we were again bounding forward, over the blue summer sea.

We arrived at Mazatlan day before yesterday, at four

in the afternoon, and after firing the usual salute came to anchor about a mile from the beach. Before I had gone in the boat I had gone to bid farewell to my sisters, who were to leave us here. Poor Annette was in tears, and Nina seemed to be sorry that she had reached home so soon. They both had prepared a keepsake for me and when I had said farewell and kissed them, Annette gave me a cross with a lock of her hair and Nina a book with her hair. And what did I give them in return? I am willing to acknowledge that I have a handsome gold locket with my miniature, which I had got in Boston for my dear Mary, and had left it in New York. Should these pages ever meet thy eye dear Mary, rest assured that in these two girls thou hast no rival in my serious affections. They are I acknowledge handsome, well informed and accomplished, and did not the remembrance of thy dear face and form cling to my memory so constantly, I know not what folly I might commit. Beware dear girls of the world, of which you know so little. You will not always find men who will be as true to the "right way" as I have been.

I went ashore with the mail boat, and soon after the other boats came with the few passengers who were going to stop here. We had considerable difficulty in landing, on account of the heavy swell and surf on the beach, which rolls up from the sea in unbroken force. When I saw the other boat approaching I hailed them to direct where to land, and as fast as they shot into the surf I caused my men to seize the bows of the boat and with her own crew to run them up high and dry on the sand.

Two were thus safely hauled up without accident, or without much water getting into them, but the third one which had no ladies in it, and which was under the command of the second mate who I do not like, I thought might take care of themselves. He came in on the top of a high roller, overshooting his balance, he struck the beach broadside to, and in a moment boat, passengers and baggage were all capsized, and rolling and struggling in the water. This pleased me very well, for Mr. Bunker had always been such a proud upstart of a steam-boat sailor, always bragging of his feats, that I was now right glad to witness his discomfort. I set the men who were bursting with laughter to picking up the trunks and passengers, but they would have seen the 2nd mate in a much hotter place than the bay of Mazatlan, before they would have lent him a helping hand.

While the mails were changing and all the boats loading up with the precious fruit and vegetables of the country, I took a walk around the place to see the curiosities and beauties of the town. I said it was in the afternoon when we anchored, and now the evening sun was lighting up a scene more calm and of more bright loveliness than I had seen before.

Mazatlan from the bay as you approach seems to be one vast ornamental garden. The neat Mexican cottages, with their white walls, latticed windows, and sharp thatched roofs are almost hid in the green groves of orange, lime and banana trees, while on the neighboring hills, the proud villas of the Spanish residents, crown as it were the soft slopes with an airy and classic beauty. From the bosom of the cluster of flowering magnolias, and lofty coconut trees the lofty spire and gilt brass of the Roman Catholic church rises high above the town, and the setting sun as it plays upon it, brings it into dazzling relief against the distant blue mountains.

I cannot describe with what entranced feeling I lay in the stern sheets of my boat, and gazed upon that shore. "Is this the home of Annette," said I "and has it been these deep shades and blue skies that have given the lilly to her cheek and the lustre to her eye? No wonder her form is so graceful, her face so fair and her mind so pure. These skies would change a very elf to an angel, or a grim spirit into a fairy."

I rambled around among the cottages and gardens and groves, looking at the neatness everywhere displayed by the people in their dress and adornments, and at the groups of half naked children at play in the shade. I visited the church whose spire had attracted my attention from the water, and also took a walk to the nearest of the pretty villas upon the rising ground. These houses are in the style of the old Andalusian architecture, light, chaste and airy, and are occupied by the few Spanish families who in the general and successive convolutions of the Mexican Republic have managed to maintain their original character and purity. I saw a party of young people on the grounds of the one I visited, dressed differently and looking entirely different from the race of people called Mexicans, who are nothing more than the descendants of the original Indian and the Spanish, and are not considered equal in mind or character to the old Castillians.

Before I returned to the beach the sun had set, and deep twilight had fallen over the waters. The mails had not yet come down, and to pass away the time I entered a little veranda, where an Indian woman kept fruit and sherbert for a few strangers who come that way. I commenced an attack on a bottle of wine and a few mangoes and while doing justice to my apetite as well as possible, the old woman entertained me with a few choice bits of broken English phrases, which she had picked up from some whalemen who had been there from time to time, and were as intelligible to me as they were laughable and witty. At about seven o'clock the agent came down with his mails and four or five passengers for San Blas and Acapulco, and among them I was surprised to see my "sisters," who I thought had reached their destination.

Mr. Mitchell, who by the way, has been more of a ladies' man than anything else, and has envied me my position with Nina, came to me and said that one of our fair friends was going on to Acapulco, and he supposed that I should now be a happy man. Yes, I said, happy in the company of either of these interesting girls, but which one was going? I was told that Annette was the one, and immediately introduced by her to her father and another sister, who were with them. The old Don thanked me as well as he was able for the care I had taken of his daughters and offered to pay me for the use of my room, but I laughed and told him and the ladies that I had received ample recompense in the pleasure of their company. "I have no doubts of it," said the devilish Mitchell, who must needs put a wrong construction on my meaning. The father now told me that Annette was going to join her mother in Acapulco who had been very sick for some time, but that she should not intrude upon me any longer as he had given her money to pay her cabin passage.

"Um," said Mitchell, who knew as well as I that all the berths in the cabins were taken up, and that not a soul would relinquish his room, not even for a lady. I said nothing however, until we had bade adieu to our friends on the beach, and had with a great deal of difficulty and some danger launched our boat and were rowing off to the ship. I then told Annette that she would not be able to get a passage without a great deal of trouble and that she had much better keep her two hundred dollars and remain in her old quarters. "But," said she, "my sister is no longer with me and you will not be pleased."—"Oh, there is Caroline and Anna and they will be your company and you may be all to yourself if you like, for the weather is now so warm that I shall not disturb you, not at night at least." She looked at me and then at Mr. Mitchell who was counting his mail in the front part of the boat, then whispered to me—"Then I will."— Ah, my dear girl beware, thou art too confiding, and I am only a sailor. May God guide thy innocent footsteps and prevent thy innocence which should be thy shield from ever causing thee ruin.

We had a moonlight row of two miles off the steamer, which when they saw our boat leave the beach, had hove up her anchor, and lay all ready to [be] off. In five minutes everything was on board. The few canoes, which had been selling eggs and fruit to the passengers had been cast off, and soon the usual routine of life had been resumed. It was my watch on deck from eight to twelve, and many were the confused meditations, the pleasant memories, and pleasant scenes that beguiled the weary hours.

At daylight the next morning we saw the high mountains that lie near San Blas, and at seven o'clock we anchored in the bay. The swell was very heavy and as I was going over the gangway, the captain called to tell me to be careful in landing as the beach was a very bad one.

"Perhaps Sir," said I, "the second mate had better take the boat." He laughed, but said nothing and I went forward to get two more men, I heard him telling some gentlemen of that officer's mishap, the evening before at Mazatlan. When I approached the beach, I felt that the captain had not warned me without cause, for I could see no probability of getting ashore without a ducking. The towns all along the coast are bad because of the heavy surf upon the beach, but San Blas is I believe the worst. There is nothing to prevent the sea from rolling directly upon the sand, and it is only in very moderate weather that a boat can land at all. The Mexicans have a sort of a surf boat, somewhat similar to those used at Madras in Hindostan, and with these they can land at any time. Mr. Mitchell became very much frightened and wanted to lay on one of our oars for landing him and his mails, but I had eight stout fellows at the oars and was determined to beach my boat if I stove her to pieces in so doing. Away we went on the top of a huge roller and in a moment more [the boat] was thrown high and dry upon the land almost out of reach of any succeeding wave.—"There by God," said Mitchell, "we are here, but how will we get off again."

Sure enough the prospect was rather "blue," and looked as though it might be a "damper" on our bodies if not on our spirits, but, "Meet trouble when it comes" was my motto and now that I was ashore, I determined to enjoy myself. Giving a dollar to my men, to buy a bottle of brandy in anticipation of their ducking, I went to look at the place. San Blas is so nearly like Mazatlan with perhaps the exception of a little less wealth, and neatness, that all the difference that I saw was that here, a bright morning sun rendered everything green, gay and cheerful, while at Mazatlan the serene horns of evening shed a milder and a more languid beauty over her loveliness. Each city has beauty that the other cannot boast of, and each is rich in picturesque beauty and enchanting views. The houses are scattered about in beautiful groves, from whence issue the songs of thousands of singing birds, and the whole place has as much the appearance of a flower garden, hung full of bird cages, as of an inhabited town. At nine o'clock we were all ready for going off. There were no passengers and after we had got Mr. Mitchell in the boat, and lashed his mail bags so that the sea could not wash them out, we took the advantage of a quiet moment and ran into a retreating sea with the boat as far as our armpits. All tumbled in as quickly as possible but they could not get a stroke with the oars before we were dashed back again, and filled with water. Poor Mitchell was half drowned and swore roundly that he would not make the attempt again; but the Mexicans laughed at him so much, that by the time we dragged the boat out again, and were ready for a new trial he was ready to risk his bones again. This time we were more successful, but just outside the surf, we had got so much head-way on, that we ran down a poor canoe with a fisherman in it. The fellow was out in a minute and had his canoe righted, but before he could avoid it he met with the same fate we had had, and was dashed in upon the beach and rolled with the canoe high and dry in the sand.

And now I will lay by my pencil and devote these twilight hours to Annette. She has been waiting for half an hour for a walk, and thinks that I have a great deal to write. And I think so too, for it is now nearly five o'clock and I sat down at my desk at two; I cannot but think often of all the loved beings, which to me are scattered all over the world. My home, my northern home, my chosen future, and the dear face of my bride, beneath the skies of India, all rise up before me and almost cause me to forget the delightful present, its happy hours, its lovely companions, and fast fleeting moments. Ah! would that treble the distance of this blue sea, lay between us and our next port of our destination.

Monday Morning, 11th August
Lat 19 10 N. Lon 104 6 W.
Three of our passengers died last night. One boy, a steerage passenger, a frenchman who was working his passage as a waiter, and one lady cabin passenger. The lady died from the effects of the hot weather upon a weak constitution, but the others died of cholera and were corpses in less than six hours after they were taken. To the timid these sudden deaths appear very fearful, especially as most people believe that cholera is contagious, but in my opinion there would be no cause for alarm, if every one would be more guarded in their selection of food, and more moderate in its consumption. These California miners have been so long where the necessities of life alone were to be obtained that now that they have reached a land of "Milk and Honey" any excesses are indulged in.

For my own part I am not at all particular what I eat, and take care not to make a feast of an unproper fruit. I have quit taking any meals in the mess room since we have left Mazatlan and have employed Nikola to bring breakfast, dinner and supper into my room, where Annette and myself enjoy them together. The door has a venetian blind to it and when it is shut the room is as private as we want it to be without excluding the air and breeze.

Thursday Evening, August 14th [1851]
Ship Oregon off—Puerto Ventosa

Alone once more. I have been so busy all day that I have not had time to think about anything but the duty on hand. But now when everything is done and I have retired to my room to write, think how lonely and cold it seems. The bright eyes and lovely face that have so long greeted my coming, the innocent tongue so ready to beguile the long hours away, and the fair hand, always ready to preform a kind office or to caress a weary head, are gone and I am indeed lonely.

We arrived at Acapulco on Tuesday morning last, and immediately commenced the operations of coaling, watering and provisioning the ship. The passengers almost all went on shore, to avoid the bustle, coal dust and confusion, that must ensue; and taking the fancy to pass a couple of days in the city, I also got leave of absence, and after taking the mails ashore, left the boat in charge of Mr. Beecraft the second quartermaster, and went in search of the residence of Annette Guion. I am afraid I have said too much already on this subject, and perhaps felt a little more, for I find that we have been together too long, and too constantly to smother the feelings in the human breast. For myself it is nothing, but I fear that on the warm heart and fair mind of the innocent girl, our intimacy has made an impression that will cause many a painful remembrance. I never thought to see so much sorrow as when I bid her adieu last evening, and I have felt ill at ease ever since. I had stayed with her in the gardens of her brother's villa till long after I should have been on board, and it was only after the gun had warned all absentees of her departure, that I parted with her and left the calm moonlight scene. God be with thee fair one.

Acapulco is a quiet and retired city, and is the seat of all the trade of Western Mexico. This however is not enough to disturb the peaceful quietness of the place, and although its vicinity to the capital renders it an important position, very little of activity is observed. The city is guarded with the huge and frowning fortress upon a high bluff which commands the whole bay and harbor and a few idle soldiers in their gay uniform may be seen sauntering about in the shady streets or queer squares. The base is almost a perfect basin, surrounded on every side by a high vine, or circle of hills, and once in the bay, the traveler can hardly tell where he entered, so narrow and winding is the entrance. In fact there is no house, light or land mark which would serve to point the place.

At two o'clock this morning, all hands on board and everything ready, we got under way, and lighted by the light full moon stood out of the bay and breathed once more the fresh salt breeze of the ocean. The cattle we now have on board are much more wild and unruly than those we got at San Diego. They have been bellowing and moaning all day, and one of them got loose about noon, and soon cleared the deck. It was with great difficulty that the men again got them secured.

I am writing a little to send home by a passenger. May God grant that it shall find everyone well, and happy, yes far happier than I am now.

How often do the words of the old song come into my mouth,

> Home, Home! Sweet Sweet Home
> There is no place like home.

Saturday August 16th, 1851
Ship *Oregon* off Sacatecoluca
The heat has become intense. It is the rainy season here and we have an occasional shower. The land along the coast and on the mountain sides, is clothed with a coat of the most luxurious vegetation, and everything seems pushed to the extent of greatest exuberance, by the hot sun and frequent showers. The nights even are no longer cool, for the quiet waters have become heated to the greatest depth and the sea breezes are almost as stifling as those from the land, loaded with all the perfume of the tropical forest. A steamer is only pleasant in one respect, no matter where the wind blows, or whether it blows at all, she is still plowing the waters as usual, disdaining alike the assistance of the breezes and the power of

the storm. But here in a climate as hot as an oven, they are not so pleasant. The boiling sun overhead, the glassy waters around, and the roaring furnaces under our feet, all combine to create a little Hell on earth, sufficient for all practical purposes. At any events it is helping that fell destroyer "Death" do his work among us. We lost four of our members before leaving Acapulco, and together with the little child we have lost three more, and many are now sick. God have mercy on their souls, for their bodies are at the tender mercies of strangers. Every morning at seven o'clock we bury the dead. The corpses have been sewn up in their winding sheets with several shot at their feet and laid upon gratings in the quarter deck ports. The American flag is spread over them to hide the unseemly looking objects. The friends and companions of the deceased collect around, and at a given signal the engine is stopped and the funeral service is commenced. At the words, "Commit their bodies to the deep," the gratings were canted, the bodies slipped from under the banner and a plunge was all that was heard of those who a little while before were full of life gaiety and passion.

Sunday 17th

Yet another funeral! This morning William Emmett, an old man who had been in California several years and had by great perseverance and hardships collected about fourteen thousand dollars, was suddenly seized with the cholera, and died in a few hours. The man was buried at ten o'clock just before the usual Sunday service commenced, and is now cut off from all the dreams he had cherished in regard to his only daughter. His last words were about her and he has given all his money and effects to a friend to have them given to her. Poor man! what good is thy wealth to thee now. It cannot make thy coral bed more soft, or warm the chill waters of thy tomb. And I might ask what good it would have done if thou hadst been more fortunate in reaching thy home. I would venture to say that thy daughter has been far more happy in her poverty than ever she will be again with her dearly bought wealth. The older I grow the more I despise gold. How little good it ever did in the world; and oh, what incalculable harm.

114

Poor young grisly bear is becoming rather an object of fear. The people have teased him so much that he has become quite cross and will sometime strike anyone a smart blow with his paw. Yesterday one of the men was teasing him and he flew at him, and tore his breeches off in a moment. He is too young yet to do any serious mischief, but still is rather a rough companion.

It is amusing to see him when the guns are fired. He is chained to them and sometimes will sit on the top of one of them so that the people will not tread on his toes. When the gun is fired, he drops upon deck as if he were shot, rolls over and over to the extent of his chain, and after he gets up on his haunches he keeps up a steady moan and winks his eye like a duck at thunder.

Caroline Patterson is lying ill and her poor sister is nearly crazy with fear lest she should die. They have moved her out of the close cabin into the surgeon's room which adjoins mine on the upper deck, and I have given up my own room and bed to Anna, who sleeps here when her sister does not require her attention. We cannot mince matters with such a crowd on board as we have, and so much difficulty of supporting the intense heat of the weather, and so but little is thought of the improprieties here.

The notorious Mr. Bunker, the 2nd officer, whom I have mentioned as having the accident in landing his boat at Mazatlan, is also lying very ill. He was taken the day we left San Blas, and has not been out of his bed since. The surgeon says he thinks it very doubtful that he will recover and I am sure I care as little about it as anyone. He is an overbearing, tyrranical, pettish scoundrel and not a soul who knows him would cast him a straw to save his life.

Thursday, 21st August [1851]
Taboga, Bay of Panama.
I have here stumbled upon a place I have never before heard of, which is isolated from all the rest of the world, and which has only been known within the last two years, to any but its original inhabitants, and yet Taboga is the very realization of all our childhood dreams of Paradise, of all the dreamy fables of a bower of human love, and voluptuous pleasures,

the very garden of the Hesperides. I cannot now describe all its beauties and fascinations however, for I only arrived here last evening, but I have no doubt that with what little I have already seen, by the time I leave here in ten days hence, that I may if I chose, tell an interesting story of this Island Eden.

We arrived at Panama yesterday evening at seven o'clock, and immediately commenced discharging our living freight of humanity, with all the baggage, treasure, mails etc. etc. If getting to sea with a crowd of passengers, as at San Francisco is unpleasant, discharging them in the midst of a calm bay, three miles from the beach, with a fiery sun pouring down on your head, and not a breath of air to cool your burning brow, is ten degrees more terrible. All is hurry, uproar, confusion and suffering. Everyone wants to be first, and all order and regularity is set at nought. The servants desert, the men get drunk, the officers curse and the ladies faint. Whew, what a time! By noon however, all had left and many are the articles that found new owners in the confusion. I lost a forage cap, three bottles of wine, and a pair of boots, which were taken out of my room while Anna Patterson was out of it, and the door open. The ship also lost a number of blankets and hammocks, and several of the men and officers sundry articles of clothing. All our wind-sail halyards, lead lines, and signal halyards were cut to pieces and taken for trunk lashing, and I believe that if they could have unrove our running rigging, or unstripped the deck pumps of boarding pipes, that they too would have been carried off. These were the bold Americans from the mines, and no wonder lynch law prevails in their regions, and all law and order set at defiance.

The sick among whom were Anna and Caroline Patterson, did not leave the ship until after all the rush and confusion was over. The ship's boat was employed in this duty, and of course I had the honor of being in charge of it. We landed without difficulty and as I was in no particular hurry to get back to the ship again, while all was so much hard work and confusion, I accompanied the two young ladies to the house of one of their father's friends to whom they had letters and let my men assist their two servants in carrying the baggage. Caroline was almost recovered, but was still so weak that before we found the place she was obliged to go into the house to rest a while, and when at length she had reached the friend's house, she had to be carried upstairs to bed. They were about sitting down to dinner when we arrived, and after the hurry was a little over I was invited to join them. The dinner was a regular South American one, consisting of green turtle soup, iguana steak, fried plantains, sweet meats, oranges, pineapple sherbert, grapes, figs, wine, etc. etc. When I say that the iguana is nothing more than a huge lizard which is caught in the woods of South America and is as ugly as a toad, some of our dainty-stomached northerners might feel a slight disgust to it, but I assure them there is not a greater delicacy to be found in all the world than a steak properly broiled from the rump of this hideous looking reptile.

The family with whom I had the pleasure of becoming acquainted consisted of Captain Phailes Henshaw, and his two daughters, and they live in the most luxurious manner attainable in this land of voluptuous enjoyments. As the Misses Patterson will not cross the isthmus with the caravan they shall remain here till the fifteenth of next month and I shall have a chance of becoming acquainted with many more people and interesting objects of Panama than I otherwise would.

When I took leave to go aboard I found that while I had been dining in the parlor my two men who had come with me were doing the same in the kitchen, besides making love to the Indian maid servants, and when we reached the boat we found it ebbing high and dry on the beach, and the other two men almost dead drunk lying in the bottom. We had to get the natives to help launch the boat, and then the two sober men were obliged to pull the boat three miles off to the steamer.

Before I came on board they had almost finished discharging the treasure, and the mail. I was much surprised to see with what apparent carelessness they handled the former. The whole $3,000,000 were tossed into a large open sailboat, which not being more than about ten tons was loaded down quite deeply. When all was on board they hoisted the sails and away they went with about three men on board and several black looking squalls knocking about the bay. The mail was used in the same unceremonious manner but there being several tons of it, and of much greater bulk than the golddust, we were much longer in discharging it. However, by four o'clock, everything was out of the ship that did not belong to her and getting up steam, we hove up our anchor and came here to this good harbor and delightful Island to recruit ourselves as well as the ship after our hot, crowded and toilsome passage.

Taboga lies twelve miles from the city of Panama, in the midst of the blue bay, and has the only safe harbor within fifty miles. No ship can be nearer to Panama than three miles and there they are exposed to every gale, and every squall that blows and a heavy sea that often sets into the bay with a strong Sou'wester. Therefore as soon as their cargoes are discharged all of them come down to Taboga to repaint and refit, in this most protected and excellent harbor. There is even a good natural dry-dock here, in the shape of a fine sandy beach, and the steamer *Sarah Sands* is now lying high and dry upon it suffering a thorough repair of her bottom.

We can get to Panama and back twice everyday by the little steamer *Taboga,* which only charges two dollars for a passage of twelve miles, and considering the great convenience this boat is, the fare is not at all exorbitant in the present golden age. And now I must stop writing and get prepared to spend the evening and the night at Capt. Henshaws, for I am foolish enough to pay $4 dollars for an opportunity of enjoying a few hours of agreeable society.

Sunday Morning, 31st August, [1851]
Panama—Bay.

We left the Island of Taboga yesterday evening after remaining there ten days, and of course becoming as much attached to its green groves and mossy carpets, retired woody bowers, and bright-eyed, black-haired, half-clothed, and timid daughters, as the length of our stay permitted. Tomorrow we bid adieu to these waters, to return again to the north. And I am not sorry to leave so hot a climate. We shall have about three hundred passengers among whom shall be Mr. and Mrs. Thorne and their daughter Emily and a whole troupe of actresses and actors for the Jenny Lind Theater in San Francisco, and the American at Sacramento. We shall at all counts be not so much crowded as coming down and as there are a number of young ladies going out to make their fortunes, I suppose it will be quite a pleasant passage. There are three other steamers here bound for San Francisco besides the *Oregon,* the *North America, New Orleans,* and *Quick-Step,* so that Panama will be pretty well cleaned out of the devils who have got that far and cannot pay their passage any further. The *Sarah Sands* also has finished repairing and is now about to sail for Sydney, New South Wales. There have been very rich gold mines discovered there, and many emigrants who had left the states, England, France, and California, have here changed their destination, and are about to embark for the new southern continent. Besides these are the *Unicorn, Prometheus,* and *Palladin,* bound down the Spanish coast to Payto, Callas, and Valparaiso, and several freight boats and sailing ships for California and Oregon.

And now what have I been doing all this time? This is a question that I might find difficult to answer correctly and precisely, but I will at least make an appology. Sometimes I have assisted in refitting the ship, and sometimes have been upon sailing parties in the bay, with the captain and his friends, and have generally made out to bring in our own boat the victor. But the greatest part of my time has been spent on shore, in the dreamy shades of Taboga, or in Panama in the pleasant society of my more refined, though hardly more agreeable friends.

I have before said that Taboga was a most lovely island. It rests like a green gem in the still waters of the tranquil bay, and its orange groves and deep coconut woods are so dense that the bright sun can hardly penetrate to the grassy banks and moss-covered rocks below, and the cooing dove and the merry macaw, and lively cricket, discourse sweet music all the dreamy day. Many pleasant valleys wind about among the hills or open upon the white sandy beach, and many little bays indent the shady shores, so retired and cool and fresh that the Indian girl, sitting upon her mossy seat and bathing her feet listlessly in the waves, almost reminds one of fairyland. But the charm of the island is in the innocent beauty, timid freedom and pleasing manners of the natives, and their unbounded hospitality to the few strangers they have seen. They dwell altogether in a picturesque little village on the shore of a quiet bay, and have no other care than to gather their food from the abundance on the island, no ambition but to be loved and no sorrow but in separation. The forms of the females are beautifully developed, their movements are unrestrained, their light and graceful display, half hiding—"Charms most lovely when but half concealed" —their looks are soft and tranquil, and their eyes large, dark and pensive. Their days are passed away in swinging in their hammocks, breathing the intoxicating perfumes of their flowers, and dreamily listening to the mourning doves, or they wander with their lover to some secluded spot, bathe his hands in the cool fountains of the rock, and weave garlands of the fragrant love flower for his neck and brow. There is not a venomous insect, reptile, or animal on this whole island. One may sleep on the velvet couch of nature without fear or harm, dream away the day with the birds and flowers and seek the shelter of the cottage town, only when the mellow twilight is gone and night has robbed the scene of its loveliness.

Oh Taboga! green be thy hills and long may thy children breath the sweet perfume of thy vales and drink in thy woodland music, and the murmur of the sparkling waters. Long may they enjoy those voluptuous skies and balmy breezes and those sweet hours of holy pleasure "which give delight yet harm not." And long may it be ere the world shall have taught thy innocent children the knowledge of one single evil. Love, they posess, sweet, tender, modest, and all yielding love; but passion, hate, jealousy, envy are all to them unknown.

The men of Taboga are not as handsome or well formed as the females, but are the most simple, kind, and indolent race I know. All their wants are clothing and food. The latter is abundantly supplied by the island and the surrounding waters, with only the trouble of going into the woods and on the hillsides and plucking either yams, sweet potatoes, or maize, or getting into their skiff and taking as many turtle, fish, and lobsters as they want. The iguana and land crabs are also abundant and every kind of tropical fruit. Their clothing hardly deserves the name; for where is the use of clothing in a country where there is hardly any cold. A skiffload of yams or pineapples at Panama, will purchase clothes enough for all the men on the island.

While we were lying at Taboga, we were supplied daily with all the luxuries and delicacies of the land. Every morning our huge ship was surrounded by canoes with eggs, turtles, limes, oranges, pineapples, yams, bananas, plantains, mangoes, etc., etc., and often with beautiful bouquets and wreathes from some fair friend.

The ten days flew rapidly by and we could scarce supress a melancholy sigh when we floated out of the harbor and lost sight of the scenes of so much enjoyment.

Panama is very different from Taboga both in size, wealth, and manners and customs. It is an old dilapidated Catholic city; exhibiting all the incongruity of wealth and luxury, and poverty wretchedness and crime. The world has set a foot here, and innocence, and peace and beauty, fled at its approach. Many of the buildings are handsome, particularly the Cathedral and the various chapels, and the place from the bay presents a beautiful and regular appearance. The tiled roofs, the glittering church spires, the surrounding green plantations of coffee and groves of oranges, and the high mountains in the distance render the prospect very pleasing. There are many beautiful sites too in the neighborhood and several most picturesque and striking ruins. Panama, fifty or one hundred years ago must have been a splendid place, but since it has become a thoroughfare for all the world it is fallen, degraded, and disfigured. If civilization works such changes as this, in every corner it invades, I would for one, prefer living in wildness and being at peace.

I have said that we sail tomorrow, and it will be an awful day with us. There is no convenience of a wharf here, and everything is done in the hardest manner. The live stock will be to bring off full three miles, and there will be a rich time on board. I expect to be about used up, but as Mr. Bunker our second mate has contrary to all expectations cheated the devil out of his due, and got almost well again, I shall show him some of the same tricks he put on me at San Francisco, and if he has not got his hands full, it shall not be my fault.

I am now going to take leave of my friends and pay these shores a last farewell. If Bunker sees me back before it is too late to man the stock boats tomorrow morning he may saddle the charge of them on me if he pleases, but I rather think that he himself will have that difficult job to attend to, as I shall be better employed. My friend Mr. Bawbee still continues to show me every kindness in his power, and would have allowed me to be absent during the whole of our stay here if I had wished. But when there has been anything for me to attend to, I have always been on board, but I confess that this has not been very often.

Ship *Oregon* At Sea
Off Ladrones
Tuesday Afternoon, 2nd Sept. [1851]

> Once more on the deck I stand,
> Of my own swift gliding bark—

As a great naval hero once said, "The sea is the only place where a man can find his true love." On shore all is disorder, confusion, turbulence; on board all must conform to rules, at once strict and salutory. On shore a man is liable to be insulted, mobbed or cheated, with impunity, but on board his rights are protected as well as his feelings, but he must fall back into his regular position, and demean himself according to his standing.

The noisy turbulent crowd which yesterday overwhelmed us, and put all order, discipline, and comfort to flight, are today as quiet, tractable, and unobtrusive as children. The pomposity of the servants, hilarity of the sailors, and importance of some of our would-be superiors, have all settled down into the usual steady routine of sea life. I did not come on board yesterday morning until about eleven o'clock, and as I expected was saluted with a—"Well, where the devil have you been all this time?" from friend Bunker.

"Ashore Sir," said I.

"Oh yes, among the girls, and here I have been looking after your duty." Mr. Bawbee who likes Bunker almost as well as I do, came along, and after telling that gentleman that the officers of the *Oregon* were not accustomed to obtain the second mate's consent to go ashore, turned to me and asked how our friends were, and whether Miss Johnson (his lady love) was at the party. Mr. Bunker looked as if he would like to pitch into both of us if he dared, but walked off grumbling and swearing. I shall have a row with that gent before long. The stock had been got on board early in the morning and, in so doing one of the largest and best bullocks was killed. He had been hoisted up by the horns almost to the yardarm, and when the tackle was slacked away to land him on the deck, it was done with such a sudden surge that it broke his neck.

At twelve o'clock the mail came off and I was engaged full three hours, in stowing it away [in the] after hold. I had four or five men with me, and one of them found a box of ale and about half a dozen bottles of claret. These were considered a prize and were confiscated accordingly. We finished the whole of them before we left the mail room, and they were a very welcome Godsend in that hot and close place. At four the passengers commenced coming on board and for a while the ship was entirely surrounded by numerous boats waiting their turn at the gangways. The ship looked like a huge leviathan with a crowd of Pygmies around it. So great was the rush that we were obliged to guard the gangway constantly and not one person who could not show a ticket was allowed on board. Many a poor devil who attempted to smuggle himself on board was sent back again, and many were the excuses and entreaties made by these wretched people many of whom had been at Panama for months, unable to get either forward or home again. One woman, on the pretense of seeing a friend induced me to let her on at the starboard gangway and although I sent one of the men to watch her she continued to either elude his observation or to promise him a reward to be allowed to remain, and she is now on board safe enough. As she is a woman she is used well and will not be sent back. The young men also who had been to the ship the day before to endeavor to work their passages, succeded in climbing up the paddle wheels and got on deck through the door in the wheelhouse without being observed. They hid themselves in the steerage and did not show themselves until this morning when they were set to work, passing coals to the furnaces. They look like young men who have been tenderly reared, and if they do not wish themselves at home again before we reach San Francisco, I am no judge of the furnace deck.

A heavy rain squall came on before all were on board, and this did not mend matters much. We got the ladies out of the boats as fast as possible but not before they were drenched through with water. Their light dresses looked anything but graceful, hanging to their persons like a pair of tight pants, and Miss Thorne would not leave the boat till her mother had found a coat to cover her with.

By sundown, or seven o'clock, we had got all aboard. The quarter deck and waist galleries were piled up full of baggage, and a fine mess it was. No one could get at their dry clothes, and the poor ladies were obliged to go below out of sight, till the trunks could be found and brought to their rooms. There was another difficulty; sometimes a gentleman's trunk was carried to a lady, and a lady's to a gentleman, and here you would find a fellow swearing that his baggage was lost or overboard, and there another disputing the ownership of a doubtful looking box or basket, with the rightful owner's servant. The deck hands took very good care to secure as many wine boxes, demijohns and fruit baskets as they could in the confusion, and the owners would look till they were tired and then curse all ships, steamers, sailors that ever were built. Oh, these are rich old times. Shakespeare could have found ample matter here for any number of comedies. Tragedy too was occasionally mixed with the rest, for once in a while a fellow would get too highly excited about his traps and would get buckled down for his pains.

At nine o'clock we hove up the anchor and bid farewell to Panama, but the confusion was so great all night that no one can tell what strange mistakes were made, or how long it may take to rectify them. There was too much noise to sleep, and too much wine to keep silence. The ship was strange to the people and it took some of them all night to find their rooms, or their own wives and family; before morning too we had run out of the quiet bay into the ocean, and the little sea there was running, was quite sufficient to wilt down the greater part of the most noisy, and wine, brandy, and late

124

supper found its way out of their stomachs, and over our decks in torrents. To cap the climax all the deck hands and firemen were drunk and even the second quartermaster Mr. Beecraft, was obliged in his watch to steer the ship himself the whole four hours.

Well thank heaven we are at sea again, and as I said have got things regulated again, for however much fun there may be in a scene such as last night's, yet there is also much trouble in it.

Ship Oregon At Sea
off Leon
Saturday, 6th September [1851]

We have now been nearly a week at sea and the time has passed away pleasantly enough. The generality of the passengers are of a good standing and pleasant manners, and employ the time in all kinds of plays, dances and amusements. Society on ship board is far different from that on shore, and conduct which is here considered correct and permissible would be scandalized at a city ball or party, or a country picnic. Everybody has become quite well acquainted and the freedom of the seas has imported a delightful freedom to the manners of our company.

We have had two melancholy accidents to occur in the last two days. On Thursday night at about nine o'clock, one of the firemen by the name of Harris, the same man who was, with another, put on board of us at San Diego from the steamer *Caroline,* had become very warm, and after filling up his own furnace with coal came up on board to cool himself and breathe the fresh air. He got on the rail just forward of the paddles and had not sat there half a minute before from giddiness or some other cause, he fell overboard. No human power could have saved him, for in one instant he was swept under the huge wheels and if not broken at once, was stunned so that he must drown in a few minutes.

As soon as the cry was raised however, that a man was overboard, the engine was reversed, a boat lowered and a careful search was made for the body. No trace was found of him but his cap, and the shoals of sharks that were gliding around, and told plainly that all further hopes of his recovery were groundless.

Again as if our victim to these monsters was not sufficient, one of our passengers yesterday morning not ten hours after the occurrence of the night before, deliberately jumped overboard among them. He had been suffering from Chargres fever, and is supposed to have become slightly deranged. Twenty people saw the act, and immediately a dozen chairs, settees, etc. were thrown after him. But no one ever saw him rise again, and when the engine was stopped and the boat sent to look for him all they found was the furniture in the water, and the dark purple place where the horrible meal had been made.

Thus two poor fellows have been cut off in the prime of life, and when they were about to enter on the fondly cherished realization of their dreams. Harris' case seemed the hardest. He had left his wife and child in Mohawk County, New York and had worked his passage as far as Chargres. From Chargres to Panama he walked the whole distance subject to every privation, stress and danger of the road. He had been in Panama nearly two months endeavoring to get a passage to California, and at length stowed himself away on the *Carolina*. When he was discovered he was beaten and knocked down by the captain, and kept hard at work for the whole passage, when within one day's run of his destination they unluckily fell in with us and he was brought back whence he started, working all the time in fire and smoke like a slave. At Panama he made application to the chief engineer to be taken back to San Francisco for his work, and as he had always been a good hand he was allowed to go. But his troubles and hardships are now over, and I hope he is enjoying that rest in Heaven which he knew not on earth.

This morning at about ten o'clock we had quite a row in the "sailor's home." One of the passengers is a respectable and quiet old Negro who has paid his passage and kept himself out of everybody's way on board. One of the firemen by the name of Bryan came on deck to get a fresh breath of air and the Negro happened to be sitting alone, upon the rail where Mr. Bryan wanted to place his own seat of honor. He told the old Negro to come out of that, but not seeing the necessity of the case, and being not in the least in the way he sat still. This enraged Bryan, who by the way is an old convict from Sydney, and going down into the boiler room, he brought up a full shovel of burning coals and dashed them into the old man's face and bosom saying at the same time, "Come out of that, you d—d old black son of a b——h." And come he did with a vengeance, for before Bryan could strike him with the shovel he had him down on the deck, and would have beaten him out of all evil notions in five minutes, had not the other firemen rushed in and dragged him off. Now again the Negro would have been worsted had not a number of the passengers taken his part, and told the firemen that if they offered to do the Negro any more vengeance they would butcher the offender like a bullock.

Bryan swears vengeance, and I doubt now how it will end, but I am well aware of one thing, we must keep order, or we might as well have a mine of gunpowder under our feet as these lawless devils when refractory.

The honorable Mr. Bunker has got himself into trouble. Two or three days ago while he, the third mate, and myself and Mr. Cummings were eating breakfast, one of the steerage passengers looked in at the door for a moment, when Bunker shouted, "Keep your head out of this room." The fellow went away, but told some of his comrades about it, and the moment he is seen on deck hence, he is saluted with groans and hisses and with a reception of his own words, "Keep your head out of this room." Today he could stand it no longer, especially as it had come to the ears of some of the girls, to whom he is endeavoring to make himself agreeable; so walking up to the fellow who is a stout Kentuckian, he asked what he meat. "Nothing, only that you are a damned puke," said he "and if you will come along with me at Acapulco, I will see if I can't fix your own shallow head, so that you will keep "it" out of "this room." Bunker replied that he did not make it a practice to fight with blackguards. "No but you can bully your own men who dare not resent. You are a damned cowardly scoundrel, and if you do not look mighty sharp, I'll make a mummy of you on your own decks." And he would too in a few words more, but Bunker thought that the best part of valor was prudence so backing out he vented his spleen on the poor deck hands. He is still saluted with all the insults that can be invented, and is hated alike by everyone fore and aft.

All this does not mend matters with the ladies or with anyone else.

Ship *Oregon* at Sea,
Off Acapulco
Tuesday evening, 8th Sept. [1851]

We have just left Acapulco, the sea watch has been set, and I have come below to think of the past, speculate on the future, and rest from the fatigue of leaving port.

We arrived in the bay before sunset on Sunday evening, and as we swept past the picturesque old fortress, and low green shores, covered with the young people of Acapulco in their holiday dress, enjoying their Sunday evening on the breezy lawns, I thought that the scene had lost no beauty during the month I had been absent, and wondered if all the inhabitants were as happy as when I had left.

It being out of the question to do anything before the next morning, I obtained the Captain's permission to go ashore, and I told him that I shall not promise to be on board again until the last gun is fired. "Very well," said he, "give my respects to Miss Guion."

I found Annette in the gardens and was delighted to receive such a warm welcome as my own eager expectations had anticipated. She had not been expecting us till the next day, and was therefore taken by surprise just the way I like to try my friends. I asked why she was not out walking on the plaza with all the gay young people and she said, "You were not here." Oh, Annette, for thy sake, would that I might always be here.

I did not return to the ship till this morning. I had hoped that I might have her a fellow passenger again to Mazatlan, but her mother was again ill, and I fear Annette will soon be an orphan. I was obliged to part again with this lovely girl, but could not bear to tell her it was for the last time, even when chided with the evasion. Among the mementoes of this dear flower of summer beauty, is the book I now hold in my hand, and in which I have just discovered the following lines in her own hand, from a translation of Almeyda.

He stands on the shores of our wide spreading bay,
Where floats the proud bark that must bear him away
And young hearts are swelling and bright eyes are dim,
For swift speeds the boat and it comes but for him.
And alas, who can tell where that loved one may be,
When back bounds his bark o'er the echoing sea?

He is gone! he is gone! one wave of the hand,
As a last fond farewell to a bright sunny land,
And away and away o'er the sparkling foam,
He has left a fond bosom a cold world to roam.
Alas, who can tell where that loved one can be,
When back bounds the bark o'er the echoing sea?

Never more, Never more, o'er the wide trackless main,
Will she bear back the lover, to Annette again;
Yet that God who can order the wind and the tide,
Thro, tempest and danger, his spirit will guide.
And, O! May I know where that loved one may be,
Each time your proud bark returns from the sea.

Poor Annette, and must it really be so? Shall I never again visit the green shores? never again gaze upon thy lovely face, breath thy own warm breath, or listen to thy sweet voice? 'Tis better so for thee and me. And now the word which I could not speak to thee alone, must be spoken to thy memory. "Farewell for ever."

Ship *Oregon* at sea,
Friday 12th September 1851
Lat 30 9 N. Lon 115 2 W
There has been quite a break in our voyage at last regarding the weather. On Wednesday afternoon, about a hundred miles east of Cape Lucas, the weather suddenly changed, the wind hauled around N.W. and the sky assumed every appearance of a storm. We immediately stripped the ship of all her warm weather appendages, awnings, windsails, etc. etc., sent

129

down the yards and lashed them on deck, stowed away all movable and dispensable lumber, battened down the forward hatches, and made everything snug as possible for a "Norther." And it was not long in coming. About five o'clock the dark masses of vapor which had been collecting over the cape, suddenly rolled down upon us, and for 13 hours we suffered a tremendous gale of wind. We kept a heavy head of steam on the boilers and drove the ship right into the wind, but we could make but little headway and she pitched at every sea, clear under the water. We had no trouble with the passengers no, everyone we had went below and were very willing to do without supper, breakfast, or dinner. Half of them were too seasick to care whether the ship went down or not, and the rest of them were so frightened that they dare not show themselves out of their berths.

Good heavens, how the sea roared and the wind blew, and the ship groaned. One would have thought that all the elements had let loose all their fury to battle with their sister elements, earth, air, fire and water, the two in our favor the others against. We sustained but little danger however, although both steam pumps were employed in keeping her free, and two men at the wheel could hardly keep her head on the sea.

We should have got through the gale without accident had it not been for two foolhardy men who went forward on the forecastle when she was pitching the worst, to secure a tarpaulin over one of the deck scuttles which was letting the water down in torrents over their beds. While out of reach of anything to hold by, a huge sea swept them off and in a few seconds they were beyond redemption. No boat could have lived in that sea, and no human power could save them. They were in another world almost before their loss was known.

We were at Mazatlan and San Blas on Tuesday last, and found everything the same in these ancient and interesting places. At San Blas, I had much difficulty in landing, and almost drowned our mail agent. The beach was even more rough than when I was here before and not having as good a boat crew I could not handle my boat so easily. Now while the mails were changing my men got into a fight with some

Mexican fishermen and before I could interfere or quell the row, one of them was almost beaten to death with their own paddles. I myself received a severe blow on the head with a stone, and had there not been so many of them I should have beaten them all off the beach, but this would not do and we were obliged to submit to circumstances, and quit fighting.

Last night at one o'clock I witnessed one of the most magnificent and grave spectacles I have ever before looked upon. We were off Redondo Island, and close in with the land. The gale had broken, and vast masses of clouds lay over the distant mountains in white and sulphurous folds. The moon which had been obscured for sometime, suddenly broke out in brilliant splendor, and the whole scene at once awoke to vivid life and loveliness. I had seen so much of calm and quietness of late, that this wild and striking appearance of the sky succeeding the storm was possessed of much interest. The sea was still running in white crested waves before the fresh wind, but the sky was clear, and its dark blue arch was set with myriads of twinkling stars. The moon in its second quarter was almost in the western horizon, while the lofty chain of mountains in the east lay dark and gloomy against the sky. The sharp peak of Redondo, arose almost to the clouds, while those dense masses of vapors were thrown into every variety of bold outline, deep shade and snowy relief. The Island itself was dark and shadowy but the weather-beaten rocks near its summit, shone wild and ghastly in the mountains. To crown the whole, one of the most distant and most magnificent lunar rainbows I have ever seen, rose high above the dim mountains. I felt that it was too selfish to be the only witness of this scene, and having heard Emily Thorne a few days ago express a desire to behold a lunar bow, I went to her berth and called her. She was not asleep and in a moment had thrown a shawl over her head and shoulders and accompanied me on deck. I led her up to the bridge on top of the wheel houses, where the view was most unin-terupted, and was well rewarded for my attention in her ardent delight. She remained with me until the bright orb that had painted the pictures sank in the west, and darkness fell over the waters.

Ship *Oregon*
off Morro Moreno
Tuesday, 16th September [1851]

I have been very ill in the last three days, so much so that I have been confined to my room, and unable to do any duty. I am much better now however, and this afternoon made out to come on deck to look at the quiet town of Monterey once more.

The surgeon of the ship William Buell, is an unprincipled rascal, and now I can believe the many complaints made of him by the ship's company and the passengers. He is not only an ignoramous in the science which he professes, but is careless and heartless in the discharge of his duty. My complaint was rheumatism and inflammation of the kidneys due to the hardships and wetting of the storm off Cape St. Lucas, and my own imprudence in sleeping four hours on deck in the night wind, with wet clothes on. The wise surgeon thought that the disease was peritonitis, and would have treated me accordingly had I submitted but as I had a lancet, medicines etc., of my own, I thanked him very politely and declined his services. I owe much of my comfort and speedy recovery to Mrs. Thorne and her good daughter, and to Mrs. Mestayer, who have been as mothers and sisters to me. But I have missed the tender care and unrestrained attention of my companions on the way down, whose sense of propriety never took fright at the trifling rules of our refined etiquette and it was in the hours of the night as well as the day that their tender hands were willing to soothe the lonely hours, as if no etiquette existed.

Hotel St. Francis, Benicia
Thursday, 18th September, 1851

Welcome again Benicia; thrice welcome are thy green shores and pleasant wind beaten hills. Thrice welcome are thy neat looking cottages and cheerful smiling inhabitants. I loved thy pleasant unbounded hills when I saw thee last and now I love them more. There are no restraints of fence, hedge, or ditch here, no trees or brush; all is clear and open, and the equestrian can give his steed the run, as he ranges the surrounding country without question or interruption.

And I have just returned from such a ride, and feel many degrees lighter, and more free than I did before. I have been over the mountains to visit the family of Don Suarez, in company with his son, my old friend Pedro, who came on board the *Oregon* last evening as soon as we arrived. All the kind family is well, and Maria Louise still more like my own dear absent Mary. But she also resembles another familiar form and I often while looking upon her, found myself wandering in the fragrant orange groves of Acapulco.

We arrived in San Francisco yesterday morning about two o'clock, and before the passengers were called to be in our way, we had warped her into Laws Wharf, carrying away two or three hawsers, however, and running into a large brig in the operation. Accidents however happen in the best regulated families and it was none of our fault, if in getting our huge unwieldy monster to her wharf we should run into and knock to pieces a saucy brig which had provokingly anchored in the way. At daylight we commenced discharging passengers, and by ten o'clock were once more cleared of all but ourselves. I had been invited to call upon the Thornes if I came to Sacramento, and as they were going to open at the American Theater there first, they hoped that before going to it I would give them an opportunity of presenting me with a box, behind the scenes. As Emily is going to make her first appearance on the stage in a few weeks, I think that I shall, if possible witness her debut.

At the request of Mr. Bawbee, almost all the ship's company agreed to remain on board till she was ready for sea again on the 1st October, and although Mr. Beecraft and myself had arranged to make a tour of the gold country, we agreed to defer it till the old ship was once more refitted, and ready for her southern pilgrimage. After discharging all the passengers and their baggage and the heavy mail we took a walk to see some of our old friends in San Francisco. Even in the little time I had been absent much change had occured in this flourishing city. New streets had been opened and new buildings had been erected and extensive wharves built. There had been no more fires to retard the growth and the infant metropolis was pushing its limits still further into the bay, further up the hills, and further along the shore.

At three o'clock all the paints, oils, riggings, canvas and marine stores for her repair was on board, and we cast off from the wharf. A three hours run brought these shores in sight, and before sunset, we had safely moored at our old berth, and gone in search of "Auld Lang Syne," our former friends.

Hotel St. Francis, Benicia
Saturday Evening, 27th Sept. [1851]
The last day of the week has arrived and we have got the *Oregon* all ready once more for sea. It is a pleasant thing to finish an arduous task on Saturday, for the night and the Sabbath following are so much more pleasant and peaceful, when the following Monday does not promise the commencement of another week of the same toil as you have just gone through. We have now been busy upon the ship ever since the morning after we arrived and even last Sunday was employed as any other day. But we have now finished, and although we have been on board but little and mostly scouring the country side on horseback visiting friends, seeing curiosities, etc. yet I am glad that everything is done and that after allowing our men a day of rest we shall run down again to San Francisco on Monday morning, where I may at least quit the home where I experienced so much pleasure, and so little care.

We were much surprised to see the steamer *Northerner* come in on Monday last with the loss of one of her wheels, her foremast, and with much other injury to her immense frame. She had met with her injuries off Cape St. Lucas in the same gale of wind we had experienced, and while we had escaped with the loss but of two men she lost all I have mentioned and one man. She also reported one ship and a brig to the northward of the cape ashore, and several others at sea with the loss of their sails, spars, etc. The *Northerner* will have to lay up at least three months to undergo repairs while we are already again for sea. Truly, poor old Ned is lucky, through all his chances, dangers and adventures.

We have also had some times of blood on board since we have been here. The men have had plenty of money and there is always plenty of liquor to be had. The head cook and the butcher got into a fight a few days ago when the latter threw a knife and inflicted some deep and dangerous wounds on the cook. The cook would then have dashed his brains out in a moment with the carpenter's axe, had he not been prevented by a strong old fellow who was close by engaged in painting. In a few hours a frightful scene occurred among the firemen and the engineers on the boiler deck. Two of them had quarreled and from words came blows of the fist to knives, iron bars and shovels. The 2nd and 3rd engineers ran to quiet the disturbance when, one of them (Bryan, the same who threw coals on the old Negro) turned upon Mr. Cummings the 2nd engineer. In defense Mr. C. picked up a shovel and aimed a blow with the back of it to knock Bryan down, but missing his arm he struck his face with the edge of it almost laying off one side of his face and ear, to the bone. The poor fellow soon fell down senseless and the row was quelled after three or four were wounded. So much for employing Sydney convicts on board our ship.

But I must not forget to tell of my own misdeed while reflecting on those of others. Yesterday evening, the second officer, Bunker, my most inveterate enemy, who has never been on good terms with anyone, and whom the captain has reprimanded several times for insubordination, came upon the main deck and commenced picking a quarrel with me, because I had been absent the day and night before, and he had been obliged to superintend the operations of my gang. I told him that I had been away on leave and that I did not know that he had any business to say anything about it. One thing led to another till he was worked up into a perfect fury and I only wanted him to commence an assault when I was determined to give him at least a trifling remembrance of his old friend.

Finding an opportunity to enrage him still more, I capsized a cask of dirty water as if by accident, over his fine gaiters and trousers legs, and this was enough. He sprung upon me like a cat and in a moment had planted his fist in my mouth. This was all I wanted, and although in plain sight of all hands on shore who however would not interfere, I gave the scoundrel as sound a flogging as ever was inflicted. I rolled him in the dirt and ashes on the deck, altered the shape of his face so that his friends wouldn't even know him and even strangled him so that he could neither call for help or sing out enough. And I am not sorry for what I have done, and would willingly go through the same operation if necessary. Bunker is a scoundrel, and everyone is pleased with his punishment. When I let him go he went to his room, and soon came back with a large coat on and dared me to go ashore with him. I knew he had been to get his dirk and pistols, and told him so. He denied it and called me a coward. This enraged me again, and I jumped on the gangway after him and was following him ashore when Capt. Pearson and Mr. Bawbee who had seen the whole occurance from the storehouse, came out and asked Mr. Bunker what was the matter. He said he had come ashore with Ely to punish him and would do it, but they told him he was a coward and a villain and then had arms under his coat. "Never mind" said I, "I will not give him a chance to use them. I will knock seven bells out of you, you whelp." But Mr. Bawbee caught him by the arm, and the capt. insisted in seeing under his coat, when low and behold, there was his Mexican knife all ready to use.

"Now," said Captain P.," in ten minutes if you are not clear of the ship, traps and baggage, I will handcuff, and have you imprisoned." "Come here Mr. Ely and take the boat to the beach for sand, and do not bring yourself or the men back till you have filled her." "Go to the purser, Sir," said he, turning to Bunker, who stood still, "and get your pay and be off."

Thus we were separated and I have not seen him since. He went to San Francisco that same evening in the *Senator,* Mr. Hull tells me, and he swore he would pay me up sooner or later. Well, he will have to be nice about it, or the next time I will not leave life enough in his body to answer a mosquito.

This morning we came near losing a man. William Everheart, third quartermaster was standing on the forecastle when feeling a sudden sickness come over him he ran to the side to vomit, but in so doing he tumbled over a pile of boards which lay on deck close to the side where the rail had been removed, and with the boards fell overboard. He was stunned and bruised and before a boat could be gotten around to him he was drowning. They picked him up however, and he is now almost as well as ever.

Not half an hour after the last occurence, one of the men who was on the stage scrubbing the outside of the wheel house about 30 feet above the water lost his balance and describing half a dozen somersaults in the air lit in the water on his back. He was a good swimmer and although the ebb tide was running with great velocity he managed to reach the wheel where he scurried up half wearied out. I think I never laughed so heartily as to see the poor devil go. He was a long, slim, Easterner, who had gone by the name of grizzly and his manner was one of the most awkward I ever saw. If it had been in the bay of Panama he would never had reached the paddle wheels before the bloody sharks had caught him. His tricks remind one of the swimmers of Acapulco who will swim alongside the ship and to heave a piece of money in the water they will dive and get it before it reaches the bottom.

Day before yesterday some of the men's time expired for which they had shipped, and they were determined to leave. Mr. Bawbee had persuaded them to remain until the ship was taken to San Francisco but they refused, and about twenty firemen and three deck hands left. Among them was poor Jack Shay, one of the best hands we had and his chum George Prentiss. They both had got drunk in the evening and kicked up a row and had even come aft on the quarter deck where we had a small party of ladies and were dancing, and would not go forward when ordered. The captain ordered them paid off, together with as many who wished, but these were the only two. At about twelve o'clock, and I was riding home with Maria Louise Suarez passing over the bridge of a tide sluice, we saw a man trying to fish up something out of the water but it was too dark to see who it was. He was drunk, and after a moment I found out it was Prentiss endeavoring to get his trunk and a wheel barrow out of the water. But he fell in rather too often to accomplish his purpose and Maria Louise having laughed aloud at his motions enraged him so much that he threw a stone at us. He did not recognize us and thinking it was just as well to let him alone we rode on. In a few minutes we came to another wheel barrow and trunk in the middle of the road and a man fast asleep or dead drunk alongside of it. I dismounted and found it was poor Jack perfectly senseless. I rolled his wheel barrow and chest out of the road and then dragged him after them so as to be out of the way of any of the furious riders of the place. In so doing a bag of money dropped out of his pocket and I thought it would be a pity to let him have it in his present state so putting it in my pocket I rode on.

When I returned to the ship the next day, I gave the money to the purser, who counted it and found the exact amount he had paid him the night before. Jack had been back in the morning to see if any one could tell him anything about his money but no one but myself then knew the circumstance, so it was supposed he had been robbed; he begged money enough of Prentiss to pay his fare to Frisco, where both had gone the same morning. I was sorry about the money, but trusting to see him in Frisco I thought that it might serve as a lesson to him. Having occasion to use a wheelbarrow during the afternoon, no one could be found when recollecting the night before, I sent a couple of men for the two I had seen on the marsh road. They found the one in the water, but the other had made its disappearance. I suppose they had put both chests upon it and wheeled it down to the steamboat landing.

But I must stop, for as the ladies say, I am engaged this evening. I know not when I shall be able to write again. Tomorrow is my last day in Benicia, and when I shall be again so settled, as to have an hour's leisure to write, I do not know. Mr. Beecraft and myself have agreed to start for the interior as soon as we have taken the ship down.

Truly, I have become a homeless impulsive wanderer, and know not where my head may next find a pillow.

Orleans Hotel, Sacramento, Cal.
Tuesday Morning, 30th, 1851
Thus far on our road to the mines, but I think we shall stop here. Tonight the American theater is opened and Mrs. Thorne, Mrs. Mestayer, Miss Albertini and a whole troup of our *Oregon* shipmates both male and female are to make their appearance. Miss Emily Thorne is to make her debut to-night in the character of "Helena" in *All's Well that Ends*

Well. By Jupiter, if the pretty Emily hasn't chosen an odd character to try her maiden prowess on, I am no judge of comedy.

I cannot spare much time for writing now, as I am anxious to have an early dinner so that we may be able to see a little of the place this afternoon. I spent last Sunday very agreeably among my friends and companions at Benicia. In the morning we went upon a sailboat excursion in the bay, and in the afternoon rode to a distant hacienda among the mountains where one of the acquaintances of Pedro Suarez lived. Before daybreak on Monday morning we were on our way to Frisco, where we arrived about sunrise. As usual we knocked seven bells out of everything in our way, stove in part of the wharf, and almost unshipped our paddle wheels. The *Oregon* is too great a monster to be handled like a ship or steamboat, and when she strikes anything she generally goes through it, or over it.

After settling with the purser we bade adieu to our companions who were to remain, and merely taking a miner's knapsack upon our shoulders, we stepped on board the *Senator* and in fifteen minutes were enroute to the mountains. We (I mean myself and Henry Beecraft) had left our chests and trunks at Benicia and had only one suit of clothes besides the one on our backs, and a blanket. We were therefore sufficiently equipped to wander over the mountains, and were well enough armed to protect ourselves at least against even numbers. I had seen poor Jack Shay, and he was delighted to find that his two hundred dollars were not actually lost, and he promised me never again to commit himself so to drink so as to lose command of himself. How long his promise will be kept is rather more doubtful, than uncertain. When we passed Benicia which was just before sundown, the whole place and country around, looked so familiar and homelike, that I found myself regretting the fortune that was carrying me away from there and heaving a deep sigh to the recollections of the many pleasant days I had spent there. After a hearty supper which by the way, cost three dollars, we went to our state rooms and slept till morning. I was awoke by the waiters who told me we were at Sacramento, and dressing as soon as possible, I sallied forth to view the place.

I found that we were in a narrow deep river with very high, steep, banks, and many ship hulks moored close to the bank to answer the purpose of wharves and store houses for the different steam boats and vessels that come to the place. The river is too rapid and too fluctuating in its height, to build stationary wharves upon it, and these old hulks answer quite as good a purpose. There is a broad, plank stage reaching from the shore side of the hulk to the top of the bunk, for the conveyance of goods to the shore, and the accomodation of the passengers. Up the stage I walked and then for the first time beheld the "Queen City" of California, stretching over the broad level plain before me. I stood upon a dyke about ten feet above the level of the streets, for Sacramento is like New Orleans, and subject to inundation. From this dyke the whole front of the city is seen to the best advantage, and I was surprised to find an appearance of so much extent substantial erection and ornamental appearance. The levee upon the river front is very wide, and clear of obstruction except the old sycamores which have been left standing, with more forethought than is usually displayed in settlements. The streets are all very wide and the parts of most of the buildings have been handsomely finished even if the rear is left unfinished. Trees have been left standing wherever they could, sidewalks constructed, and the whole arrangement of the city seems to be made as much of a view of a handsome appearance as the interest of the inhabitants. In the appearance of a place I am always pleased to see a little labor, or a little wealth sacrificed to beautify the whole, and for that reason I soon formed a very favorable opinion of Sacramento and her citizens. There are but very few brick houses as yet and there still remain many of the original canvas ones of the early settlers, but wood is the principle building material, and although rather a dangerous material to build a whole city of as has been shown in the fatal fires of San Francisco, yet there is more room here to avoid crowding and it makes a very handsome house when well painted.

There are four large hotels here, The Orleans, United States, Lady Adams and Crescent City. I am staying at the Orleans and it is decidedly the best hotel in California, and is proud of good fare and good beds, good rooms and comfortable furniture; it is not behind many of our good hotels in the states. But when you come to look for the servants, you find them few and indifferent. Indeed the salary required by these functionaries in the country is so high that only the best established can afford to keep them. The gentlemanly manager of the house, Mr. Curtis, does his utmost to render his guests comfortable and were it not that occasionally you have to help yourself at your meals, or bring your own water to wash, the guest might fancy himself at the Tremont or Lovejoys.

Placerville
Friday Morning, 3rd Oct. [1851]
Yes, sure enough I am now upon that far famed ground which had so recently acquired a golden name throughout the world, "the Gold Region of California." Placerville is the center of a very rich neighborhood, rich I mean in minerals and precious metals, but wild, mountainous and barren in appearance. We arrived here last evening at about ten or eleven o'clock from Sacramento which we left at five in the morning in a large stagecoach drawn by six horses. We had seen everything of worth there and having fallen in with two boys who had belonged to the *Oregon* (Harry Kaigh and Dan Clarke) who wished to accompany us, we bid our friends adieu and soon were dashing across the vast plains of Sacramento. Placerville is about 55 miles from Sacramento and the road, for the first thirty miles is good, passing through a level country thinly covered not with large oaks or pines but with undergrowth or bushes. Being the dry season, the ground was as bare and as innocent of vegetation as the sands of Sahara, and the only green thing to be seen was the half withered trees, almost smothered in the dust of the road. The road itself was not confined to any particular track but every teamster selected for himself what part of the plain he fancied. Here and there a roadside inn offered its hospitality to the traveler but as we increased the distance from the city these became more few and at further intervals. At the distance of five miles from Sacramento we passed the confines of Sutter's Fort better known by the title New Helvetia. This has been an extensive and strong fortification well adapted as a safe residence and

convenient depot, from the enterprising individual from whom it has taken its name. The tall and deserted buildings with their high walls looked so lonely in the midst of that naked plain that even the bright morning looked less gay in the neighborhood and the few birds seemed discouraged to sing a cheerful song in the trees. The whole establishment looks like a ruined monastery. We saw a number of grey squirrels during the day. They are precisely like our own busy tailed grey squirrels at home, only instead of hopping so lively from tree to tree, and chattering from their hollow nests in the boughs these squirrels are obliged, on account of the scarcity of trees to run upon the ground and also to live in holes under the surfaces. Some of the passengers who had rifles amused themselves by occasional chase after one of them, and by the time we arrived at Mormon Island where we dined, we had collected enough to have made our dinners could we have waited for them to be cooked. From Mormon Island to the end of our journey the road was very wild and uneven. Sometimes every one of us was obliged to dismount, and walk up a long steep ascent, where the empty carriage was a heavy load for the horses, and sometimes everyone was glad to leave the carriage for his own safety. We reached the town of Colona on the South Fork of the American River just at sunset and here we saw the first diggings. A large company of miners had been engaged all summer in turning the river from its old channel by means of a dam and tunnel, and now they were reaping the rewards of their labor in the golden harvest in the old bed of the river. There were more than a hundred men employed here, and a rougher, wilder or dirtier set I never saw. Thinks I to myself, "Are these the men who have left their native homes in the comfortable life, to seek a fortune in these distant mountains? Are these the fathers, brothers, sons, of many tender beings at home, who little dream of the actual condition of their friends in California?" If these men were to return to the states in their present garb they would excite a greater sensation than a menagerie of wild animals. Their clothes are of coarse material, ragged and of one uniform color, that of dirt; their hats slouch down over their faces which are almost the color of their clothes, and their beards are long and matted. They scarcely look at you as you pass along, so bent are they upon their engrossing tasks. Poor devils, your toil is spent in search of a useless bauble, your hours are lost in the acquirement of the earth's most unsubstantial production, and your lives are wearing away in misery to yourselves, in absence from your home and friends, and in total neglect of every precept and conjunction of your maker.

Colona is pleasantly situated on the banks of the river, with towering mountains rising in every direction around. It consists of but one street and the rough log houses that line it on either side are of the most primitive construction. Only one or two of the largest can boast of a board front. At Colona we were obliged to leave the stagecoach in which we had come this far, and as there were no other passengers for Placerville but our four selves the stage agent sent us forward the remaining distance in a light carriage with two remaining horses. It was a beautiful moonlight night and as we had long exchanged the level plains and scattering oaks for the high mountains and towering forest of pines and firs, the scenery was most romantically wild. About half the distance between the two towns, we broke the hind wheel of the wagon and although it still supported us yet we dreaded that at every rock or at every hill it would go down. It would have been but little matter however for except carrying our knapsacks, the vehicle was of very little use in these mountains. At length we came in sight of Placerville, and had just passed the "gallows tree" (so named from its having been the instrument of several lynch executions) and were descending the last hill when down came the wheel pitching us out in the dust and spilling all our baggage in the road. We had not far to go, and in a few minutes we had shouldered our traps and leaving our driver to remedy his own case, proceeded to the Placer Hotel and were doing our devoirs to the really excellent supper our lady hostess set before us.

Placerville, El Dorado County
Sunday Afternoon, October 12th, 1851
I am once more in a house with a roof over it and a floor to it. It has been ten days since I first arrived at this place and since that time I have traversed the whole of the region of

which it is the center. In the afternoon of my last date, our party started off with knapsacks, arms and brandy bottles, to make our projected tramp, and see for ourselves life in California. Walking is the only means of locomotion in this part of the world and we consequently prepared ourselves accordingly. We struck into a mountain trail that led across to a locality called Coon Hollow, and having been told that it was four miles we expected to make it before sunset. The distance must have been double what we were told however, for the darkness of the night surprised us in the deep forest and the coyotes commenced their serenade to the moon now hid in fleecy clouds, without a cabin, a light, or even a road to be seen. To go forward was impossible in our case, and to seek for a place to sleep was our only resort. The climate of this country is very fine, and the ground at this season is as dry as possible. Although we had been wading several deep creeks and our clothes were wet, we had no fear of rheumatism nor in fact any other fear to mar our pleasure, in the novelty of our first encampment on the mountains of California. We spread our blankets beneath huge pine trees, and although we had forgotten to provide ourselves with tinder for lighting a fire, we depended upon our arms for protection. Clarke undertook to keep a watch but, waking up in the night, at the noise of the coyotes I found him as sound asleep as any of the others. Oh! how grand and majestic was the scenery of these mountains. Not a single soft feature could be perceived in the landscape. And the frowning cliffs, and dark vallies and towering pines, seemed but a piece of the broad blue arch that afforded us our only roof. How fresh the air was on that mountain! No dampness, no impurities, no stagnation.

We arose early in the morning and feeling the calls of a hungry stomach rather sensibly we made haste to pursue our journey. Upon gaining the end of the mountain we were upon Coon Hollow with its log huts, dirt heaps and noisy brook, opened immediately at our feet.

Going to the only place in the digging where "Prospectors" could be accomodated we were soon making a hearty breakfast off a piece of salt pork, some sea biscuit and a cup of what they called tea without any milk or sugar. This is good fare here, and if a man can get that, he is master of all the necessaries, as well as luxuries of California. Those who travel about from place to place, either looking at the count or hunting richer diggings are called by the miners "Prospectors." This class is very numerous and it is a frequent occurence to meet a solitary man in the mountains with his little mule loaded with his blankets, pickaxe, shovel and wash basin with perhaps a few necessary cooking utensils, while he is armed to the teeth, and both toiling onward to some more profitable place. Many whimsical fellows spend all their time in this way while some are satisfied to remain in one place and dig away without being tempted to seek a better place. The diggings at Coon Hollow were very rich and the miners are throwing out vast heaps of dirt, in readiness for the rainy season which will set in about the middle of November. Gold cannot be separated from sand and dirt without the aid of water and in the dry season it is too far to convey the dirt to the water with the few and clumsy vehicles that are yet here.

In this small rude village, I found a brother chap of mine engaged alternately in dealing out pills and powders to his patients, from his dirty little hut, and in using the pick, the shovel, and the cradle in the capacity of miner. His name was Foster, from the state of Vermont and while with him he showed me all the hospitality that was in his power. There is a baker's cart comes regularly through Coon Hollow in a round of the neighboring settlements, from Placerville and supplies to the hungry miners what they call bread and pies, in exchange for their dust.

We left Coon Hollow the same day we had arrived and entered a canyon (a deep cleft in the mountain) which took us straight to Webberville a distance of three or four miles. Here was a little better appearance than at Coon Hollow and we were able to obtain tolerable good accomodations at the hut of Mr. Webber who had first settled in the place. What I mean by good accomodations is enough to eat of the coarsest food, plenty to drink of tolerable liquor, and a place on the ground to spread your blankets. There is a creek running through the place, and great quantities of dirt are carted from the adjacent diggings to be washed.

Early on the morning of Sunday, the fifth, we left Webberville and having provided ourselves with some smoked bacon, and biscuits and our brandy bottles being replenished we felt ready for a long tramp. We made a circuit through the most populated part of the district first, examining all the different methods of mining and cleaning the gold, and spending our time as pleasantly as possible. We penetrated about twenty or thirty miles to the eastward into the very shadow of the lofty Sierra Nevada and the farthest frontier of the gold country. On Wednesday we were at Murderer's bar on the South Fork, and on Friday and Saturday we were at Chillian bar on the American River. There we assisted an old man by the name of Wendell who had given us food and shelter to throw out and wash about $40 of gold, and our companions Kaigh and Clark were so pleased with our success that they immediately built themselves a hut, and are now hard at it, digging for gold on the banks of that lonely river.

Beecraft and myself have become tired of this kind of navigation and having seen the whole of the district, the various modes of mining and the life the miner leads, I have come to the conclusion that whoever makes a fortune in the mountains of California has abundantly earned it. We arrived here this morning, en route for the plains and tomorrow morning bright and early we shall abandon our pedestrian mode of traveling for the more expeditious, though rather less pleasant carriage and six.

In the meantime I have the afternoon before me and as my lady hostess has supplied me with pens ink and papers I can do no better than write it out. There are two entirely different preparations employed in obtaining the gold here, each adapted to the peculiar state in which it is found. Quartz mining is effected by great labor in quarrying the rock in which the metal is deposited, and entails much expense upon the miner in the purchase of the proper machinery for crushing, smelting and refining. It is always carried on by a large and wealthy company and under ordinary circumstances pays better than, any other mode of mining. Riverside diggings are more worked than any other, because they may be worked at any season of the year, by one or a hundred men in company, and with no other expense than a pick and shovel, a wash basin and a cradle or long Tom.

The cradle is only a box set on rockers with another

146

box with a seive bottom in it fitted upon the first. The sand or dirt containing the gold is shoveled upon the seive in the upper box, and water is poured upon it. A rocking motion is given to the machine while the water is constantly poured on, and the grains of gold like the grains of wheat in a winnow mill, fall through into the lower box, while the muddy water, sand, gravel, etc. run over the sides like the chaff and straw of the same familiar machine. After a quantity of dirt has thus been run through the cradle, perhaps all that one man is able to dig up in a day, the upper box is lifted off, and the gold dust, together with much heavy sand, stones, etc. is carefully taken into a large tin wash basin and gradually cleansed of all dirt and impurity except a little black sand almost as heavy as gold itself which will not wash out with water. This is then dried altogether by a fire, and after the miner has had his supper, he finishes his day's work by carefully blowing away the sand from the pure gold, and weighing and taking care of the precious dust.

Sometimes where several men are working together, in a position where plenty of mining water is to be had, they employ a shute made of long board through which runs a fresh stream of water, and into which the dirt is thrown as fast as it is dug out. A drip box or reservoir at the bottom of the shute, catches all the gold, but lets all the dirt and sand go over in the cradle. By these means much more may be done in a day than with a simple cradle. This machine is called a long Tom. Mining thus by the side of a river or near a brook is comparatively easy, but where the dirt is at a distance and has to be carted or the miner has to wait for the rainy season to swell the mountain rivulettes, it is not so easy or profitable. Then again in some localities there is such a heavy variety of black sand mixed up with the gold, that the poor miner is obliged after washing it as clean as possible, to dissolve the gold on mercury, and in this country where there is no other currency but the dust, it is still less valuable than in the cities. I say that the dust is the only currency here, and every man has his small try scales to weigh it out. An ounce is worth $16, one dollar is half a drachm, and a half a dollar is fifteen grains. Below a half a dollar the Californian never goes and I might say that there is nothing in the diggings that has a less price than fifteen grains of gold. In Placerville however, there are plenty of coin and plenty of means of getting rid of it too. Everything is very dear here, and there is no end to spending money. Indeed you never think of opening your mouth here without putting your hand in your pocket. I said before I thank providence for I once more have got a roof over my head. I certainly do thank providence that I have thus far passed through so many dangers and hardships and exposures, without harm, but I do not know that I am more comfortable here than under the pine trees of the mountains or on the banks of the rock bound rivers. We have slept almost every night in the open air, and have sometimes occupied many hours in descending a ravine or in creeping along a precipice, in constant danger of a break-neck tumble, or of a deadly bite of a rattlesnake. We have also been passing through a wood where the grizzly bears were numerous and where a few days ago a poor fellow was torn to pieces by them and his companion, scalped and torn in the most shocking manner. We have encountered many parties of fierce looking Comanchees, and even lit our campfire in sight of their own, without ever having received harm or ill, with the single exception of poor Clark's losing one of his boots, which he had left at a little distance from him and which the thieving coyotes stole. These animals make a great noise at night and will come quite near a sleeping man, but they never do any further harm than carry off your saddle or boots or other leather articles that may lie at a little distance. I have woke up at night and seen half a dozen around us, and they look so much like a wolf that one is inclined to dread them; but a word and they are all off like foxes.

I felt very much interested in the old man Wendell of whom I spoke before.

He has been in the country near three years and in that time has made and lost three fortunes. His son was with him at first, but when they amassed about 20,000 dollars, by hard work and keeping a bake house to supply the settlement with bread, his son entered a large damming company and persuaded his father to invest all his capital in it. The company had worked all summer and had eventually got ready to commence operations in the dry bed of the river, when a heavy rain came and swept dam, tools and cradles and everything else away. This ruined every man of the company and in despair, the young Wendell joined a company to go home overland. They had reached as far as the valley of Nevada, when they were attacked by Indians and all but one or two murdered. The old man grieved for his son a while, and then commenced anew but with no better sucess. When he had got together about ten thousand dollars, he was induced to join another company for damming the South Fork and after two summers work they found that the returns for their labor would not be as much as a quarter of the capital invested. After all this discouraging experience the old man is still hard at work again, and he says that unless someone robs him he will not lose his money so foolishly again. He has a wife and daughter at home, and is looking forward to joining them in two years more. Poor old man, I wish thee well. It is a matter of surprise to me that more robberies are not committed among the miners themselves, for there is no other care taken of the gold than to put it in a box in their cabin, pull to the door and remain absent all day. I have seen old Wendell put away his bag containing at least three thousand dollars, in a box, without a lock, where every man who worked for him could see it, and start off to the next diggings as unconcernedly as if he had not a penny in his possession. The reason however, that robbery is not more common, is that the punishment is not like the slow-coach justice of official bodies but is meted out surely summarily and immediately. I mentioned having passed a tree near Placerville called the "Gallows Tree." There is many another tree in California that has obtained the same notoriety, and although I am not at all in favor of capital punishment for any crime, yet if life must be taken by man, I would have it taken for one offense as well as another, and by the people themselves as I am sure it has a more beneficial effect in checking crime. For an example of this we might well look back to feudal times of old, when every man went armed, and insult was as severely punished as robbery or murder. This is exactly the present state of things in California. Not a man do you see without his bowie knife, pistol or revolver. Swords would be carried were they not in the way, but the ready bowie fills their place. In every village of this golden country we have from one to a hundred houses dedicated to the purpose of gambling. In San Francisco and Sacramento these buildings, many of them are the most extensive and expensively furnished and finished in the city and even here in Placerville we have two very large and attractive temples of fortune. But in the miners villages they are the huts in which is also kept for sale, the rum, and tobacco for the community. Nevertheless humble the appearances of these places, I have seen hundreds of thousands of dollars of dust change owners here in as short a time as the more refined hells of the cities. Here the banker sits with his cards in his hands, his table loaded with gold, his pistols before him, and his knife in his bosom; and here comes the poor miner who has filled his bag with the precious dust only to lose it in the excitement of the game. I think I have spoken once before of hearing in San Francisco the rattle of the dice, and of the call of the bankers in every hour of the day and the night; and I might say that in Placerville at least the gamblers had no day nor night. All hours are alike to them. There is even another type of business driven on here quite as profitable to the managers, and quite as demoralizing to the community as gambling. I mean prostitution. There is a house here owned by a young woman from New Orleans, who has succeeded in bringing to this retired spot about a dozen Sandwich Island girls and although she has not yet been in the place one year, she must be worth a hundred thousand dollars. It could scarcely be otherwise considering the high price of everything in California, and more especially where there is a monopoly. To speak plainly one night's enjoyment of the society of the charming mistress of the house, costs the man the moderate sum of one hundred dollars, and the same indulgence with the girls, fifty dollars.

Oh! Babylon!

And now to return to the other side of the picture we will enquire for the schools, places of worship and churches. That is a blank page as far as these diggings extend and I am told that it is the same throughout the country. There is I think one building in the city of Sacramento devoted to the worship of God, but I must confess that I did not see it, so unostentatious is its appearance, and there are also in San

Francisco three or four more Roman Catholic Chapels. I have myself seen but one minister of the gospel in the whole country, and I am sorry to say that he was engaged in a ten-pin alley to set up pins. So I have come to the conclusion that religion in this country has come to the lowest ebb, or at any rate much less sought after than gold. Blind mortals, *"to neglect the only object for which we are placed on earth,"* for the pursuit of a shadow and an empty bauble.

As for lawyers I fear their chances are far more dull here than they are at home. Every man is his own lawyer, judge, jury, and executioner, and where the nature of the case demands more than one-man power, he calls on his neighbors to help administer the justice.

Doctors seem to be the only learned profession that thrive in California; and the market is rather overstocked with them too. Their shingles are to be seen in every little village of logs, or camp of tents you meet, and woe be to the man who falls under their hands, both in regard to his chances of eventual recovery and the price he will be obliged to pay for it. There are doctors to be sure, but whether they are all M.Ds. or Christians even, is a matter of much doubt to me.

There are a class of men here who call themselves merchants, and who undertake to supply the necessaries of life to the scattering. These are sold at an immense advance on the already immense cost, and the *merchant thus* soon makes his *pile* and returns home.

All kinds of tradesman are paid enormously for their labor, and it is at once a fortune for a man if he happened to be possessed of a set of carpenters or blacksmiths tools and knows how to use them.

As for schools, the people must wait till there are any children, before they need to go to the expense of erecting schools. Children do not emigrate to California—and there are also too few of the fair sex to ever think of populating the country with native born inhabitants. I have seen but two women in this town; one is an active, cleanly, and pleasant hostess who makes her guests as comfortable as lies in her power, and the other is the lady of whom I have spoken before.

I must now put up my writing and go to supper. When

I shall have another opportunity I do not know. I do not wish to leave the country until I hear again from home, but I do not know in exactly what manner I shall spend that time. Beecraft is going to San Francisco to superintend the fitting out of his vessel for Sydney, and perhaps I may yield to his solicitations and take her there. At all events I am ready for anything.

Sacramento City
Saturday Oct. 18th [1851]

Another week has passed away, and with it some new adventures of my own. I left Placerville on Monday morning last, in a large coach almost overloaded with passengers. One of our fellow travelers was the lady of whom I spoke in my last note and who was going to San Francisco on *business*. She was really a goodlooking girl, and had I not known her character would have thought her to be quite respectable. However we did not stand upon moralities in a California stagecoach and as she was witty and talkative the ride passed away very well. One chap by the name of Underhill became quite smitten by the lady and when the coach drew up at Crescent City in Sacramento, he offered his services to escort her home.

We took another road entirely in returning from that which we had gone to the mines, and it was much more pleasant. The Company dined at the White Rocks, and a rich dinner it was. Pies, milk, cheese, stewed tomatoes and good bread and beef was about the sum total of our fare.

In the afternoon we passed a wagon train from the states, of about twenty teams. Each wagon was drawn by about six to ten yoke of cattle, besides these a few horsemen were driving some three thousand prairie cattle for sale in the large towns. The men all looked weary and worn out and the cattle tired and lame. They had come a long way and had even a wilder appearance than the miners. We were the first white men they had seen since leaving Missouri and the manner in which they had stared at us would have induced us to believe we were the first *Christians* they had ever seen. Some of our party had made out to get drunk before we reached Sacramento and we had quite a merry cargo to astonish the people with, who lived along the road. When the road wound out

152

of a mountain valley, upon the bluff of the high land, that overlooks the broad valley of the Sacramento we enjoyed a noble sight. The level country at our feet stretched away to the north and west for many miles in the midst of which, at the distance of ten leagues the winding Sacramento with its delta of green shone like a painted figure in the brown picture. The mountains near San Francisco and Benicia were plainly visible although distant more than a hundred miles, and the Pacific itself might have been seen at certain points had it not been for the slight haze in the sky. We all got out to walk up the steep and long hill, and [as] I was the first, I was fortunate enough to start a red deer. Bang, bang, went my pistols and bang, went an old hunter's rifle behind me but the deer escaped and as we had no dogs it was useless to attempt to follow him. At a place called the cold spring, we saw a man who a few days before had been hugged by a bear. He had been hunting for the same fellow, who had been seen several times in the nighborhood, and had done considerable mischief to this man's cattle. As the hunter was going near some bushes the bear suddenly came out and looked right at him, growling all the time. The man took aim but fired too soon and only wounded the bear who rushed upon him and in a moment had broken two of his ribs, bitten his arm through and through, and torn open his bowels with his claws.

The poor fellow notwithstanding all this torture had enough strength of mind not to give any sign or motion of life, and the bear letting him go smelled of him and then pursued the dog who ran home as fast as he could. The alarmed family and companions of the man, immediately started in pursuit, and in a few hours by the help of the dog found him almost dead upon the spot he was attacked. This was two days before I saw him, and he was still alive, although I doubt his fate at this time.

We arrived in Sacramento about six or seven o'clock in the evening, tired to death and almost smothered with dust. Long before we had arrived there we had observed an enormous column of smoke arising directly over it, and we had expected to find the whole city in flames, but upon nearing the river, we found that it proceeded from the woods on the

other side of Sacramento, which were in one immense conflagration. Here I bade adieu to my friend and traveler Beecraft who was in a haste to get to his ship and get it in readiness for the trip and who was going to return to San Francisco, by that evening's steamer. I would have accompanied
him, but as I had not seen as much of Sacramento as I wished,
nor of the inhabitants either, I determined to remain a few
days and if possible until the time arrived for me to quit the
country. So after receiving the offer of the *John Potter* from
my friend, I shook him by the hand and hurried to the
Orleans, where a good supper and a warm bath put me in the
best position possible for a good night's sleep.

On Tuesday morning bright and early I was out, listening to the songs of the birds in the sycamore trees on the
levee, and watching the beauties of the early day. As soon as
the shops were open I went to the barber and submitted myself into his hands for half an hour. Then I went to the tailors,
and for the exact amount of 50 dollars purchased myself as
respectable a suit of black broadcloth as was to be found in
California. Thus metamorphosed from the "Prospector" to
a gentleman, (at least in appearance) I set out to call upon
some of our friends. I found Miss Thorne in the height of her
glory. She had appeared on the stage several times since her
arrival, and had received merited applause. I was much
pleased at this, and much more so because it had not made
her vain or elated. Emily is a very good as well as a very
pretty girl. In the afternoon as I was looking at the people
going on board the San Francisco steamers, who should I
meet but my old friend Cyrus Linton of Newton Bucks Co.
Pa. He did not know me and I am not surprised at it, for my
own dear mother would not recognize the sunburned phiz
and heavy frame of her son. I soon brought him to his recol-
lection however, and we were soon ensconsed in a back room
in his store, busily engaged in summing up our lives since we
had last seen each other.

The last time I had seen him was in Philadelphia when
I was a student of Medicine, with far different ideas then of
ever being here in California at this time. Since that time he
had fallen from a high building, made a cripple of himself
for life and finally came out here, and is now doing well on

the salary of two hundred a month, and chief clerk in Clarke and Milne's auction and commission establishment. We spent the afternoon together and in the evening went to the American Theatre to see the playing of our friends and also Chaufrau in the character of "Mose" in the "New York b-hoys."

On Wednesday I became acquainted with Dr. Crane of New York, and at his request I engaged to superintend at his drugstore in the absence of the assistant who had gone to Marysville Island, and I am to receive $100 a month as long as I wish to stay here. So here I am in my old licence dealing in the poisons and remedies of many a poor Californian, and in all the various articles used by men of the craft. Our business is mostly wholesale, and amounts to a good round sum every day. Dr. Crane tells me this is a dull season of the year, and yet our gross sales since I have been in the establishment have amounted to the daily average of about $1500.

Tomorrow afternoon, (Sunday) there is to be a bear and bull fight at the pleasant little village of Washington on the opposite side of the river, and it is expected that crowds of spectators will be in attandance. In this country all kinds of racing and skylarking of this sort is always put off till Sunday, as that is the only day that people can spare time to go and see them, another indication of the moral standings of the inhabitants. These bear fights have become quite the rage here of late, and whenever a hunter can succeed in capturing a live bear, his pile is half made. I intend to go and see the fight tomorrow and then will be able to describe it.

Yesterday one year ago was quite an era in my life, and little did I think then that in one short year on the very anniversary of the day upon which I wound up a business I did not like, that I should be engaged in the very same business again, in a distant country. But so it is, and so it shall ever be with me. I have not known from one day to the next where or in what manner my lot should be cast.

Sacramento City
Wednesday Morning
October 29th, 1851
I am about to leave the pleasant city of Sacramento, and I will devote a few hours to the perpetuation of its memory in

155

my random journal. I have passed two very agreeable weeks among the people of the place and have formed altogether a good opinion of it. There is more good society in Sacramento than in any other town in California. It is better adapted to a residence than any other with the exception of Benicia, and its situation is pleasant and healthy, adapted well to either commercial or social pursuits.

The ground upon which Sacramento city is built is low and level, and although in the rainy season it is wet and muddy, and the river like the Mississippi at New Orleans is liable to overflow its banks, the settlers have remedied this defeat in a great measure by dykes, drains, wide and well planked streets and avoiding the crowding of their dwellings. The city is regularly laid out in squares with a broad levee fronting the river and the whole place is well shaded by the fine buttonwood trees which have been left standing on the levee, and the forest oaks that are scattered through the streets. The river as I said before is deep with high steep banks on either side. There is a pleasant little village on the opposite side called Washington, and this is the Hoboken or Mantua village of Sacramento. A little steamer runs between the two banks and ferries the few foot passengers and fewer wagons that go across.

The dwelling houses of Sacramento are comfortable and well finished. The hotels are good, and the storehouses are substantial structures. There are still however many of the original houses remaining, and these give the place a most curious appearance. Something like that of a country town during a large exhibition filled to overflowing with people and crowded tents and booths in every vacant space. But the grandest edifices here as well as elsewhere in California are the temples of fortune (ruin rather). These rise at every corner and seem to be their own sign boards, for they may be known at once for their size, style and richness. It is easily accounted for, in what manner these concerns drive so profitable a trade. The majority of those who come to California are not the best principled in the world, and soon finding that their chances of finding wealth is a mere lottery they feel inclined to stake their all upon the game of chance instead of hard toil and severe privation to gradually amass their pile.

156

In nine cases out of ten they are losers and even where a man has been fortunate in play it is generally the ruin of him in a social point of view.

I have seen many young men who were in a good way of business, and who were surely gaining wealth, go into a gambling house, for the purpose of merely looking on, and not return till every penny they had in their pockets was gone. No wonder then so few are very fortunate who seek to better their fortunes in the golden land; no wonder that the gamblers' halls eclipse in magnificence the houses of the law, of pleasure, or of God. Yes this is a land of gold, though at the same time a land of weak heads, black hearts, strong passions, and lawless power.

I said I had spent my time very agreeably here, and so I have. Although our business has been heavy I have had plenty of help and plenty of spare time on my hands. We never opened the warehouse till nine o'clock, and were always closed at sunset. There is a large library in the establishment and none need go there without entertainment. Friend Linton would sometimes drop in for an hour and have a smoke and chat, and sometimes I would return the civility. Our stores were but a few doors apart. Sometimes Seymour, Dr. Graves, would come down and amuse us with his lively conversation and occasionally bring the daughters of Samuel Brannon Esq. along with him. Our evenings were mostly spent at the playhouse, where a "box behind the scenes" was at least always waiting for me.

While I have been with Dr. Crane I have boarded in his family. (A California bachelor's family is small) and I am sorry to say that I have often been locked out of the house and have been obliged to seek quarters at the New Orleans as otherwise. A few nights ago as myself, Messers Mestayer, Anderson, and Bond, were returning to our houses in company, Mr. Anderson who was a little elevated commenced a song. He had not got far when we were accosted by a policeman, who required him to be silent, but as Anderson did not see the necessity for all that mock modesty, he continued. The "Charley" now advanced and laid hands upon him, for the purpose of arresting him, but Anderson was in quite another humor and he had no sooner touched him than he measured his length at the ground. The fellow got up and drawing a pistol deliberately fired it at Anderson's body and the ball taking effect in his side, the latter fell as we supposed for dead. We were close to the poor fellow's boarding house and after ascertaining that he was not so badly wounded as we had feared we carried him in assisted by a whole crowd of people who had by this time arrived. But the policeman had by this time decided it prudent to take himself off and nothing has since been heard of him. The mayor has offered a reward of five hundred dollars for his arrest. But he might as well hunt for a needle in a barrel of hay. Anderson has had the ball extracted and is doing well, and we have made our dispositions before a magistrate of our knowledge of the occurrence. So much for singing a song in the streets of Sacramento. One man nearly killed and another made a fugitive from justice for life. The policeman was an Irishman by the name of Riley.

While speaking of the police of Sacramento I may as well say that they are a tolerably well organized body chiefly employed in watching the streets in the night, and the store-houses of the merchants by whose contribution they are chiefly maintained. One of the fruits of their labor has been the formation of a chain gang of all the vagrants, thieves, and all the other petty offenders of the district. This gang is kept constantly at work from early morning till late at night in repairing the streets or river banks, cutting down trees, or carrying burdens from one part of the city to the other. They all go together guarded by a policeman with a double barrelled rifle, and the clanking of their heavy irons may be heard half a mile. I like that kind of punishment decidedly, as the community not only gets rid of a set of troublesome characters for an indefinite time, and gets their street and public works kept in repair at a small expense, but the public, and particularly those disposed to do evil have the penalty of transgression constantly before their eyes and ringing in their ears.

I must not forget to mention the bull fights that have taken place in Washington on the two last Sundays, and which have created quite an excitement here. On Sunday a week I started directly after dinner for the ferry boatlanding. This little vessel had for the last two hours been busily engaged in transporting the crowd across the river. She had been making about four trips an hour each time carrying about three hundred people, and after the whole assembly had crossed it was estimated that there were upwards of three thousand men upon the ground. I was there early and got a good position to see the fight. The pen or arena in which the affair was to come off, was an large enclosure of about a sixteenth of an acre, formed of large upright posts set close together and firmly in the ground. The stages and seats were placed outside the pallisades and high enough to look down in it. There were many drunken people present and many horse races, fist fights, etc. as a prelude to the grand performance. A little before the fight was to commence a half drunk Spaniard fell over the pallisades into the arena. The spectators immediately raised the cry that the "Bear is coming" and the poor fellow jumped up half frightened to death. He first attempted to climb up the posts, but from fear or intoxication he could not succeed. He then ran around the ring, crying and begging to be taken out, but there was no door but the one the bear was to come in through, and nobody would give him a rope. At length when the fellow was almost frightened out of his drunken fit, one of his friends hauled him through a small opening in the pallisades, which was as tight a squeeze as he had ever had, since the day he was born. At three p.m. the large black California bull was let into the pen and after he was well excited by every irritating means that could be thought of, his antagonist that bear was also let in. The animals eyed each other for a while, when the bear began to show symptoms of a wish to avoid the contest but the bull at length made a rush at him and tossed grizzly into the air. The bear was an enormous one weighing about eight hundred pounds and as this kind of play did not please him very well he proceeded to put a stop to it. When the bull came again to the charge, the bear caught him by his shaggy throat with his jaws, and hugging his neck with his fore paws succeded in bringing him to the ground. He then commenced tearing the bull with his hind claws, and the scene was awful; for five minutes the combatants rolled in the dust, struggling and roaring most fearfully. The bull seemed getting the worst of it and his cries were most heart rendering. The bear seemed too busy to make much noise but now and again when the bull succeeded in giving him a thrust with his sharp horns, he would utter a deep smothered but determined growl, but the bull was fast wearing out, and the first opportunity he got he broke away from the bear and nothing would induce either of them to engage each other again.

The bull was dying and as that bear was thought to be too weary and too much hurt for another bull, they were both drove out of the pen. The next bull was as wild and as fierce as the first and as the bear was a much smaller one, the contest was of short circumstance. The first pass that the bull made at the bear he thrust his long sharp horn into his side and after that the only fight that could be obtained was the chasing of the bear around the arena, and an occasional snap by the latter. The performance wound up by turning in upon the bear a lot of dogs, some of which were killed and the others so much frightened that they would not fight. I confess that during the heat of the fight between the bear and the bull, that I was deeply interested but upon leaving the place to return, I felt quite disgusted with the whole affair. Last Sunday there was another fight at the same place. The large bear that had killed the bull on Sunday previous was again victorious, in two encounters, but another and quite as large a one was killed. The bull gored him unmercifully and getting his head between his horns and the pallisades he crushed his under jaw. I was not present at this "entertainment" but my friends told me it was about equal to the one I had seen.

The hour is approaching when I must bid adieu to these shores, and already the runners for the various lines of steamers are singing the news along the levee. By the way, these runners are the most amusing individuals I have seen in the country. They are witty gassy men who are employed by the rival companies to obtain passengers for their boats. The steamers usually all start at two o'clock p.m. and the people from the interior who come in on mules or stages generally care little about which of these boats they take. As soon as a party is seen to approach the landing, they are beset by the whole pack of runners, who in loud voices and unchosen language commence the attack, running down all lines but their own, and praising it up to the skies. All talk together or contradict themselves and each other, as fast as they can speak, making all manner of fun at each other and of the lines to which they are attached. But the best of the whole matter they always keep in a good humor and as they tell all manner of lies they are in no way irritated on being told of it. Yesterday they had quite a woods meeting of it on the levee in front of our stores. A large party of miners were coming down the middle of K. St. on their way to the steamers. They were just from the mines and were loaded with their knapsacks, and were going home in the mail steamer of the first of November. The runners soon discovered them and at it they went. The party stopped under some trees on the levee and seemed inclined to hear the arguments on all sides. Runner No. 1 spoke as follows: "Gentlemen, You are going down to the bay after making your piles in the mines, and you want to go safe. You don't want to go in any old rat trap that will blow up and kill you all before you get two miles, nor you don't want to go in an old box that will take two or three days in getting there and then the mail steamer will be gone and you will lose your passage. Gentlemen, take the advice of a friend, and don't trust yourself on board that old *Confidence,* nor yet on the *New World,* which will surely be blown up one of these days for her boilers are a hundred years old, and were used to boil malt in before they were put in her, and the . . ."

Runner No. 2: "You're a liar, you're an old fool!"

No. 1: "And the other never went more than two miles an hour since she was built, till they stopped the leaks in her boiler with putty, and now she goes about three."

No. 3: "Hold on there you old fool, you must be talking about your own old craft."

No. 1: "No I ain't! The *Senator* gents, is a magnificant boat, and nobody was ever sucked in that traveled on her. Go on board the *Senator* gents and you will be in San Francisco before daylight in the morning."

No. 2: "Yes day after tomorrow morning."

161

No. 1: "Have a good supper, sleep on a good matress, and all for $5. Here are your tickets gentlemen, only $5."

No. 2: "Look here gentlemen dont mind what that fool says. He is so big a liar that nobody that knows him believes a word he says. The *Confidence,* gentlemen, is the newest best, fastest and most comfortable boat on the river, and I would not trust my life on any of the others. The *Senator* is an old comdemned hulk that has been painted and varnished over, and had an old horsepower boiler put into her, and the . . ."

No. 1: "Ha, ha, ha. The fellow must be drunk or else his head is swelling. I say you had better take a dose of pills."

No. 2: "And the *New World* is a d——d site worse than the *Senator.*"

No. 3: "Ride him on a rail! Why gentlemen these two fellows are the biggest liars in Sacramento and if you go in their boats you are sure to be robbed or cheated, for anybody that will lie like them chaps, will murder a man for his money. The *New World* is the best boat in California. She goes around Cape Horn in just six weeks from New York, and she can do it any time. Only five dollars for a passage on the SPLENDID STEAMER *New World.*"

No. 1: "That fellow gets paid for every word he speaks and for every lie he tells so you neither care anything about him or the *Confidence* man either. I saw them both together an hour ago eating boiled cabbage and ale; I don't get paid anything for what I say gentlemen and it is only out of pure love for mankind in general that I want you to go in the best and safest boat. Here are the tickets gentlemen, only five dollars."

No. 3: "GO HOME you old Jackass before your throat gets sore, and the captain of the *Senator* has to pay another doctor bill for you. You will come to the insane asylum yet. Come gentlemen, I'll show you a beauty, just come and look at the *New World.*"

No. 2: "Now I hope you don't think these gentlemen are as big fools as either of you are, do you. They would look pretty about the time all of you got on board, if your rotten old decks were to fall through, and land everybody in the lower hold. NO! NO! They are going on board the *Con-*

fidence. Come on gentlemen, I think I have a little "Old Tom" on board and you must be thirsty after your dusty tramp."

No. 1: "Hark at that will you! Why gentlemen that fellow was only let out of the chain gang last week for stealing an old woman's night cap to make a bustle for his sweetheart. I hope you will not go and drink with such a jail bird as that. Talking about drinking, I think they are just now wetting their whistle on board the *Senator* now. Come Gentlemen I am dry. All for five dollars you know."

And so the noisy laughing crowd followed the jolly old runner, who winking his eye at No. 2 and 3 as much as to say, "Suck our thumbs," led the way over the bank on board the really fine steamer *Senator*. No. 2 and 3 could not stand this defeat calmly and so they called after the returning party:

"You'd better not drink any of the liquor that fellow gives you, it's poisoned."

"We will report you when we get to San Francisco in the morning."

"Keep your eyes on that old scoundrel."

"Say you'd better come on take a look at the *Confidence* before you pay your passage on that old Box. She is the best boat on the river by far."

No. 1: "Shut up your mouths you are drunk," "You are a couple of liars," "Go to bed," "You can't shine . . ."

Such scenes as this are going forth every day about the time the steamers start, and it is often the most laughable farce in the world, when they chance to get hold of a chap particularly green or in a hurry. They are like the New York cabmen however, and if you stop or hesitate, you are at once beseiged, but if you pass on and say nothing you are not troubled.

I must now however stop; it is near two o'clock and all my baggage is on board the steamer the *Senator*. I have become anxious to hear from home, and I am sure of doing so by the next mail which is expected in, in two or three days. I have therefore quit my employment, with Dr. Crane, bid adieu to my numerous kind friends, settled up my accounts, and am now going to San Francisco to look out for a ship to

India, by the time I am ready to go. I have abandoned the idea of first going to Sydney, even as master of the ship, as I might have difficulty of getting from there to India.

Farewell to Thee, Sacramento! Like all the other places in which I have found kind friends, I feel a pang in saying the parting word, Adieu!

San Francisco
Sunday Night, 2nd Nov., 1851

It is past midnight, and I have just returned to my cabin after walking the quarter deck for two hours, thinking of the various scenes, past and future, that so constantly arise in the mind of a wanderer. The half moon has not yet set, the air is mild and pleasant and the sea wind is rolling vast masses of white fog cloud over from the ocean, and singing and sighing through these dense forests of masts and riggings. Ever and anon the air resounds with the fluttering of many wings, and the shrill startling cry of the wild fowl as they sweep by the large flocks for the inland lakes, or become lost in the dense fog. Silence reigns over the sleeping city, and save the sounds of the air and the waters, no other noise breaks the thread of absent thought.

I left Sacramento at two o'clock on last Wednesday afternoon, in the steamer *Senator*. We had a pleasant run down the river and arrived in this city before daylight the next morning. The Sacramento River is very narrow throughout most of its length and though very deep it requires the most careful management of a vessel to prevent running on shore. The *Confidence* and *Henry Clay* left their docks at the same time and the former led us a merry chase before we could drop her astern. We had an excellent supper on board and though there were but few cabin passengers we passed away the time very agreeably. I became acquainted with M. P. Barney Esq. a resident of Sacramento and one of the earliest settlers here. He was conveying a vast treasure to San Francisco, to be sent home on the first, and during the evening he gave me a history of his early experience in the country.

We passed Benicia almost eight in the evening and although it was dark, I saw enough of that familiar place to recall pleasant recollections of my residence there. Before retiring to rest, I walked into the ladies' cabin more out of curiosity than expecting to find anyone there but what was my surprise to find there Mrs. Samuel Brannon and one of her children. I had not known there was a lady on board, much less, one whom I knew and as she did not wish to retire, being obliged to leave the boat as soon as we arrived I very willingly kept her company. Mrs. Brannon, and indeed her whole family are turned converts to the Mormon religion, and although I myself am of no particular religion whatever, yet I found enough to converse and argue about, to pass the remainder of the night quite pleasantly.

In the morning I went to the Pacific Hotel and got breakfast. After and while eating I was much struck by the apparent suffering and sorrow of a young man who kept walking around in an adjoining room, wringing his hands, and giving many other signs of distress. I later learned from the landlord that his only brother and companion had died the night before in the house, and that the young man was now here a stranger in a strange land, without even the means of discharging his own brother's funeral expenses. Poor fellow how I pitied him his dreary and sorrowful condition.

I had not long to look for a ship to India. There were at least a dozen here, all ready to sail for Calcutta, Singapore, Hong Kong, as soon as they had procured crews. There were the *Southern Cross, Game Cock, Witch of the Wave, Eureka, Flying Island,* etc. etc. all splendid clippers, but for a comfortable passage in any capacity I would prefer a different sort of ship. The *St. Thomas* of New York, a large new ship of over a thousand tons, built for the New Orleans and Havre packet trade, was my choice. As soon as I saw the ship I went on board and inquired of the captain, an old Quaker looking man, if he wanted an officer, and where he was going. He told me he was going to Calcutta and that if he could get a good second officer he would discharge the one he had. And I immediately made a bargain with him and as I would much rather do service on board a ship than go as passenger and be tired to death doing nothing, I agreed to go to Calcutta in the ship as second officer, for the sum of one-hundred and fifty dollars for the run. This being settled, Captain Merril desired me to come on board as soon as was convenient as he was in a hurry to get out and would require my services at once. I told him I would come on board the next morning, and here I am once more a sailor and this time I hope in a good and comfortable ship. Capt. Merril is an old-fashioned man and one would sooner take him for a preacher than a sea captain. He is kind and considerate in his address and so far I like him very much. Mr. Elder the chief officer is a young man from Maine. He is a good specimen of a Yankee sailor and we shall get on well together. The ship is new, is a fast sailor, and is one of the handsomest ships in the port. She will carry double her tonnage, and will not fall far behind the clippers in making the passage. My station on board her will be very easy, as we shall carry a third officer whom I shall require to do all the hard work of the second officer in ordinary ships. In fact Mr. Elder tells me that captain Merril never gives himself much trouble about his ship, leaving the mates about to do as they like.

I came on board the *St. Thomas* on Friday morning and have been engaged with the old second officer Mr. Jackson who had not yet left, in overhauling the marine stores of the ship, and getting things in order for my own use. The cargo is nearly out and we shall be off in about a week. I am certain of letters for me in the mail which arrived here this morning but as I had given directions at the post office to have my letters forwarded to Benicia, and I had forgotten to countermand the order, they have, I have no doubt gone there and will be back again in a few days.

I have been much amused since coming on board the *St. Thomas* with one of our boys, the only one left after the sweep that took place after the ship had gotten in. His name is William Henry Keeler, and he is one of the laziest boys I have ever heard of. He will work hard for half a day at some light job, merely for the sake of shunning a harder, both of which might have been done in an hour. Elder tells me that he has not been worth the salt all the passage out, and was often found in his berth with a pipe in his mouth fast asleep during his watch on deck. If he chances to fall in my watch in the passage, I shall give him fits I know.

The ship *Challenge* from New York came in last

Thursday. She is the largest clipper and most splendid merchant ship ever built. Her tonnage is two thousand and six tons and she is a monster indeed. After she had come to anchor in the bay, many people boarded her to look, and it soon became known in the city that the crew had been treated in the worst possible manner, ever since leaving home. Some of them had been lost by the meanness of the captain and the mate, and some of them were lying in the forecastle disabled from the blows and the inhuman treatment of the master. Captain Waterman was well known to seafaring men, as one of the hardest men that ever commanded a ship, and before the ship was hauled into the wharf on Friday the excitement was so high, that could Waterman have been found he would have been gibbeted in five minutes, by the exasperated sailors on shore. His friends becoming aware of these intentions took the precaution to remove him and secrete him in some safe place till the excitement should die away. The mate, George Douglass was also an object of much hate and when the ship just touched the wharf she was boarded by several hundreds of wild seamen, determined on the immediate destruction of the mate and the captain. Douglass saw the danger just before he had gotten the ship to, and leaving everything go, he rushed over the side into one of the small boats owned by one of his friends by the name of Land, and who was now the waterman of the place, and reached the shore in safety. The seamen finished mooring the ship as she was left in great danger (Jack never likes to see a fine ship injured) and then took every man out of the ship but the carpenter who had been so badly beaten that he could not be moved. A diligent search was instituted for Captain Waterman, Mr. Douglass, and Land, the waterman who had now incurred almost as much hatred as Waterman himself. In the course of the day, Mr. Douglass was discovered in the bottom of a baggage wagon which was on its way to Monterey and in spite of his entreaties and protestations, he was brought back to the city and would have been executed at once on the yard arm of his own ship, had not one of his friends interposed and obtained for him a fair trial before the court. In the meantime the men of the ship had been before the mayor and made their depositions and a reward of $500 had been offered for the captain and mate. The men who had captured Douglass received their reward, but the captain was "non est inventues." The mob forcibly entered the houses and offices of the consignees but were unsuccessful. The boatman Land also succeeded in keeping out of the way till this morning, when supposing the storm had blown over he came forth with his little boy, and was seen on Long Wharf. A number of sailors and wharf rats immediately surrounded him and the cry was raised, "Hang Him, Hang the Rascal." A rope was brought, the end made fast around his neck his hands lashed behind him and in one minute more he would have been run up to the freight shears, had not his little boy, only six years old caught hold around his father's knees, and cried and begged so piteously that there was not a man found who had the heart or hardihood to seize the rope and finish the business. So the time was thus spent, and in the meantime the little fellow had so worked upon the feelings of the men, that some began to be in favor of releasing the man and forgiving him, while the more violent had but little to say. Thus in ten minutes that poor little boy had saved his father from certain destruction from the infuriated mob, whom he had offended. How small sometimes is the arm that produces great results! How little often serves to turn the tide of popular passion. That old man has to thank his son for his life, and long may they both live to enjoy each other's love. The little fellow's name is Charles Land and a brave little fellow he is.

Last evening Mr. Elder and myself were taking a walk, and among other means of passing the time we went into the Eldorado to witness the play and to look at the new paintings that were displayed there.

There was a dense crowd around one of the tables, and we soon found the banker who owned it was intoxicated, and losing money very fast. We stood watching the game a while, when a slight dispute rose in regard to the cards. The game was French Monte and the banker swore that they were stacking the cards against him. Two or three of the bankers from the other tables commenced flocking in with their pistols in their bosom, and we expected that in a moment more we should have a row. The play proceeded however, but with the same fortune, when as the stakes had become

168

immensely high, the intoxicated gambler jumped up, seized his revolver, and swore the stakes were his, as he was cheated. He made a sweep for the money, and would have bagged the whole of it, had he not been seized by the throat by one or two of his adversaries who in the melee upset the table and scattered the money in every direction. Now the row commenced in earnest, and as we had nothing to do with the matter we came to the conclusion to beat a retreat. Before I reached the door however, the loafers and lookers on had commenced picking up the gold, and putting out the lights to avoid detection, and the bankers had begun to clear the room at the point of their knives. The drunken gambler had had his pistol taken out of his hand, and before I had lost sight of the interior the bankers and managers were making a clear sweep of everything in the saloon. I had lost Mr. Elder, but met with him on the wharf close by the ship hastening on board as fast as possible. He said he should never go inside one of those places again, and I rather think it will be his best policy to keep his resolution. I have no doubt that several thousand dollars changed owners in that saloon last evening, quite unlawfully, and also against all gamblers rules of right and wrong. I saw one fellow make a grab at a pile of "slugs" and then make for the door, and I suppose he made out to get quite his share of the spoils. I have not heard whether any serious inquiry was made into the row as yet.

Harbor of San Francisco
Friday, 7th November, 1851
We are at anchor in this noble bay and all ready to go to sea. The cargo was finished last evening and this morning at six o'clock the harbor masters came on board and after unmooring from our berth at the foot of California Street wharf, we warped out to our present position and let go the kellog. I expect that we shall be off in two or three days as the crew are all on board, and nothing detains us now but a final settlement and average which Captain Merril is making with the owners of part of the cargo which was damaged on the passage by heavy weather.

I say that our crew is on board but I am by no means sure of it. They are a great set of men but we have had the greatest trouble in the world to keep them on board. We dare not even send them ashore in the boat with the captain, as they will desert and get drunk as sure as fate. We also are obliged to keep a strict lookout, lest any of the shore boats come alongside and take them off. Jack is always ready to spend the last cent of his money before he leaves shore, and the sharks and grog house keepers are always ready to supply the means. Our boy Bill, of whom I spoke before, thought he would play us a nice trick a few days ago, so one night he got someone to assist him and effected his escape from the ship, together with all his clothes and indeed a few that did not belong to him. Yesterday morning however he came back again civil enough, and begged to be taken on board again. Captain Merril is such a fatherly old man, that he did not refuse and so master Bill is back again. He ought to have had a severe thrashing for his pains, but never mind, *I'll* teach him navigation for his thoughts to digest. He found, I suppose that California is not so fine a place for a friendless boy as the *St. Thomas* and our fine old captain.

The steamer *Columbia* passed us this morning on the way to Oregon. On board of her we saw Mrs. McAllister and her two children, who came out on this ship from New York, to join her husband who is now in Oregon. She has been living with us till yesterday and I like her very much. She is one of the careful motherly women who are seldom seen beyond the family circles. Her husband is doing well in Oregon and I wish them a happy, prosperous life in their new home.

Sunday Afternoon, 9th November,
Bay San Francisco

Oh how truly has it been said that this life is a life of trials and suffering, and when our skies are lightest and our bosoms lightest, the dark clouds of sorrow or adversity are likely to arise, and darken the mental day. I have been waiting in this country nearly four months for letters from home, and for the last month have anxiously expected them in each mail, but Oh! I never expected such news as I received to-day. My dear little brother Clinton is no more. He has gone to join his brothers and sisters in the next world, and I shall see his dear, dear beloved form no more in this. Oh my dear brother I never knew how deeply I loved thee until now, Thou art lost, I never knew that thy tender and gentle soul had twined itself so tightly around my heart, till I learned that our earthly connection was severed. Dear, dear, little brother, thy little cares and sorrows are over in this harsh world, and I must devoutly and humbly pray an all powerful God to gather thy tender soul among the happy chosen of Heaven, and guard thee from all future cloud and storm.

There were but three of us, and soon after the death of Little Clinton, my only remaining brother Silas was taken ill. Oh my dear parents I can only guess at your feelings.

My poor little brother Clinton Ely, breathed his last on the 23rd day of May last, of a scarlet fever, while I his wandering brother was cruising over the South Pacific, thousands of miles away, and all ignorant of the sickness of those I best loved on earth. And so pass away the pure, the innocent and the beloved, and so remain the hardy, the careless and the thoughtless.

Did I believe in the existence of spiritual warnings and communications, I should remember with awe and wonder, the melancholy hours, the long period of depression of spirits, and the many troubled dreams of home, which oppressed me about the date of my brother's death, and which on referring to my journal, I find to have made a serious impression on my mind. On that very date too, I found while looking over the remembrance of home, a copy of verse which my dear mother had given to me, and which I read with peculiar and deep emotions. But I know not what to believe when the mind is a channel of such strange wandering thoughts, and the subject of so many mysterious whisperings. Certain is it that the mind often receives a mysterious and unaccountable intimation of distant events, though in so confused a manner as to render the knowledge of the means or agency, or the shadowy truth itself, too uncertain to rely on. Oh! God! Our lives are in thy hands.

I have been spending the morning in writing letters in answer to the three I have just received and in administering as much consolation to my bereaved parents as possible. Wherever I may go, or in whatever land I make my home, I shall always remember this day as the most sorrowful one of my life. When I first opened the letter and sat down on the post office steps to try and read it, I cared little whether I saw another day dawn or heard another human word.

But tis past now, and I earnestly and humbly pray that although heavy and sad this trial is it may be one of the inscrutable and all wise instruments of our merciful savior to chasten and redeem our little family.

Harbor San Francisco
Thursday 12th Nov. [1851]
Still lying at anchor in this noble bay surrounded by the immense fleet of vessels of every nation which have been lured to these banner shores by the great lodestone of the human race "Gold." The weather since Sunday last has been in connivance with my spirits and it has rained almost constantly so that no business could go on. Oh how welcome have these stormy days been to me. I have been able to remain in the retirement of my cabin and meditate upon the sad intelligence which has so lately reached me. They are the first of the rainy season too and the parched ground which for so many months has been baking under the summers sun is now plentifully soaked with water. I am glad I am about to leave this country. I do not like rainy weather and I shall make haste to get out of it. This however is the first rain storm I have seen for many months, and both on account of its novelty and its kindly sympathy with my sorrows, I have gladly welcomed it. This morning however the storm had ceased. There is a delightfully cool breeze from the hills and plains and every taint seems to have been washed as it were from earth and heaven, so pure, so bright and lovely is the face of the morning.

Thus it ever is. The sky is always brighter after a storm, and many a dark gloomy morning turns to a bright and lovely day.

We had expected to have gone to sea this morning and I am disappointed we did not. The pilot came on board and we commenced heaving up the anchor, but in breaking it out, we broke one of our windlass brakes, and will be obliged to remain till tomorrow to have it repaired. In my present frame of mind I particularly long for the quiet and solitude of the ocean, and although I shall be leaving the American shores behind me, I shall also be nearing the end of my voyage.

The men too give us much trouble and though altogether as fine a crew as ever reefed a topsail, yet they are full of money, full of rum, and full of having a "last spree." We had to man the boat ourselves this morning and I went ashore to take a last farewell to California. Although literally a land of gold, it is a land I never care to see again.

Ship *St. Thomas* at Sea.
Saturday evening, 15th Nov. [1851]

I'm afloat, I'm afloat and the river is free,
I'm afloat, I'm afloat, on the dark rolling sea.

Thank heaven I am again on blue water! We got our anchor up Thursday morning last after a great deal of trouble. We had become so deeply imbedded in the clay bottom of the bay, that it was impossible to break it out with the windlass. We hove as long as we were able and then tried another plan. The cat block was hooked on the chain at the water's edge and the fly block of the fish tackle was hooked to the cat fall after the latter was hove as taut as possible. The fish tackle fall was now led to the capstan and thus an immense power was obtained. We hove the ship's bows down at least two feet before the anchor broke out and when it did so, the ship surged as if a sea had struck under the bow. Then came a long seige of working out of the bay in a dense fog and headwind. We did not get outside till well on in the afternoon, and then not till the pilot had like to have us upon the rocks. The entrance to the bay is very narrow, very deep, and the tide runs through it with such violence that the most active work is required to beat through with a head wind. As soon as we were out, the wind was fair for us, we discharged our pilot and made all sail on a wind, to the southwest. The ship was light and in fine sailing trim and the way we sped through the water was astonishing. The only fault that we discovered was that she was too cranky and at every puff of the breeze we laid almost on our beam ends. There had not been quite enough ballast taken on board in San Francisco, and as we were on a wind we felt it more than we should have again, while running before the trades.

But not withstanding all of this we were coursing over the waters at a rapid rate and before the sable curtain of night had fell, o'er land and sea, we had lost sight of the last distant mountains of our native land, the land we are proud to call Columbia, Columbia the land of the free and the brave. A man's feelings upon leaving the shores of his native land for a long time, are hardly describable. As I paced the unsteady deck that night, or leaned over the taffrail watching the pale moon arise from a clear and watery horizon, I might have exclaimed with Fairchild:

> Blow scented gale! the snowy canvass swell
> And roll thy silver eddying current on,
> Grieve me to bid the last fair point farewell,
> That ere we say adieu my native land, is gone.

But I forgot all poetry in more absorbing thoughts. I thought of the fair flower that was ere this transplanted from the cold soil of America to the vales of India, and I looked eagerly to the eastward and counted the hours, of time and the league of trackless waters that must intervene before I could once more place her on my bosom. Many a long watch must I keep on these waters and barren decks before I clasp my Mary to the breast.

The hours of a lonely silent sea watch, are always sweet hours of meditation to me. In such reveries as these I have passed many an otherwise dreary watch away, and eight bells had often found me still deep in the thoughts of home and absent friends and Heaven.

Ship *St. Thomas* at sea
Sunday Evening, Nov. 16th [1851]
Having just arisen from the table where we have been indulging in all the dainties afforded by a free and generous ship I feel but little inclination for writing. It is not time to attempt a composition after a full and hearty meal, as the gratification of the apetite always interrupts the free and easy flow of a person's thoughts. However as we have been favored by such

an obstinate and provoking calm today, I cannot help abusing the weather a little bit.

This is essentially one of Paddy's Hurricanes. There is no wind, yet it is not exactly calm, it neither blows from one point of the compass yet neither three or four but we have an occasional puff from all points. It is not rainy nor yet is it clear, but in making attempts to be both it maintains a happy medium of a scotch mist with a high land draught. It is not cold, [nor] yet is it at all warm, but the air is of that raw and penetrating nature which sends a shudder over your body the moment you are upon deck. In short the weather is most disagreeable, the winds good for nothing, and the whole face of nature, dark, cold and sullen. But never mind—we have had a splendid run off the coast, and we shall soon leave all the unpleasant weather behind again, as soon as we reach the trades, and then for the sweet smiles of the Pacific.

We spoke the *Australian* this morning from Van Diemens Land to San Francisco, and as I had some letters written to various friends to post at Honolulu, I embraced the speedier chance of forwarding them to California.

In spite of wind, weather and water, we get along first rate. I have become very fond of our old captain, and as Mr. Elder is one of my kind of men, and Mr. Scott the third mate is not a bad fellow altogether, we are as one family. The men, now that they have not the shore and all its fascinations in sight are contented and happy, always obeying the slightest order night or day in the most prompt and seamanlike manner. They spend their day watches in telling yarns about their cruises in California, in dancing or singing to the tune of a violin which I had bought one of them before we left. Mr. Elder also has a very large music case, and in the soft twilight hours of the lovely climate we certainly feel as much pleasure as our natural life allows.

Who is there, that would not, if he could, trade the busy life of toil and care of a businessman ashore, for the quiet, regular, and orderly one of the mariner. To the man who can find pleasure only in a crowd, and can enjoy himself only in the midst of hundreds of his fellow beings, the sea is not a proper sphere, and such a man would be very unhappy on a long sea voyage. But the man who is not afraid of his own conscience, who dreads not to be left alone to its silent communication, who delights in his own thoughts and meditations, and who rarely finds those thoughts less interesting than the empty conversation of Watery society, should be a mariner and live in the grand solitude of Nature, with his God, his Saviour, and himself. True it is that one of the greatest enjoyments of the human race is lost at sea—the companionship of the opposite sex. But this is only a custom, and woman ought to be allowed to traverse the ocean as freely as her sterner partner. When such is the case, when our mothers, wives, sisters, and daughters contribute their smiles and glad presence to the scene, "Old Ocean" shall henceforth be my home, my earthly paradise. Ah! Mary, when shall I put thy fond promise in execution? When shall we two, rove the blue waters together.

> Ship *St. Thomas* at sea
> Lat 21 15 N. Lon 158 10 W
> Thursday, Nov. 27th [1851]

This is my twenty-fourth birthday and little did I think one year ago today that I should spend the next anniversary in the Sandwich Islands.

We left Honolulu about two hours ago, and are now coursing away westward again, at the rate of eleven and twelve knots an hour. The afternoon sun is shining brightly upon the western slopes of the green islands we have just quitted, and the trade winds bring to our nostrils the sweet perfume of those fair gardens of luxuriance. What a lovely picture! They seem to rise like a cluster of green everglades from the blue sea, and their hilltops are so clearly defined against the crimson sky, that the whole scene seems more like a highly colored painting than the usual careless attitudes of nature. I am now willing to believe the boast of these simple islanders, that "Hawaii is the fairest and happiest land of God's Creation."

We have been at sea two weeks today, and considering the prevalance of the northwest winds on the coast, have done exceedingly well. We took the trades in 25 30 North, and from that time we have had constant fair winds, and good weather, moving ten and eleven knots almost constantly. We made the Island of Maui the day before yesterday in the afternoon, but darkness set in before we were able to distinguish any landmarks of importance. We stood boldly on however with everything set that would draw, and at almost ten o'clock were within six miles of the land. Here we ran the narrow escape of almost losing the noble ship and perhaps our own lives. Capt. Merril was certain of accuracy of his observations by noon, and by our reckoning he was steering for the passage, between the Islands of Maui and Wahoo, but one reckoning was wrong and we all mistook the low neck of Maui for the proper passage.

It happened the wind had hauled round southwest in the evening and we were standing W.N.W. on a wind directly for the bay which has been the most unfortunate place on the island. At a little past ten we discovered numerous lights directly ahead which we supposed to be the villages near Honolulu, but which in reality were fishing lights on the coral banks in the bay. The breeze was fresh and we were moving eight knots. In a few minutes after we had made the knots we found we were in a strong current setting to the N.W. and carrying us right away to leeward. We braced sharp up and endeavored as much as possible (as we afterward learned) to rush into the very jaws of destruction. At eleven o'clock we had drifted too far to the northward to fetch into the bay, so the ship was just about under easy sail so that by morning we should be far enough to windward to fetch the bay (Straits as we suppose).

It was only the accident which saved us. In the morning we were sure enough right off our bay, but oh, wonder of wonders, the passage which we thought we were about to pass was fifteen miles away to the northwest, while now the bright light of the morning illuminated the scene we discovered that the place into which we were so boldly steering the night before was only a deep bay, almost running through the whole width of the Islands to its western shore and there only crossed by [a] low sand neck. We could also see several coral reefs stretching across the bay upon which many a good ship had been lost in the same manner as ourselves had come so near.

The old captain took a long look at the certain destruction we had so fortunately escaped, and then sung out, "Square away the yards Mr. Elder, we will leave this place." All sail was made before the wind and at eleven o'clock yesterday we were in Honolulu.

The reason of our mistake was this. The ground on the beach part of the bay, as I saw, is quite low. So that in the daytime the sea is seen beyond it but the land on the beach side is high; at night it resembles that on each side of the Honolulu Straits. Thus in approaching the bay in the night anyone is very likely to be deceived as no land is seen ahead and the seaman fancies himself alright and safe until he either strikes upon one of the coral reefs or runs ashore on the coral bay. Current too is unequal on these islands, and no one knows how much to allow for drift, in running down upon them. In this manner at least two vessels are lost each year, for once enter the bay with fresh trade wind, and no power can save the ship. Had we been two hours earlier or two hours later we should have been irretrievably lost, but just as we were entering the bay the ebb tide was at its strength which together with the vessel current set us away so suddenly that we were unable and then in fact rather unwilling to make the passage. Here again poor Ned is saved although madly rushing to his destruction.

Honolulu is truly a lovely spot and those who have described it have not exaggerated its beauty. It is situated on the straits between its own islands, Wahoo and Molokai with a southern exposure and high ground to the north of the plain or flat upon which it is situated. The town is laid out regularly and there is a great number of buildings. The house of my friend Samuel Brannon stands preeminent among the dwellings, for extent and beauty, and I was much pleased to find the old gentleman at home, enjoying himself with his wife and daughter, the same who had been passengers with me from Sacramento to San Francisco, in the *Senator* several weeks ago, and who had come out in the *Gamecock* from California a week ago. They intend making Honolulu their home, and although they are Mormons by profession, the place could not have better citizens. The streets of Honolulu and

178

the roads about the Island are finely shaded with coconut and cabbage trees, bordered with flower gardens, orchards and graperies, while the fields are rich with the agricultural productions of the island: rice, wheat, sugar cane, plantains, yams, sweet potatoes, pumpkins, onions etc. They all flourish in great exuberance, while most of the tropical fruits are in profusion.

The American population of these Islands seems to predominate and although the French and English are doing all they can to retain the side of favor with the Hawaiian King, yet I think from appearances that our own star is in the ascendant. The natives who call themselves "Kanakas" are a mild and pleasing race, rather slavish and spineless, but possessed of far better qualities of mind and heart, than most other pagan nations. I regret very much that I did not see their king, "Kamee—amee—ah" who, I was told is a remarkably intelligent, and shrewd person. However I had the pleasure of kissing one of his daughters and that is worth as much as the sight of her father.

There are a number of my countrymen here, and many interesting places of note, but I was obliged on account of the shortness of our stay to forego making but very few acquaintances or visiting many of the landmarks of the place. Either Mr. Elder or myself were obliged to be on board constantly to prevent the men from deserting, and when we did go on shore we were obliged to keep such a strict watch on the boat's crew that there was little pleasure for us. The men had all received $1000 dollars advance in San Francisco and could they have got a chance they would have left us here, with that money and we should be detained in having them retaken again. That part of the Hawaian law is at least very good. If a seaman deserts a ship in any part of the island he is immediately hunted up by the king's police and restored to his ship again, or placed in irons. We lost no men however, for we were always particular that no one should go in our boats, but the best of them and even those were searched.

Determined to have one night on shore, to say at least that I had slept in the Sandwich Islands, I hired a native boat to take me ashore last evening so that I might not be bothered by our men. I soon fell in with some of our friends that I had seen during the day, and away we went to see the sights and have a night of it. I soon found out the drift of my young companions however, and told them that I entered no house under the cover of night, that I was ashamed to be seen about in the day, and notwithstanding that a Kanaka maiden was a very pleasant companion for those who desired her society, yet I had friends whom I wished to see. A young man by the name of Courtney accompanied me to the house of my Sacramento friends where I found them all very glad to see me, and very sorry at the same time that my stay was so short. I remained here all night, took breakfast this morning of a sort of stuff called "Poa" and bade them farewell at ten o'clock to go on board. I found everything in confusion, Mr. Elder had gone ashore with a lot of Kanakas for some goats, and in the meantime our third officer Mr. Scott had made a great mess about decks with the fruit and vegetables he had been hoisting in. I have been engaged almost all afternoon in setting to right what his stupidity has capsized. Even old Captain Merril as quiet a man as he is took note of Mr. Scott's clumsiness and mentioned it at dinner to me. We hove up our anchor at three o'clock, and have now been under way about four hours. It has grown dark while I am writing and the blue hills of Hawaii are no longer in sight.

We had very near been carrying off two Kanaka girls with us, who had come on board last night and who had kept such close quarters in the forecastle that no one but the men knew that they were aboard. Had it not been for the boy Bill who came to me just as we were sheeting home the topsails and disclosed the matter there is no doubt but what we should have had these beauties with us all the passage. As it was however we hauled them out of their quarters, and sent them ashore in a canoe. Mr. Elder was quite rough with them, but I pitied the poor things who knew no better and who moreover were quite goodlooking.

I must now get a cup of tea, eat a plantain, smoke a cigar and prepare to take the deck from eight till twelve. The wind is whistling now through the rigging and sails, and I shall have a merry watch all to myself upon the deserted decks. Good night. . . .

180

Ship *St. Thomas* at sea
Saturday, 6th Dec. [1851]
Lat 18 2 N. Lon (4 p.m.)
    179 52 E.
"For the first time in my life I am in the Eastern Hemisphere"! We crossed the 180 Meridian of Longitude from Greenwich an hour ago and we are now but eight miles to the westward of it. Thus in the short space of a few hours we have lost a day. Before we crossed the Meridian the day was Saturday, as I have dated this note, and as we should find it were we to sail back to America, but since we have crossed the Meridian it is:

Sunday Evening, 7th December,
as we shall find at arriving at Singapore or any of the Asiatic cities. We are obliged to alter the date thus, as our nautical calculations would be inaccurate did we not do so, and although strange as it may seem to those who do not know the reasons, we have lost a day, and December of this year will contain for us but 30 days.

The men are growling because they have been "done out" of their Sunday as they say. This morning they went to work as a Saturday morning, and this evening we tell them it is Sunday evening. "Now mind boys," says the old man, "you shall have your plum dough, killed pig, and holiday tomorrow."

Ship *St. Thomas* at sea
December 10th, 1851
One year from my home this day! One year ago I bade all my dear friends adieu, my father, mother, brothers and all. One year ago, I left them and that which has been my home through life, to wander about the world and to seek a new one in a more congenial climate. And here I am, at home truly, but on the blue ocean with thousands of leagues of water in every direction around me. Verily this is a great change I have made since the same day of last year. I left Pennsylvania, a poor weak, diseased and suffering invalid, without home, friends or hope, and with but distant ideas of recovery. I am now here a strong healthy, and I may say happy

181

man. When I look back and view the great changes each successive year has wrought in my life, I almost fear to ask myself, "Where shall I be next year?" Oh! God, I am in thy keeping. Deal gently with me, not for my sake, but for the sake of my parents and only brother.

Ship *St. Thomas* at sea
Sunday Dec. 14th [1851]
Lat 19 3 N. Lon 161 54 E.

What a bright, a beautiful and lovely day! The fresh trade wind came careening over the blue ocean as sweet as the breath of may, and playful as a young lambkin. The sky is of that clear blue only met with in this summer sea, and the sun shines with a mellow splendor upon us. How happy are my feelings today. I'm not aware of ever having felt so well satisfied and contented as I have been since joining this good ship.

Tuesday, December 16th [1851]
Lat 19 10 N Lon 160 20 E

For the last two days we have been the subject of much changeable weather. The winds blow from every quarter, the ship is constantly overcast with clouds by day, and it is only by night that we are able to get observations of the heavenly bodies to calculate our position. This morning at eleven o'clock I took an altitude of the pole star, and made our latitude forty miles further to the southward than, by our dead reckoning. We must have had some strong currents, and indeed we might expect them and gain also as we approach the Ladrones.

This morning one of our men by the name of Peter —a boat builder of New York, fell through the forehatch way into the lower hold, and injured himself very much. He was carrying a bucket full of water down the ladder into the between decks for the grindstone, together with a plane bit to grind, when his foot slipping, he fell about twenty feet, striking his head upon the water tanks in the lower tier. He is a good man and I am sorry for his accident as it is the second or third that has befallen him already. He seems to think that he is a doomed man, and says that he wishes to God that he had broken his neck and that he would give all that he ever expected to be worth if the fall had killed him at once. I have bled him and I hope that he will get safely over it. This is the same man that was so near dying of Delirium Tremens in San Francisco, and the habit of drinking seems to be his only bane. Otherwise he is a good workman, and excellent sailor, the best helmsman in the ship and is very well educated. He came out to the South Seas fishing in '41 and from there went to California.

Our boy Bill, of whom I have before spoken, gives not only myself but all hands on board a deal of trouble. He is in my watch and I can do but little with him. I have ropesended him often to no purpose, and I have made him walk the deck the whole of my night watch, with handspikes in his shoulder like a soldier, the laughingstock of the ship's company. I have kept him up in his watch below and made him slush down the masts fore and aft and I have at times ridiculed, reprimanded, and remonstrated with him, but all to no purpose. He will still lie, steal, cheat, shirk out of his work and do whatever he attempts in the very worst manner. If he escapes the gallows it will be by the means of some such accident as befell him a few days since, caused by his own slovenly carelessness. I had sent him to seize on the fore topmast, backstay crane lines, one morning and he occupied the whole four hours about it. In the next dog watch I had occasion to set the fore topgallent studding sail and as usual I made Master Bill take the tack aloft and reef it. This time it got foul of the backstays and upon his going out on the crane lines to clear it, the seizing which he had put on as usual in the most careless manner gave way, and down he came, tack, halyards. and all, nearly killing himself by the fall. Another specimen of his lubberly habits occured today. The main topsail bunt lines had been hauled too tight on deck so that they lifted the foot of the sail and chafed it. I sent Bill with a piece of sail twine to overhaul them and to stop them just forward of the block. He lost the twine in going aloft, but thinking the rope yarn just as good as he had one in his pocket, he took four turns with that around the two parts of the rope, and after making all fast came down. An hour or so afterwards I went to the topgallant yard with my glass to

183

look at a distant sail when as I was coming down what should I see but this bit of sailorizing.

If we should have wanted to reef our topsails in a hurry we should have been in an awful mess. The whole ship's company could not have started the buntlines. Never mind, I shall make him keep his watch on the main yard royal tonight for the good of his eyesight. If the boy tried to learn anything I should have compassion on him, but he does not even try to keep himself neat and clean like a seaman besides his other failings.

Wednesday, 17th December [1851]

A rainy day; I cannot call it stormy for the air comes down warm, gently, and without wind, like some of our southerly August rains in old Pennsylvania.

Oh how gladly would I visit that happy valley home of mine once more before other changes might occur to render the visit a melancholy one. They have winter now in all this cold region among my native hills, and so closely do I keep the thoughts of everything connected with that native spot, fresh in my mind, that even here while enjoying the mild warmth of the latitudes, or fanning my heated brow with my summer hat, I can see those hills covered with the white snow and the whole country alive with the merry jingling of the bells, dashing of sleighs and shouts of skaters.

Mr. Elder our chief officer is almost as young a man as myself, but has the advantage over me in being married. He is from Brunswick Me. and is a very intelligent, interesting and pleasant companion. It is a pleasure to sail with such men as him. I have passed Mr. Scott over into his watch as I can get along much more comfortably without as with him, and this allows Elder and myself much more time together. He often remains upon deck with me during my first watch, till I am relieved by the starboard officer at twelve, rehearsing all the events that have occured in his busy life, and I in turn relating many which have befallen myself. There are many incidents which must necessarily occur to one who wanders for many years in foreign lands, and had I commenced making a note of everything ludicrous, marvelous or melancholy that has ever come to my knowledge, I should now have a rare encyclopedia of fun and earnest.

We employ our days in cleaning and painting the ship, and in the ever necessary work of adapting our sails to the variable force and direction of the wind.

Monday 22nd Dec. [1851]
Lat 18 58 Lon 149v 17 E

Yesterday morning between ten and eight o'clock we were passing the Ladrone Islands between the Isles of Ascension and Pagan. Beautiful green islands! How bright and calm and lovely you looked lying in your beds of ocean blue, with your sweet scented breezes, woody hills and flowery brooks and how happy and picturesque seemed your people as they were roaming about your deep shades or standing upon your silver shores. The day was fine and after the long continued rains, everything looked far more fresh and bright than usual. Today also the weather is fine, but the barometers are falling and we may expect more wet and ugly weather. Until yesterday we have had six days almost constant rain, so that we were obliged to discontinue painting the ship, and our men have been employed in various necessary jobs of sailor's work, and in catching water. We have secured at least a thousand gallons of pure rain water, and our men are allowed to use as much of it as they like to wash clothes etc., etc. It is all very fine however to wash our clothes, but as for getting them dry, that is an impossibility. We have all our clothes wet, and we turn in wet and turn out smoking. Our friends at home might think this of rather doubtful benefit, but we receive no harm from it, and all the inconvenience is the feeling of langor and lassitude.

We have at length finished one hard job, planing the main deck, and I am not sorry for it, for planing a pitched deck is not as easy as planing a board and our fellows have got very tired of it. It is done now however and looks as clean and white as a new shingle. If we could ever get it dry we should give it a clean coat of varnish, but that is about like our clothes with as little chance of drying.

Our between decks are not finished cleaning yet, and that is a great rainy weather job. They become very much coppered from the steam from the cargo coming out from New York, but as we have no cargo in now, we have a good chance to clean them. The men have been trimming ballast today, to get her more by the stern, so now she is three feet ten inches deeper aft than forward, quite enough I rather think. Capt. M. thinks however that she runs better in that trim than on an even keel. At any rate we are now slipping along at the rate of ten and eleven knots. Since yesterday we have been running W.N.W. and Capt. M. is determined to go to the north of Luzon in preference to taking the Straits of Bernardino into the China Sea.

Christmas Day—1851
Lat 20 1 N. 141 23 E.
A lovely warm and breezy summer's day after the rain. The soft east wind blows just as much as we can carry studding sails to and we are jumping over the foaming waves with the speed of an Arab. For three days the rain has been pouring down in torrents, and I have not got one stitch of clothes of any kind but what were wet through long ago. My bed is the same, and anyone might think we were comfortable surely, and so we are. There is no use for oiled clothes in these rains for it penetrates anything. In my morning watch this morning it cleared away and as if in honor of the day, Dame Nature had vouchsafed to make it bright and beautiful.

And now a merry Christmas to every one. Our tars are having a holy day, and they have enjoyed it like sensible men, in drying their wet clothes, bedding etc. We also have got the quarter deck hung full of our own wet garments, and if the wind and sun lasts all day we shall be blessed with dry clothes and beds once more. Oh, how merrily we are going along again, and how merrily do the white shirts and blue trousers and clean jackets flutter in the wind. They put me in mind of a sunny lawn at my own dear home of a summers morning when the newly washed clothes are fluttering in the breezes to dry. But it is not summer time there now. It is the Merry Christmas time. The time of doughnuts and minced pies, sweet cider and apples and of sausages and buckwheat cakes. But little however of the familiar appearance of that happy scene is here. The clear frosty winter nights, the blazing kitchen fires, and the lively sound of sleigh bells are replaced by the heat and sunshine of the tropics by fans, windshield and awnings. The halcyon, the stormy petrel, and the crested gull follow constantly in our wake, picking up in the daytime the small pieces of food that are cast overboard, and in the night sweeping round and round us in lofty circles, ever and anon startling our dreamy senses with their discordant screams.

Would that I possessed the power in looking over the vast distance that intervenes over this and my native land, that I might know how all my dear friends, parents and brother are now. September 13 is the last date I have from them. How long seems the time that must elapse yet before I can receive dates but little later. Truly the life of the wandering son is hard indeed.

Sunday 28th Dec. [1851]
Lat 20 2 N. Lon 122 12 E.

We are among the lovely islands which lie to the northward of Leuconia called the Bashee group, and most lovely the scene appears indeed. The day is beautiful and bright as Sundays usually are, and all nature looks gay and cheerful. The green islands with thin white coral cliffs, deep luxuriant forests, and silver sandy beaches look like so many emeralds in settings of gold, upon a field of ocean blue. The most of them are low and perfect paradises of tropical luxuriance, but there is one which we are just passing, which is the only exception to the general rule. It is Richmond Island and is a barren weatherbeaten coral rock of curious outline. There are also many others always in sight, the shade of whose palm groves and mimosa bows reaching almost to the water's edge, looks very inviting this warm day. The trees are beautiful in their wild proportions and they are filled with singing birds, parrots and monkeys. The ever green slopes and moss grown glades are the haunts of droves of the Indian gazelle, and the gentle waves make no harsher sound than the low murmur as they break upon the shores. The pretty little verses of Sir Thomas Moore, are ever recalled to my mind while sailing in these seas:

187

Oh, had we some bright little Isle of our own
Far off in a blue summer's ocean alone—
Where the bee banquets on in the bright sunny bowers
Gathering sweet incense from the open blown flowers,
Oh had we . . . etc., etc.

and I think had I those with me whom I might choose I myself would be content to make these peaceful islands my
future home.

Tuesday Morning, Dec. 30th [1851]
Lat 16 33 N Lon 115 06 E.

We are in the midst of the green sea of China with its thousands of reefs of sunken coral, and myriads of fickle currents,
about three hundred miles from Cape Boliano on the coast
of Luzon. The weather is hazy yet mild and serene, and we
have had no rain for two days. I hope also that we shall have
no more, as nothing is more unpleasant to the mariner, than
rain at sea. The color of the water has been changed since
we left the Pacific day before yesterday and although it is
fresh and green almost disclosing by its transparancy the coral
sinks and beds of white sand at the bottom, yet to the sailor's
eye nothing is so pleasing as the dark blue of the open ocean.

The wind which has been so light for these two days
past is freshening fast and we are beginning to run off the
knots in glorious style. Speed thee my gallant bark; I would
thou had the wings of the falcon, so anxious am I to reach my
destination. This is the season of the northeast monsoons in
these seas, from Japan to the Indian Archipelago, and we
shall have a fair and strong wind all the way to Singapore.
The typhoon season is over and we have nothing to fear but
the ever busy coralline, the numerous pirates, and the more
unpleasant but less dangerous rain. We are not far from Can-
ton and were we so disposed we might run over there in a
few hours, and gratify the great curiosity that everyone feels
to visit the land of the Celestials.

Mr. Elder had been passing away some of these fine
nights largely in spinning me a yarn about some of his frolics
at Bowdoin College, Brunswick, and though I much more
love to listen than to talk, his yarns have brought to my recollections many a similar prank of my own.

How happy would it be were all seagoing craft as well regulated as this. There would then be no insubordination and mutiny, no domineering tyranny, no gross abuse of the law of God. Every man would be well used, every one do his duty cheerfully and all enjoy the pleasures of life together.

Wednesday Evening, Dec. 31st [1851]

It is New Year's eve and a curious way I am spending it. Sitting in my room endeavoring to write, and far too busy in keeping myself steady, my ink and books from sliding away, and my lamp from capsizing to think about that which I wish to say without the task of writing them. The ship is rolling fearfully and has for the last two hours. We have the monsoon very strong now though perfectly steady so that we can carry just as much sail as she can bear. There is however a heavy sea, and as the wind and sea are both dead aft, and our ship almost flying light, there is nothing to prevent our rolling. We carried over studding sails this morning on both sides, but we were obliged to take them in as they rolled under and endangered our booms. This evening I have seen her dip the ends of the topmast studding sail booms into the water on either side a dozen times, first one side then the other so that anyone may know how we get along on deck and how our loose barrels, buckets etc., etc., dance a hornpipe when they get adrift . . . one who has never been to sea would fancy that it were impossible to do anything on board, while ships were rolling that way. But we not only suceed in doing all that we want, but a good deal more. We are running at the rate of nine and ten knots an hour, and that is not bad. We make as much sail as ever she will bear; we keep everything well lashed so that nobody's bones are broken unless he breaks them himself by a fall or slide down to leeward, and we eat our meals in true sailor fashion holding on to our plates and glasses as fast as we can, occasionally getting a round of hot beef, or a soft plum dough slid into our laps. The steward has as much as he can do to keep everything in his pantry from going to destruction, and the cook is cursing because he cannot have his boilers more than half full at a time. The captain has gone to bed for it is too much work for an old man like that to keep on foot in such weather as this, the man at the wheel has lashed himself to the spindle to prevent being thrown away, and Mr. Elder and myself have the whole ship to ourselves. Drive her, bullies, drive her. She must walk three hundred miles in the next twenty-four hours or we will carry every stick of timber out of her.

But I was beginning to say that this was New Year's Eve and I have got upon something else altogether; but I must now go on deck. It is eight o'clock, and I shall have to "rock the cradle" till twelve o'clock. "A happy New Year to you All." I am just about going to watch for the advent of it.

Twelve o'clock midnight
I have just been relieved but before I turn into my cot, I must say a word merely for the novelty of it. I have kept the vigil for the New Year, and now it is upon us. The old year with all its load of sin and sorrow, has gone from the face of the world forever, and the new one has come, bright, fresh and hopeful, to commence his new life when the morning dawns. God grant that this may be a "happy New Year."

January 1st, 1852
New Year's day! What a varied train of emotions does this reflection cause, in the bosom of a thoughtful man, especially should he be as in my case a wanderer from a loved home. Another year has passed away leaving us that much nearer the grave, and another year has commenced which in its close, may witness the death of all around us, of those most near and dear at home, and even of myself, now so well in health, full of life, hope, and anticipation. How have I passed the long year that has just gone? I have passed it actively and adventurously in foreign climes, though mostly afloat upon the ocean. During this period I have changed from a weak and fragile youth, to a man of strength and vigor, and my ever ambitious spirit is not now curbed by physical [inability]. I thank God for this change and earnestly seek a continuance of his blessings in years to come.

But has my spiritual being improved as happily in proportion, as my physical strength. Alas, I fear not. I have serious thoughts and much distress at times, in reviewing my thoughtless, careless and sinful course, but I feel the time has not yet come to lay aside all the worldly care and ambition and devote myself to the good purpose, for which only we were I believe, placed upon the earth. It is true I endeavor always to do right and where passion does not interfere. I feel that I lead an upright if not exemplary life. But I have mentioned the word which is my very bane, *Passion*. This irregularity of mind controls my deeds, and actions far too powerfully. Love, anger, ambition, and self reliance are my besetting sins and as the robust powers of animal life, are strengthened in man, so also are these passions in the soul. I would that I were placed with my beloved family, upon some of these lonely islands of the sea, where temptation and vanity are never felt, and sin never known; where sorrow and repining are never known as the acts and spoils of scheming man.

I have experienced a trying sorrow too, during the past year, in the loss of a dear little brother who in my absence, has been moved to a happier world, and even now while thousands of miles from my country I know not whether he is the only loss that I have sustained. Oh God, forbid that other sorrow should be added to our already great one. But "Thy will be done" for thy will is wisdom and thy deeds are justice and mortals should not blindly repine.

We are still coursing onward to southwest under every rag of canvas we can set, and still rolling madly. The monsoon is more steady than any of the winds we have had, keeping constantly to the N.E. and keeping a steady 11 knot breeze. The weather is becoming more warm, though the sun is almost constantly obscured by flying masses of vapor. I suppose this must descend somewhere and I am looking for the recommencement of the rains daily.

We have had the first unpleasant circumstance to occur on board today. All of the men have been keeping all of their money in their own chests quite carelessly, and today one of them lost four half-eagle pieces. A man by the name of Tom Randall was at once suspected of it, and his chest and clothes searched, but none of the money was found, although one of the men claims he saw him heave it overboard when they first commenced a search. It has made much suspicion and ill feeling among them, which however I hope will soon pass away. Most of the men have brought me their money to keep that it may at least be safe, and it is curious that in every ship I have belonged to, I have always gained the confidence and regard of the ship's company, and have been free from any contention of any kind on board. True, the 2nd mate of the Oregon was no friend of mine or indeed anyone else, and we hated each other fiercely, but he was more of a devil than he was a man and a very sneaking low devil too. I have near a thousand dollars now of the money belonging to the men, and if any one gets into my chest he is welcome to it.

Our boy Bill is just the same as ever. I have found out a new mode of punishment for him. I give him two hand-spikes, one on each shoulder like a musket and make him walk the poop fore and aft, when the ship is rolling so that one can hardly stand on his feet. Many is the tumble he gets, but he might avoid it all by trying to do right.

Peter has got well, and has gone to work again, he is the best and steadiest man in the ship, and although he is a little deficient in real sailor work, yet he abundantly makes it up in his activity in everything else, and his excellent steering.

Capt. Merril has no mercy on a sojer and despises likewise one who is impertinent or out of place. He is one of the most eccentric men I ever knew, and his curious speeches are often too much for the risibility of my nature.

Sunday Morning, 4th of January [1852]
Off the Anambas

All night long I have been on deck alone, and the ship has been howling along at the rate of 13 knots an hour, groaning in every timber, and steadily plowing her foamy weight through the great seas, like some huge ocean monster in his mad flight. Mr. Elder has been very ill due to the heavy rain which has been driving over the seas for near two days, and I have to sail the ship myself. At daybreak this morning I made Pulo Pisang, and Pulo Timoan, directly ahead, not more than fifteen miles distant, and if the wind holds we shall be in Singapore straits before night. It has been a fearful night, and everything in the ship which was not lashed has gone adrift and smashed to pieces. Chains, dishes, barrels and buckets went first then the grindstone and carpenters tool chest, the cooks coppers and stew pans, spare spars and windlass breaks, and even the ballast in the hold has shifted. The sailors have had their chests stove to pieces, and in my own cabin I have had a regular blow up. I had been making beer, and having corked the demijohn too tightly, the violent rolling of the ship got up rather too much steam, and the consequence was the boiler burst, and we lost our beer. There was about three gallons of it and it washed from side to side in a perfect torrent wetting the steward through and through who was sleeping between the table legs to prevent his rolling about, and soaking everything in its way with the sweetness. This morning the steward has been obliged to take up all the cabin carpets, and wash them. The old captain sleeps it out quite comfortably despite the commotion. He has made the carpenter fix him a new berth in one of the after compartments with such high sides that he cannot roll out, and there he lies night and day as contented as possible. He knows his ship is in good hands however—Ahem! Well as she has been handled I expected to see any moment her top studding sail go or the ship broach to, so heavy is the mass of the sail we carry.

Afternoon, 3 o'clock

We have just had a narrow escape of running the ship ashore, where we should, in the sea which breaks upon its rocky shore, never have seen another hour. The weather is very thick and we could not see three ship lengths ahead. We had just gone down to dinner leaving the third mate Mr. Scott to look out on deck, when a man on the flying jib boom sung out "Land ahead," when we rushed upon deck, where Mr. Scott instead of putting the helm hard up at once, had let go all the lee braces, and the ship was almost in the wind. "Hard up, Hard up, Let go the spanker sheets, flatten in forward," were hastily thundered and as hastily obeyed. The ship slowly paid off and almost in the breakers and so near the rocks that we could have hove a stone on them. In two minutes we were clear but in all my life I never ran quite so narrow a chance as that. It spoiled the old captain's apetite for dinner, but it will take something worse than danger to trouble mine. It is raining in torrents yet and I have no dry clothes to put on. If

I had there would be little use in it for I cannot leave the deck now and we are in rather too ticklish a place. If it were clear we could now see Cape Romania but it will all be a blind man's buff in entering the straits. Good luck to the brave ship. I hope we shan't loose her.

Tuesday Morning, 6th Jan. [1852]
Off Bintang Island.

Here we are thrashing away to windward in order to gain entrance to Singapore Straits, instead of being now at Singapore two days. We have had a rich treat these two days I admit, a treat that I never care to have again. On Sunday afternoon after just escaping being dashed to pieces on the weather side of Pulo Aor, the weather came in very squally and thick with occasional strong puffs from the N.W. We took in all our studding sails and hauled her up for Pedro Branco, which we should have made about five o'clock but we saw nothing anywhere until a few minutes past five when as we were rolling away before a northeast squall with everything straining fore and aft, one of the lookouts sung out "Land!" "Where away?" "On the bow." In a moment more the fog and mist lifted so that we could see, not the lighthouse rock of Pedro Branco but the bold black cliffs of Bintang directly under our lee and not two miles distant. The strong current which after sets by the straits in the N.E. monsoons had carried us to about ten miles leeward of the entrance, and there was no use in thinking anymore about Singapore in that weather, as we should lose ground all the time if we undertook to beat back. There was but one of two things to be done either to stand over towards the coast of Borneo, under as much sail as we could carry on a wind, or to douse everything in an instant and let go the anchors where we were. I should certainly have preferred the first resource as being far the safest, but as we should have lost a little time and perhaps gone a long way to the strong current Capt. Merril decided to come to anchor.

"Heave the lead." "Ay, ay Sir." "What water?" "Seventeen fathoms." "Let go sheets and halyards." "Hard down with your helm." "Stand by the starboard anchor." "All hands stand by to light-too chain." "Let go the anchor!!!" Thus in less than three minutes the huge ship was eased of her canvas, brought round into wind and the anchor let go in seventeen fathoms of water, but with a heavy head sea and every appearance of a gale of wind. There was no need of all hands standing by to light-too chain as the whole 90 fathoms of it, ran out like lightening as soon as the anchor hit the bottom.

We were now more than fourteen furlongs from a dead lee shore, upon which a strong and increasing gale was blowing and a tremendous sea and current setting. All our canvas fluttering and thundering against the masts, the ship was pitching madly to her anchor and taking on board vast quantities of water, and to crown all, darkness was setting in. It was not a situation to be coveted by even the most enthusiastic lover of adventure, for if the gale increased we were sure to go ashore; all the anchors in the world could not have held us, or if they could it was only to sink us where we lay. It took two hours as hard work as ever, I had to take in all our wet and heavy sails. Sometimes the men would get the topsail all snugly rolled up in a lull, but in a moment a terrifying blast would send it thundering away again, in spite of everything. By the time we were done furling the sails the gale had increased to a fearful force, and although it was dark as Egypt, we knew the ship was dragging her anchor, from her trembling, and unsteady jerking. We let go the other anchor and sure enough, as soon as it was upon the bottom, the cable drew out ahead with as much strain as the other. We paid out the whole of our second chain, and weather bitted, stopped and unshackled both of them ready if necessary to slip them in an instant. I am sure the ship was drifting still as I could plainly feel her surge at each heavy sea, and Mr. Elder swore that he could hear the breakers at every lull of the wind. As for seeing anything it was out of the question altogether for besides the darkness, the spray from the sea was absolutely blinding. Sometimes our forecastle bowsprit and jib booms were buried in the sea and then as she rose, a hundred tons of water would rush aft carrying everything away before it. It is well that we had everything well lashed, on account of our rolling so much lately, for if things had been fastened as usual we should have lost all our spars, deck tanks and everything else.

195

At ten o'clock, the gale still increasing and the barometers still falling, Capt. Merril gave orders to strike topgallant and royal yards and house topgallant masts. Good heavens! what a task. No one can form the slightest idea of the danger, difficulty, and imminent peril, attending this operation upon that terrible night. I myself would have sooner cut away the masts altogether than attempt what must almost be sure to lose them and the men aloft along with them. No one shrunk from his duty however, and in an hour we had completed the job, safely and carefully, without any other loss than our heavy main topgallant yard which with the sail attached, broke away from its lashings in the main riggings before it was well secured and went to "Davy Jones." I do not believe that a ship's yards and topgallant sails were ever housed before, in such circumstances without more loss, and the oldest sailor we had said that he had never seen the like attempted where the ship was pitching so violently. The sea was now making a regular beach over us fore and aft, and it was impossible for any one to remain in the forward part of the ship. An old hand was kept constantly on the lead in the lee gangway, and from time to time we were cheered by his cry, "She is dragging again Sir." Capt. Merril went below for there was nothing to be done. If the anchors held us we might ride out the gale in safety, but if we dragged much further or one of the cables parted, we were lost. It was a trying night for me. No one could do anything and we were all collected on the poop deck, where every man during all the hours of that night was left to his own thoughts. Mine were bitter indeed, and I over and over prayed that were I to be lost upon these rocks that some kind spirit would keep my dear parents in ignorance of my fate, or else lighten the load of sorrow which they must feel for their loss. I have never feared death myself in any form, and were I not the child of two tender and loving parents, I should never hesitate to meet it on every occasion, but I remembered the recent loss of my dear little brother which must have been a sore trial to them, and I knew that if I was now to be lost, their grief would be too great to bear. Upon the barren coast of Terra del Fuego and Staten Land, I have looked shipwreck and certain death in the face without shrinking and even with a kind of mild interest, but since I have learned of the loss just mentioned, I feel I have no life to lose with impunity.

As morning dawned the gale lulled a little and we began to hope the worst was over. The barometer had commenced rising and the sky was clear in patches. When the light had got strong enough for us to see around us we found ourselves close to the rocky shore, where the still tremendous seas were still breaking with a force that would have rent our ship to atoms in an instant. The carpenter sounded the pumps and reported four feet of water, which was much less than we had feared she had made. As the day advanced the wind fell, we pumped out the water and as soon as the sea had subsided so that it did not break over the ship, we cleared away the wreck of lumber on our decks and secured our topgallant masts so that we were enabled to work the ship if necessary without getting them on end again. At ten o'clock the gale had so far abated that we were enabled to commence heaving in on our cables, at one o'clock we got the first one to the cat head, and at half past three had hove almost short on the other one. The top sails were loosed, close reefed, and set, the storm jib hoisted and the anchor tipped, and we soon were making our way from the spot which had been near our graves. I cannot but blame Capt. Merril for getting into all this difficulty, for it was in my opinion the height of impropriety to come to anchor on a dead lee shore in the height of the N.E. monsoon, upon a gale of wind and in a spot where the whole force and current of the sea has the greatest power.

This is the third narrow escape we have had of losing the ship and our own lives, and I sincerely hope it may be the last one. At the Sandwich Islands first, at Palo Aor next, and now here on the coast of Bintang. There is certainly a screw loose somewhere. Since I am criticizing I will mention two other things where I think he is wrong. In running down the China Sea, we have as I said been directly before the wind, and rolling very heavily. Most ship masters would have hauled their ship up two or three points one way, for a few hours and then the other tack for as long, making quite as much distance, and keeping the ship steady and easy. But instead of that we have as the sailors say, "Almost rolled her guts out," kept two men constantly at the wheel, and strained the ship in every joint, without having made any more than had we pursued the other plan. True it is that we have had a fine run, from the beeches to this place and had it not been for the gale on Sunday evening we should have made the distance from Bashee to Singapore near two thousand in two days, and it is also true that the China Sea is no place to box a ship about much out of her course, but still many a time we might have eased the ship without any danger whatever.

Another fault I have to find, was the manner in which he directed us to get our anchors at Bintang. When we had hove in short, in the first chain, I think it would have been much better if we had then run in the slack chain on the other anchor, but instead of that we tripped our first anchor without ever starting the other side at all and the consequence was that we had another two hours hard heave against wind current and sea to get what might have been bowsed in, in fifteen minutes. Besides that we were very much in danger of snapping the other chain short off when the ship brought us all standing to her anchor after a clear drift to 90 fathoms. As it was it almost threw the men from the windlass breaks by the violence of its surge, and shook the ship to its very keel. The old captain who was below came running on deck to learn what was the matter, and not feeling in a very good humor after all our hardships I told him very plainly what the matter was. But all things must have an end and I hope that this voyage of ours will soon again become pleasant. There is no fun in nearly losing your life besides having to contend with the mad elements for forty-eight and sixty hours at a time, wet and cold tired and hungry. Such however is the life of a sailor.

I said that we were beating back again over the ground we have lost, but up to this morning we would make but little on account of the very short sail we could carry. This morning at four o'clock however we made Pedro Branco light three points on the lee bow and were once more cheered at the prospect of getting into the port. The current was too strong though, and we were reluctantly obliged to wear ship again and here we are just about to stand in there again; I hope we will fetch in this time and it is a pity if we don't, for we have shaken two reefs out of the topsails and set a fore and main topgallant sail. It is now ten o'clock and if we have no ill luck we shall be to anchor in Singapore before night.

Singapore, Tuesday evening.
We are at anchor in the harbor of this "City of the Sun" safe from all our dangers and forgetful of all our hardships. How different is the weather here from what it is outside these straits where we were this morning and where we have been for the last three days, only fifty miles distant. It seems like emerging from the cold storms of March and April at home, into the heat and sunshine of the hottest dog days of August. For the last few days we have been constantly as wet as water, and the strong winds seem almost to pierce through our bodies, but this afternoon after entering this harbor we soon commenced hauling off our clothes, first our wet and heavy monkey jackets, then two or three flannel shirts, then trousers —and now we are in our old summer rigs again. Dungaree trousers, cotten shirts, and straw hats.

At ten o'clock this morning we wore ship for the last time and stood in under everything we dared set. At twelve o'clock we were within twelve miles of Pedro Branco and for a long time it was very doubtful whether we should weather that rock. We stood on however and just as the captain had sung out, "Ready about" the wind favored us a point and in ten minutes we had cleared the rock by only a cable's length and were safely in the straits. Ten minutes after passing the rock our main topsail split in the middle and went to glory, thus like a true and faithful servant having to perform all his duty, to die when his services are of no longer importance. Had we lost that sail a half an hour early we should have been in Singapore this blessed night. The sea which was so heavy outside, subsided as soon as we had passed Pedro Branco, and we were soon boarded by a Malay pilot who brought us in.

I said we were at anchor in the harbor. We have just finished furling the sails and cleaning up the decks and now (8 p.m.) are preparing for a good night's rest. The full moon is shining brightly on these oriental scenes, the palm shaded islands and the picturesque town before us. Everything is new and novel to me, and for the last half hour I have been gazing with rapture upon the scenes which have often visited me in my youthful dreams. An East Indian Island city, embowered in the dark shade of the palm, coconut, and orange trees and bathed in the silver beams of a dark tropical moon. Oh what a lovely picture. I shall dream of a heaven on earth tonight and I will wake in the morning to realize my dream.

Tuesday, 8th January, 1852.
Straits Singapore off Pulo Pisang

We left Singapore this morning at nine o'clock, and have been beating up these straits ever since. The weather is most lovely though very warm, and nothing could be more pleasant than sailing up these waters among the many green islands and spicy shores. The coconut groves are filled with broad-leaved green plants, bright gorgeous flowers, and flocks of singing birds. The pepper vine fills the air with its aromatic fragrance. The coffee tree and nutmeg surround the huts of the natives along the shores, figs, mangostines, pomelas, oranges, limes and plantains line the gardens and hedge the green rice fields, and most plantations of ginger, and pine-apples are seen on every sunny slope. The sun is obscured by a slight haze, but the sky has the color of copper and burns the skin as quickly as the hottest sun that ever shone in Pennsylvania. When I was in Panama last August I thought that weather could not be hotter than we had there, but I find that these lands lie beneath a far more fiery sky than those of Panama. One would think that such excessive heat would parch up the soil and destroy the vegetation, but it has the very contrary effect. There is plenty of rain and a seed has only to be put in the ground and in a few hours it is a growing plant, developing itself with the most astonishing rapidity and luxuriance. True the lives of tropical plants is short in proportion to its high stimulation resembling in this the lives of men, in the same climate, and there is no tropical production which attains a quarter the age of our sturdy oaks of the north, nor no native of an Indian land who sees the advanced age of the Laplander or Scandinavian.

But I have forgotten to say anything about Singapore, and in fact I was not ashore long enough to obtain much information or see a great deal of the place. Early Wednesday morning I dressed up in a "Go-ashore suit" of clothes, and leaving the ship in charge of Mr. Elder went to take a look at the town, and hunt up some friends. My first adventure was capsizing the Sampan in getting into it, and giving myself a ducking. They are the lightest boats I ever set myself into, and the least move one way or the other turns them over as easily as a cork in the water. I got another suit of clothes on, and this time being more careful succeeded in reaching the shore in safety. I landed at the boat quay, and was at once surrounded by the entire population of the place offering their services to take me wherever I wanted to go. They were all Malays who had learned to speak English, and a milder or more picturesque looking people I never saw. Entering the house of Messrs. Dare & Co. I inquired if they could show me the house of the American consul Mr. Ballastier. Mr. Dare sent one of his Peons with me, and gave me the use of his own palanquin, as the distance was quite considerable. I found Mr. Ballastier who was glad to meet me, in his garden, enjoying the cool of the morning, and eating green figs and claret for lunch. He immediately laid aside all other business and devoted the day to my entertainment. We conversed about local matters of geographical and historical interest till after tiffin, when we went to visit Sir George Malcom, Governor of Singapore. This gentleman devoted the whole evening to us showing us all over the governmental house grounds on the hill, through the citadel, public gardens, and his own gardens, and would not allow us to depart without dining with him. The Government house had the most delightful and airy structure on the island, and nothing sems to give its present master so much pleasure as entertaining visiting strangers. He pressed me to remain a few weeks in Singapore before proceeding to Bombay, and when I explained the impossibility of that he gave me a warm invitation to visit him again after I had become established in Bombay. Sir George, Thy hospitality is as liberal as thy attentions are delicate and I know not whether I shall at some future date avail myself of thy invitation. The streets, gardens and avenues of Singapore, and the roads round the island are all well shaded with every variety of tropical fruit. The English houses are large, comfortable and airy, and their country bungalows perfect little Edens. The natives are rather wild looking, but generally orderly and very clean and

201

neat about their bamboo cottages. Their greatest enemies are the tigers which infest the surrounding jungles in great numbers. Every week someone falls a victim to these ferocious animals, and even yesterday everyone was engaged in lamenting the fate of one of the Zecmanders of a neighboring town, who had been destroyed by a tiger close to Singapore. There is a premium for their scalps, but the Malays are so deadly afraid of them that they will not hunt them. There are a few ladies in Singapore, and it is the greatest study of the inhabitants of this remote spot to enjoy their lives as much as possible; there are but few of them, and almost every day they meet in a dinner party or a riding excursion together. At eight in the evening I went with my friend Ballastier, to the bungalow of Mr. Woolcot, an American gentlemen, the partner of Mr. B. in the firm of Woolcot and Company, and the only American besides Mr. B. in Singapore, excepting a few half civilized missionaries. There were a number of gentlemen collected here and all the ladies of the place, to whom I was introduced. I cannot say much for the quality of the society, but of course it was the best in Singapore. The inhabitants of these remote spots are almost shut out from the world and their manners, customs, conversation and habits, soon attain a local pecularity and freedom quite foreign to all established rules of European society. But there is as I said no comparison here, and we take what we meet to be the best.

I remained at the bungalow of Mr. Ballastier last night, who I must not forget to say has a lovely daughter 16 years of age, the child of a Malay mother. Her manner was also infused with the lanquid freedom of the climate and I almost lost my heart at the fair shrine of her bewitching beauty. The night was one of the loveliest moonlight I had ever seen and long after the midnight hour, the lovely Marion remained with me in the garden talking all the nonsense and good sense that she ever learned. When I retired to rest the servants secured the gauze curtains around my bed and one of them remained in the room for an hour waving a punkha which was suspended in the curtains right above the couch, and I think he would have fanned me thus till morning had I not told him to leave the room. I don't think my fair companion retired at all, for I heard her voice in the next suite of chambers, humming a song long after I had sent my attendant away.

I do not think my dear friends at home, where the winds of winter reign in all sincerity can fancy that at that very time we were lying almost without clothing at Singapore, and a servant fanning our bodies as we slept. And this the seventh of January.

After an early breakfast I bade my kind friends adieu, and hurried on board the ship, expecting to have kept the ship in waiting several hours, but they had only just finished taking in our fresh supplies and were engaged in driving the hundreds of Malay bum-boatmen out of the ship, who had come to sell all the curiosities of the place, and fruit, eggs, tobacco etc., to the sailors.

The *St. Thomas* looked like a huge leviathan surrounded by a brood of pigmies, while all these sampans were around her, and it was useless to attempt heaving up the anchor till everybody had been driven away, birds, cages, flowers, monkeys, shells, coral, tobacco pipes and all. We had a Malay pilot on board and easily passed the Rabbits and Coneys, St. Johns Island and the Caramons. We shall be up with Pulo Pisang by four o'clock, where we shall discharge the pilot and have the more open straits of Mallacca for our navigation. I have been writing a letter to Dr. Lee, which I shall give to the pilot before he leaves.

Friday, 9th January, 1852
Off Tanjon Tuan, Sts. Malacca

A lovely morning! The sun shines bright upon the green groves and blue hills which skirt these smooth waters, the parrots and birds of Paradise are fluttering through the air, and with the glass we can see whole troops of monkeys clambering among the trees on the shore. The air is loaded with the scent of the spice trees upon the hills. The sky is of the cast peculiar to these regions, and the whole landscape is essentially Indian in the general contour and more minute details.

All night long we have had a strong fan breeze, but now it is falling away, and I fear we shall have one of the calms so common in these waters. At about one o'clock this morning we passed the P.&O. Cos. steamer *Erin* on her way from Hong Kong to Bombay, but when the breeze failed us, she overhauled us again, and is now almost two miles ahead. I wish I were in her, and then I should see my new home at Bombay in ten days.

At the same time that we got underway at Singapore, there was also a Portuguese frigate and an English brig, getting under way. They were both deep, and yesterday in beating to windward they beat us all to pieces, as we were almost flying light, and could not hold our own. But through the night we passed them like a shot, and now they are hardly distinguishable from the tall palm trees, on the shore far astern.

Speed thee my gallant bark, I shall yet maintain that we shall accomplish the passage in seventy days.

Sunday Afternoon, 11th Jan. [1852]
We are lying entirely becalmed between Pulo Jarva and the Sambellangs. We have had no wind since we lost the breeze on Friday morning, and all that we have made since has been by catspaws, and tides. At every flood tide we are obliged to let go an anchor to prevent losing what we had gained by the ebb. The rain is almost constant, and what few intervals of clear sky there are the sun pours down upon us in a perfect blaze of fire. There are as many as a dozen sail of vessels in sight at once, some working one way and some the other, without the least perceivable breath of wind. Some of them go along with all their sails cleared up, and hanging in graceful festoons to the yards, as if they were at anchor in a port, while others do not even attempt to take in a sail even while at anchor and float along either stern first, head first, or sideways, letting go a kedge when the tide is unfavorable, and heaving it up again at the next turn. It is a curious scene at night to see so many vessels lying motionless on the dull glassy deep. No sound is to be heard except the roll of distant thunder or the faint song of some ships crew heaving at her anchor, or the low wild chant of the Malay seamen. We pass and repass each other as silently as if no one were on board, and all our work is letting go and heaving up the anchor, and

in stearing clear of some vessels already at anchor, or floating down upon us while we are at anchor.

The days are very hot and showery, but the nights are lovely and mild. The soft air is loaded with a thousand sweet perfumes from the shores and the moon illuminates the adjacent hills and forests with silver brightness. It is not unpleasant to be thus becalmed, yet it is not a sailors nature to count the absence of the breeze. "Wind wind, we cry when most becalmed, and wind, still when it blows."

Yesterday morning we floated over the 2½ fathom bank on the north side, not a ship's length from the buoy, with only two feet to spare between the bottom of the keel and the sand. There was not a breath of wind and we were perfectly safe in doing this although had we been drawing a foot less it would have been a dangerous experiment. *To tell the truth however, we did not know we were upon the bank till we saw the buoy right alongside.* Great navigation this, I must confess.

Mr. Scott is getting worse and worse every day. When he is called to relieve the watch, he seldom if ever turns out till the third or fourth call, and then just as likely as not sitting down on the timber heads or skylights and going fast asleep. The captain has thus caught him once and given him a blow up, and if he finds him asleep in his watch on deck again he will disrate him as sure as that he is a jackass. The sailors all hate him and I should not like to mention the name they have given him, in speaking of his lubberly, thick headed blunders.

Monday Afternoon, 5 o'clock
Off Pulo Java

A large Malay proa is bearing down upon us before a light wind from the Sumatra shore. Ever since she has been in sight they have had her crowded with sail, and as many as twelve sweeps out on each side. She is now within two miles of us and we can see her crowded with men. They are nearing us fast as we are almost becalmed while they are bringing down a breeze with them. There is no mistaking these gentlemen, they are pirates without question, and there is but one of two things for us to do, either to escape if we get a wind, or to beat them off if we don't. We could easily do either, but should it come to an engagement, some of us must certainly fall victims to them, shot before we could drive them off. In less than an hour I myself may lose my life and lie a bleeding corpse upon our decks, fit only for food for sharks. But I am as eager for the fight as they themselves. We have all our muskets and pistols loaded, cutlasses stacked, and pikes placed in their racks. Our guns are all double shotted and if anyone is sufficiently experienced in the art of gunnery we could sink their vessel at one broadside. Like every other chance I take, this may be the last time I shall ever take my pen in hand. God's will be done. Should I die, and these lines ever meet the eye of a friend, let him know to my father, my mother, my brother, my dear own Mary, and the few other dear friends I have that my last thoughts are given, my last blessing breathed.

Wednesday morning, Jan. 14th, 1852
Off Junk Ceylon, NEbE 20 miles

Tis Life to feel the wind of night
Careening o'er the main
Tis life to breath the salt sea gale
And the spray from the foaming waves.

Once more the open sea is before us; the blue bay of Bengal lies spread out to the westward in all its free beauty, and the straits of Malacca with all its stifling heat, vexations, calms and dangerous neighbors are behind us. We took a fresh breeze on Monday evening, when the pirates who were chasing us were about a mile distant. The good *St. Thomas* however spread her snowy wings and soon left a long distance between us. The villans followed us a long time, as long as there was any hope of overhauling us, and then fired off two heavy swivvels in pure and impotent rage. We kept the wind all night and in the morning there was nothing but the blue mountains of Malacca in sight.

All day yesterday we kept a light southerly wind, and last night at about eleven o'clock, the dark monsoon clouds began to arise from the north, and this morning we again have the monsoon in all its freshness. Hurrah! for the open sea once more. Yesterday morning early we went ashore at Penang more to oblige me than anything else as I wished to see several people for whom I had letters. Capt. M. and myself stayed most of the day. We had took the boat in at the southeastern passage, and just at night we came out at the northern. Mr. Elder had got a wind while we were gone but was lying to off the island waiting for us about five miles off. We were more than an hour pulling off to him, and then "fill away the main yard."

I can say less of Penang than of Singapore. It seems like a very quiet pleasant place, with but few European inhabitants and a great number of pretty Malay women and half-castes. There were but two vessels here and it seems to be a place as yet uncontaminated by the world. The natives are free and independent looking, and the town and country around picturesque and comfortable. There are no Americans here for a wonder, and nobody in fact but the chief magistrate, a few civil and military officers, and two or three merchants. The pleasantest feature of Penang is the half-caste asylum or seminary there, kept by a lady by the name of Hall. It is a refuge for the children of European fathers and native women, who when their fathers return home would be left in peculiar circumstances but for some institution of this kind. Mrs. Hall has about thirty girls of all ages from ten to twenty-five. They are mostly handsome and well educated and any one who wants a wife can be accomodated directly there. It is certain that the house possesses more attraction to the young men than any other, and some of those that I saw were really accomplished and interesting.

We dined with a gentleman named Mr. Dawson who showed us much kind attention, and when we left to go on board the ship he sent two Malay sampans with us loaded with pineapples, mangostines, figs, plantains, sweet potatoes, etc., etc., as a present. I also received another present while at the seminary from a beautiful girl of a half-blown cashmere rose, and this I prize more highly than all the two boatloads of fruit. She seemed to be a lovely girl but could speak no English. She was the daughter of a French man of Pondicherry on the Cormandal coast, and was a beautiful and tall brunette. I fully intend visiting Penang at some future date when I shall have time to stay and enjoy its pleasures. Till then "au revoir."

Saturday Morning, Jan. 17th
Off the Andaman Islands.

We came in sight of these islands this morning, and the great Andaman, now bears west forty-five miles distant. We are bounding along close hauled like a charger, heading about N.N.W. with a steady and pleasant monsoon. We shall not however be able to weather the Andaman group, but I hope that two or three tacks to windward will bring us clear. We had hoped to hug the weather shore as far as Cape Negrais but this is now impossible, but if we weather "Landfall" island—we shall do well.

Just before sunset last evening we came up with Banen Island, a detached volcano in the middle of the sea. It was not in violent action, but after dark we could plainly distinguish a high column of illuminated sulphurous smoke resembling flame, and giving the most curious appearance to the rough black rock itself. Occasionally a jet of brighter light would shoot high up in the air and the whole scene was to me peculiar, interesting and novel.

The sunset last evening too possessed extraordinary beauty owing I suppose to the sulphurous fumes from the volcano which had spread over the western seaboard, and the morning moon although in her last quarter was sufficiently luminous to produce a beautiful and distinct bow.

We caught a porpoise this morning which must have weighed 6 cwt. He was an immense fellow, and after he was harpooned it required all hands to haul him on board. When opened we found his stomach all filled with small fish in various stages of preservation and decomposition. Some were very good such as squids and sunfish and the men picked out a bucket full and had them cooked. They were much better tasting than the porpoise himself. As a specimen of the various uses sailors put things to I will mention this porpoise.

His skin the men have made into Sou-westers his paunch they have stretched over a cheese hoop and have made a very fine tamborine, his entrails they have cut up, and twisted into good catgut for my fiddle, his jaws have offered them about a pint of good clear oil for embrocations, the bone is kept for a curiosity and the flesh is already half eaten up.

Soon after we had caught the porpoise we saw a beautiful sea serpent close alongside the ship, we were going too fast to catch it, or shoot it, but we got a very good view of it. It was about four feet long and about two inches in diameter, and was beautifully spotted with bright red, yellow, and black spots and rings. One of the men threw a piece of coal at him and he dove to the bottom immediately.

There are also a number of sea turtle here but they are too shy for us. They are like the green turtle of the West Indies, and almost everyone is attended by two or three fish which attach themselves to the under sides somewhat like a sucker on a shark though much larger fish. They are the "Indian Remora" of Dr. Wilson.

Sunday Afternoon, Jan. 18th
Lat by pole star 14 04 N
Lon 93 10 E

We are now out in the open Bay of Bengal, with the Monsoon as fresh, water as blue, and sky as clear, as a sailor can desire. We never can lay any higher than N N W but even with this, we should be able to reach the sands of the Ganges without tacking.

We passed to windward of Landfall Island this morning at 10, so close that we could see men and animals running about on the beach and in the coconut woods. We have been beating all night to weather this and have only just made out to do it. At 11 a.m. we saw the little Cocoas bearing N E 30 miles distant, but now we are out of sight of everything and I want to see nothing more till we reach the sandy shores of Sangur.

Capt. Merril broke the third officer last night, and I only wonder that he has refrained so long. He has all along conducted himself in a most lubberly like and un-officerlike manner, and of late while keeping Mr. Elder's watch, while he was sick he has repeatedly gone to sleep. This offense is always sufficient to disrate an officer, and although Merril is a very quiet and easy man, yet he cannot stand being imposed upon. Once in the China sea, Capt. did not hear any bells struck, and coming on deck found Mr. Scott fast asleep on the skylight, no lookout on the forecastle, and the sails hardly doing any good for want of trimming. He passed this over and many other things, but night before last when running by Barren Island, Capt. Merril had told him to call the mate and at 11 o'clock and if the wind was no more favorable we should go about. Feeling somewhat uneasy he did not go to sleep as usual, and not hearing anything on deck, he waited till long past eleven and then went on deck. There he found Scott fast asleep on the timber heads and the ship three points off her course. The man at the wheel said he had been there ever since eight o'clock and there was no lookout. Capt. Merril roused Scott, showed him the course the ship was taking, and told him the time of night, and asked him what kind of a man he thought himself. He told him to let that be the last time he found fault.

Not withstanding this the very next night, (last night) he went to sleep again and this time while the ship was running in directly for the land. The Capt. was on the alert however, and about the time he thought the ship was far enough in, he went on deck and sure enough there she was not a mile from the beach the lookout just coming aft to report it, and Scott fast asleep.

"Go below, you infernal lubber." "Go below and sleep till you are blind." "Darn you, you'd had us ashore, ah." "Not a word! go below and don't let me see your face in this ship again." "A sailor eh!" "You're not fit for a sojer!" "A mate, eh," "You're not fit for a scullion." "D——n you." "Bout ship there." "Bear a hand." "Bear a hand. This scoundrel had run us almost ashore."

I never heard Capt. Merril in such a rage before. But he had sufficient provocation to enrage a saint, and I only wonder that he did not have the lubberly jackass seized up and flogged. We went about in three fathoms water and the ship draws 13 ft. 6 in. In half an hour more we should have been high and dry on the beach, had it not happened that our capt. came on deck just in time. Scott sulked off to his stateroom, and there he has been ever since. If he comes out I am sure that he will get a kick in the seat of his trousers from someone before we get to Calcutta. The steward has took him his meals ever since he has been there and this is no small duty for his appetite is as great as his resemblance to an ass.

The islands we have just passed are considered the most beautiful and fair of any in the East, and fully can I corroborate the truth of the supposition so far as I have seen. They are alone in the midst of a large bay of the size not large enough to afford the foundation of a foreign settlement, yet large enough to accomodate several hundred of the most mild and peaceable natives of the Indies. East Andaman is the largest of the group and has a good harbor on its northeastern side where vessels may lie in safety. There is a small village there also and the place has been called Port Cornwallis.

All day yesterday and today we have been standing off and on on the shores of these islands. They are thickly wooded with trees of tropical growth and bloom with flowers of every hue. Their groves are full of bright winged singing birds and their waters of golden fish. There are no rocky shores here! The beaches are fine white sand of which only to allow the summer waves to break and curl, and fringed throughout by the dark forest where one may look with pleasing thoughts of cool grottoes and calm retirement and again in the background, blue hills with their slender towering palms, lifting their heads like sentinels above the surrounding forest, give a character to the landscape that I have never witnessed before. And then the weather! Oh what lovely weather; the air possesses that peculiar clear lightness, met with only in a few places upon the earth. The sea rivals the sky in azure coloring, and the waters are laughing in little foaming waves over which hundreds of little nautilus are sailing their devious voyages.

Oh would that all those who are dear to me on earth, might translate themselves hither to participate in the pleasures of the sunny summer evening.

Wednesday Afternoon, January 21, 1852
We are yet at sea, but near the place of our destination; it is now five o'clock and had we a wind, there would be a pilot on board us tomorrow morning early, but it is as heatless and innocent of wind as a dead land, and oh how hot. We are one hundred miles S.W. of Sangur, lightship and this calm is

rather too provoking. It is the first we have had however since leaving the straits of Malacca, and we have been improving it in cleaning and painting and in stripping her of chafing gear. It is wonderful what a vast quantity of mats, parceling, rounding, service, battens, scotchmen, etc., etc., we have had upon the ship. There are seven port casks full of parceling and half a boat load of battens. I love to see rigging well taken care of and never spare the canvas. We have used up two whole mizzen topsails since leaving California for parceling. We look as neat as a new pin, now that we have got our working suit off, and all we want is wind! wind!!

When we left San Francisco everyone said the ship would be one hundred days in going to Calcutta, but I have always maintained in ten weeks or seventy-five days, and I still maintain it. We are now out 69 days, and if we have a wind which I am very much in hopes of we shall have a pilot exactly on the seventieth day.

Poor Scott, is now obliged to go to the galley for his food. Our steward who is a shrewd chinese boy from Amoy has got tired of carrying his food to him, and yesterday he told him that the captain had given orders that he should wait upon him no more. He still however occupies his stateroom, but no one speaks to him, and he looks very sad and lonely. He occupies his time in reading, trying to study navigation, and in making a little ship. The pineapples and plantains of which we have yet a number, were going so fast while they hung in the main cabin that we have been obliged to move them into the after cabin where Master Scott can not get after them. Really the fellow has the hankering of a child with the capacity of a walrus.

It seems that I have come to the end of this chapter, and I must therefore give you a hymn before the "commencement of the next lesson."

I bid you good morning, good day, or goodnight,
At expense of perhaps one deep sigh,
Since I know a few hours will renew my delight;
But oh! I can nae bid goodbye.

EPILOGUE

JUDGING from Edward's letters home and from his consular reports, he was happy in India. He and Mary married, but unfortunately, had no children. Their life, nevertheless was a full one, with Edward maintaining a medical practice as well as a commercial enterprise. In addition, he was this country's diplomatic representative, and as such, involved in a long-standing struggle with the British East India Company.

On August 28th 1854, Ely wrote from Bombay as follows:

General Franklin Pierce
President of the United States

Honorable Sir:

In addressing the President upon the subject of my letter, I feel warranted, not only by the great importance of the measure I am about to recommend, but by the knowledge of your own anxiety to improve the terms of our Commercial intercourse abroad, and to raise the standards of our national estimation with the people of every country.

Since my appointment in 1850, to my present office, I have on numerous occasions experienced difficulty in obtaining from the local authorities of the East India Company such assistance and support, or even "attention" as the Consul of a friendly nation has a right to expect, and in several instances, I have had the mortification to see the interests of our Merchants and Shipowners trading at this port allowed to suffer unnoticed, because of the apathy, carelessness, or jealousy of those servants of the Government to whom I have applied for Justice. My own experience is corroborated by the complaints of all the Consuls of the United States in India who have ever attempted to execute their duty in a faithful manner, and if the grievance has never before been laid before our government, it is because those officers have either despaired of effecting a reform or found it more to their own interests to remain silent.

The obvious reasons for such a want of friendly acknowledgment of the claims of foreign commercial officers in India are plain indeed, and cannot fail to be recognized upon a careful examination of the nature of the East India Company's Charter and general system of Government.

A government organized entirely for, and by, a gigantic "Joint Stock Company"—and administered solely by a body of men interested in—and responsible only to—the same company for their deeds, can possess little in common with the Principles of other Governments.

The "East India Company," is in fact an immensely overgrown, self-governed monopoly, embracing in its dominions such vast extent of rich territories, and such heavy weight in the Councils of the British Government, as to render it in reality an almost independent Sovereignty; at least the most important Dependency in the World.

I have been repeatedly informed by officers of high rank in the Service that many provisions of the Commercial treaties between Great Britain and other nations, are disregarded with impunity by the authorities here; and my own experience has taught me that a prominent feature of the Government is a jealousy and intolerance pervading almost every branch of the service.

In consequence of these conditions together with various others, incidental to remoteness from home, the nature of the Climate, the Customs of the Country, etc., etc., the prosperity of our commerce with India must, until a reform is effected, depend in great measure upon the influence of the incumbent authorities and the successful influence of the local officers of our own government.

The faithful exercise of Consular duties in India is at present so undeniably irksome and expensive to the incumbents of the several Consulates, that—(with all due consideration)—I fear that cases of evasion, if not of actual injustice often occur, to the evident detriment of both the Government and the Commercial interests of the United States.

With a view to the improvement of these important relations with the Company's Dominions in the East, I have had the honor to recommend in a former report to the Secretary of State, the appointment of a "Consul General" of the United States to "British India" who shall be invested with such Diplomatic powers as will enable him to negotiate directly with the Supreme Government, thereby placing our interests in more responsible hands, and upon an established footing, and superceding the necessity of protracted and often irregular correspondence in simple cases where advantage is seldom obtained.

I now have the honor to enclose a copy of the revised charter of the East India Company which will continue in force until the year 1874. A perusal of this patent will afford a clear idea of the immense freedom of the Company, while isolated geographical situation of the vast extent of territory subject to its control, will suggest the advantage of maintaining at the seat of Government, *a duly qualified Diplomatic Agent*.

I have also the honor to enclose several kind recommendations of myself as a candidate for the proposed appointment, which, as coming from our own fellow citizens, I want most respectfully to submit to your attention.

In soliciting your favor in conferring upon me an appointment which I deem of the utmost importance and from which I anticipate a vast benefit, I would beg to assure you that should I receive it, I will take care it shall never fail to render a valuable return to our Country.

I have the extreme honor to be
Sir
Your most obedient servant
Edward Ely
Consul

Despite his aggressive attempt to secure the appointment, the post Ely suggested was not created, and so he continued to struggle with the East India Company as United States Consul until the dysentery epidemic of 1858. Edward, being a physician, plunged into action with typical abandon and disregard for his own safety and health.

As the epidemic waned, Ely, weakened by fatigue and continual exposure, contracted the disease and on the 17th of January succumbed. When the news of his death reached Mary, the shock was so great that she dropped dead.

The word of their death was sent home, but it was not until 1885 that his family learned the details of Edward's burial.

James Allison, our grandfather, while a student at Harvard College, attended a formal dinner at Boston Navy Yard given in honor of a visiting admiral. Over brandy and cigars, the admiral recounted tales of his travels and adventures, only one of which will be retold here. While a junior officer aboard a vessel pausing briefly in Indian waters, the admiral had been privileged to witness extraordinary honors bestowed upon an American, Edward Ely. In recognition of his tremendous service during the epidemic, and in particular for the many sacrifices he had made in caring for the victims of the disease, the British Navy had buried Edward at sea, and "manned the rails," an honor the admiral had never before or since seen bestowed on a civilian.

It is fitting that we end this chronicle by again referring to the March 16th, 1858 issue of the *Bucks County Intelligencer*.

". . . The latest arrival from India brought to his family the melancholy intelligence of the death of Doctor

216

Edward Ely, the American Consul at Bombay. This will be mournful news to his extensive circle of friends in this country to whom he was justly endeared. . . . He was cut off in the vigor of early manhood, in the midst of the active prosecution of duties upon the results of which were based fond hopes and anticipations for future years.

"Dr. Ely was a young man in whom Bucks County may justly feel a pride; for while he lived, at home or abroad, he shed lustre upon her character."